# Party
# Basics

Everything you need for the world's best party

Cornelia Schinharl   Sebastian Dickhaut   Kelsey Lane

# Party Basics
# Table of Contents

Front Flap: Makes Enough for How Many? — Basic Quantities
Back Flap: Basic Class, High Class and No Class — Basic Etiquette

# Party
## Defined

When does a meal become a party? When 1 candle is burning between 2 lovers eating 3 courses, or when 20 friends step up to a buffet? Both are parties—food prepared out of love and food that can make people dance with joy. Sometimes all it takes is someone cooking for you to make you feel in a party mood—or throwing a party yourself because you love to see people enjoying themselves.

Now here's the point—guests need hosts—people who shop, cook, set the table and clean up afterwards. People like…you! "You mean I'M the host? No way!"

Is it really so bad? Having a house full of people who start feeling great about themselves, you and the world in general? That should make you the happiest guest of all, even at your own party. What could be better than being in love, dancing and feeling happy? Nothing we know of.

We put together this guide so you can create that "I'm glad we're us" feeling. Basics from invitations to cleaning up and culinary creations that will make people ask, "What's this? It's delicious!" and "How did you make it?" We've examined basics from all over the world and since they extend from San Francisco to Slovenia, the recipes are an international "hodgepodge" that tend to be geared toward smaller quantities so that you can throw your own party for two or a buffet for 20 according to your own pattern (by doubling and tripling the recipes when needed). So now, let the whole world be happier than it has ever been before. Let's party! That's all there is to it.

# Know How

# Party?
## That's It. But How?

Isn't Peter's birthday coming up? That could be fun but, as usual, he won't want to celebrate it. But Barb, she likes to shake things up once in a while. Oh, but she just broke up with Carl. Then there's Rose and Nancy—they're always up for anything and besides, spontaneous is best. Although last time, Nancy's hot dog bagels and warm champagne left a little to be desired. So now what? Maybe I should wait for my own birthday and throw a party?

If you have to put so much thought into partying, you can forget spontaneous parties. Inviting friends over for a casual evening of making things out of paper (I'll explain later) can be almost as low key as cuddling up with another person on your balcony. All you need to do is think of something, do some planning and then celebrate it the way you want, while being flexible. In other words, plan a party and invite fun Peter, Barb and Rose and Nancy because they're always up for anything. Start chilling the champagne.

# 17

Good Reasons to Party

# You

# You & Me

# Guests

# Me

# Children

# Colleagues Colleagues Colleagues Colleagues

# Calendar

# Food

Family

Surprise!

Drinking

Weather

smile!

Hello

Goodbye

Congratulations!

Construction paper

# 17 Good Reasons to Party

## You

A likes B—a lot. A wants B to know it. But A doesn't know B very well. What should A do? "Make something to eat!" That's pretty brave since meeting over homemade food is not only the smallest but also the trickiest kind of party. Has A anticipated B's tastes? Does B like the same things A does? And how the heck did dishwasher detergent get into the pasta water? This could mean the end of the relationship before it has started. But it could also be that in surviving a disastrous "You" party, the two people end up really appreciating each other. And then if A makes pasta every year on the anniversary of their first meal, B can say, "Oh, this really tastes good. Did you cook it in dishwasher detergent?" Love itself can be a party!

## You & Me

Do you like one another? Has your relationship survived pasta fiascos and other disasters? Have you even whispered something about "love" and "you"? Then quick, go public and tell people before they find out through the grapevine. But don't go knocking on doors with glowing faces, saying "We're in love!" Throw a party instead because everyone understands parties, even if they don't believe in marriage. An engagement is certainly reason to party. Or celebrate moving in together. Or if it hasn't gotten that far yet, at least invite people over as a couple, like the royal family. Which means, of course, that it's OK if it's a little formal.

## Guests

Some people don't need a special date or a family event as an excuse to party. They just get the feeling that it's about time to invite over a nice group of people and fortunately these people have the time to come. And no wonder! Hosts who celebrate simply for the sake of their guests are the best. The invitation itself communicates a feeling of "I'm glad you're you" that lasts for the duration of the party. That's why such hosts excel in the almost forgotten art of entertaining, where parties are thrown in honor of others. If an uncle arrives from South America or if a friend doesn't have time to plan for her own birthday, these people throw them the best party they've ever had.

## Me

Yes, you, because guests often come because of the host: because she's a good cook, because he's a nice guy, because we always have so much fun at their place, or simply because it's your birthday. Your birthday is your own Christmas, a date that comes around at the same time every year when friends can tell you they're glad you're you. You can throw yourself a birthday party, which can be sedate or lively, however you feel and whatever you want. Sure, there are some people who think it's stupid to celebrate their own arrival into the world. But they're sure to be the first to show up and stay until the very end.

## Children

After the game of Pin the Tail on the Donkey at the children's birthday party, why did you feel so gratified when the neighbor's kid wrapped his arms around your legs, looked up at you with a shining face and stammered, "This is the best party I've been to in a long time!" Because last year the same kid asked, "Are your parties always this boring?" For a host, throwing a successful children's party is like being dubbed a knight. If you manage to sustain the good moods of an excited mass of little people whose ways of thinking, talking and eating are completely different from any reasonable grown up's, you'll be able to throw a welcome party for Martians or a cold buffet in the Sahara with one hand tied behind your back. Nothing has the power to make you happier—or more worn out.

## Colleagues

Eight hours of solid work? Hardly. Count on colleagues to come up with many reasons to celebrate: new hires, birthdays, retirements and such. For many office parties, it's enough to have champagne and canapés or bottled beer and finger food. When celebrating for a specific purpose (e.g. to promote team spirit or thank your boss), it's good to do something more specific and creative—but don't go overboard. It's better to hold something in reserve than "kiss up" too much and become the focus of office gossip as the "boss's pet project." And when mixing your work with your private life outside of the office, be careful which friends and which colleagues you choose to invite.

## Calendar

Celebrating because it's a holiday—isn't that old-fashioned? Yes, and isn't it wonderful? Even hipsters can be brought around. Idea 1: Make it sound cool. Invite them to go on a picnic for May Day OR celebrate All Saint's Day instead of Halloween. Idea 2: Celebrate international holidays, such as the Chinese New Year, France's Bastille Day or Carnival in Rio. Idea 3: Celebrate natural phenomena, such as the summer solstice or have a harvest festival. Idea 4: Celebrate today because it happens to be a holiday – try an Ash Wednesday breakfast or a St. Nicholas' Day tea. And if none of this works, there's always New Year's Eve! Idea 5: Celebrate just because it's today.

## Food

"Esteemed guests, we rejoice in the interest you've shown in celebrating with us at the Fancy Host Country Club. Please permit us to offer a few seasonal culinary events: Spring Herb Festival, Green-Violet-White Asparagus Feast and the Berries & Roses Party. Other popular programs include our dance around the large roast in the Gold Room and the Souvlaki Sirtaki—the dance of Zorba the Greek." Hey, what's all this about? The food sounds good (but the programs?) Let's get out of here and really party! Are the chili peppers on Annie's balcony ripe yet? You bet! Let's go!

# Family

Do you really have to show up? You'd better, because family celebrations are sacred festivals and you need a good excuse if you're going to miss your nephew Phil's christening, your sister Annette's wedding or your dad's 80th birthday party. Besides, it usually isn't as bad as you think it's going to be. Feelings tend to be expressed more openly in such close-knit groups, which is a rewarding part of families. Also enriching are the few holiday rituals that are unique to your family—you'd miss them if they were gone.

# Surprise!

A couple decided to get married alone in Hawaii. Since they didn't want to disappoint their friends, they threw a party for 150 guests before leaving. Before it was over, everyone was supposed to gather for a group photo. But instead of a photographer, an Elvis impersonator appeared with the bride and groom in all their splendor. Elvis sang the wedding ceremony and the couple sang "I do, I do, I do!" (True story.) It was fantastic! Parties that surprise the guests can be great. But "surprise parties" are another matter. Would your guest of honor really want a surprise party? If she's a quiet, shy girl, she may not appreciate it if Elvis and 150 guests showed up in her living room.

# Drinking

If you party to get drunk, you'll get as much out of it as someone who's lactose intolerant yet polishes off a whole gallon of ice cream – nothing but bad memories. That said, having something good to drink is a good reason for a party. Celebrate the arrival of the Nouveau Beaujolais, Novello Rosso or simply do a tasting of French Chardonnays. A welcome invitation: "I just brought back a wonderful Barolo from Italy..." Wine not your thing? Include some in your drink menu in any case, but don't overlook hard cider and imported or local micro-brewed beer. Gourmets can even invite friends for a first flush Darjeeling tea party or to celebrate the first roasting of Jamaican Blue Mountain coffee.

# Weather

When spring returns, it inspires you to spread your wings and your heart rises like a hot-air balloon. Start out slowly by serving breakfast on the balcony or patio with wild garlic omelets and bread with marigold-butter (made by finely chopping edible marigolds and mixing well with a little salt into softened butter). When summer finally breaks out and makes you feel even more intoxicated, have a picnic on the dock while your feet dangle in the water. As autumn slowly descends and you can taste gold and silver in the air, take a sunset stroll, roast sausages over an open fire and drink micro-brewed beer. Then when winter again turns white and your ears are ringing like sleigh bells, hold hands in a mountain cabin over a snack of Christmas cookies and hot-spiced wine.

# Smile!

Have you ever thrown a party out of obligation? "Huh?" Ok, ok. We mean, for example, to say "thank you." You made a small dinner for the neighbor who fed your tomcat while you were on vacation (and whose eyes happen to be the same shade of green as the tomcat's...). Or "I'm back." You threw a party for your friends when you came back from being stationed in a submarine for three months. Or, during one of your nastier moments, you had a soirée and only invited all the people who owe you invitations. But if you really want to practice a random act of kindness, throw a "Smile" party to cheer people up, a get well party or, for the best mood of all, an "I'm glad you're you" party.

# Hello

Being new can make you shy, especially at parties. Good hosts can ease the situation, provided guests are open to new horizons: Who are all these people who have come? What do you want them to see of you? Revealing too much right off the bat isn't always a good idea—this goes for hosts, too. So you might not want to invite all your neighbors to your housewarming party; try easing them into your life gradually, instead, by inviting them over for coffee first. Revealing too little isn't the greatest either so above all, try to keep an open mind. One time when it's okay to pull out all the stops is called a "welcome back party" for old friends or acquaintances. When someone finally returns from their lonely island, going all out is just right!

# Goodbye

Let's get this straight: A good going away party is like a roller coaster ride—steep ups and downs with a few calm moments in between that give you a fresh take on the amusement park of life. The most brilliant toasts and finest gifts can provoke the loudest sobs; an otherwise superficial conversation can suddenly plunge into the deepest depths. Just to make sure everything stays on track, a going away party should be somewhat organized. It's best that the main characters are relieved of all responsibilities. And here's a little piece of bon voyage wisdom: A going away party where no one cries is a crying shame.

# Congratulations

Congratulations parties are among the most pleasant of all celebrations because the unpleasant part is already behind you. Congratulations on your 18th birthday (puberty is as good as over). Congratulations on your successful debut (stage fright was yesterday). Congratulations on your new job (you can finally stop reading the want ads). A decent congratulations party also combines the best elements of "goodbye" and "hello" parties because the person has something behind her, something ahead of her and success on her side. At a really good congratulations party, everything seems possible—you can put off reality and the rat race until tomorrow.

# Construction Paper

You're sitting in the bus, and you notice something bright in a shop window. You jump out and find out it's just contruction paper. Why not? So you buy some and take it home to start creating. Then Edna calls and asks what you're doing. "Construction paper," you say. She says, "Does that still exist? I'll be right over!" You both get hungry and call Sven, who loves to cook and will whip something up quickly. Then you call Maria and Carol because they like this kind of thing and they'll bring the beer. One thing leads to another and the next thing you know, you're making the coolest ships in bottles out of construction paper and beer bottles. In other words, make up a reason to celebrate!

# My Guests and Me

Guests seeking fun and gracious host. Must enjoy planning and celebrating. In exchange we will party, party, party.

"Ah, isn't it great? The sun is shining, the food is delicious and nobody has anything else to do; we're all feeling fine, we all like each other and the wine is exceptionally good. Life is a party, at least when there's something to celebrate like there is today. Why can't every day be like this? Why can't I throw a party like this at my place sometime?"

A nice thought, but make sure you think about this realistically: if you have a party at your place, you'll be busy on behalf of other people. Initially, at least, all you'll have to show for it will be onion tears under the kitchen lights, not summer sunshine and exceptionally good wine. But if you enjoy giving this gift to your guests, there's a good chance you'll be offered the job of good host or hostess. The qualifications of the good host are that they love their guests as themselves and it does them good to do good unto others. They're guest-friendly.

## The Party Questions

Guest-friendly hosts prefer to direct rather than take center stage. Exactly what happens depends on several questions: Why do I want to throw a party? How? With whom? When? Where? Although "where" is often a foregone conclusion—at your home. Having it at your place sets an upper limit on the number of guests, which can be scaled down, if necessary, from a stand-up reception to a dinner for two. The type of party depends, in turn, on the type of guest—coffee and cake for your aunt and uncle, a Thai banquet for six colleagues who are cooking fanatics or a pig-out buffet for 20 close friends. It can also be fun to mix guests—a lot of close friends, a few family and a couple new acquaintances—and then let things take their course. Provided the people show up.

That leaves us with the question of "when", which can be tricky if you already have a clearly defined "why." "Do you want to come Thursday at three for a birthday party?" "Hello, I have to work!" "In the evening then?" "OK, but only till ten." "Saturday night?" "Karen's parents are coming—it's been planned forever." "Monday?" "Football, you idiot!" It's best to pick out a few potential times and then narrow it down. What days would be good for you? When is there no football? There's more competition for weekends and people don't have as much time at the beginning of the week. Ask guests ahead of time which days they prefer. The earlier you start and the more important the party, the greater your chances of having your invitations accepted. You always have to reckon with a 10% refusal rate, or even 25% for large parties. But if it's 50% or more, you'd better start questioning either your cooking skills or your personal hygiene—or whether there was something wrong with the invitation. Or maybe you're barking up the wrong tree.

## Clear Invitations

If you want something, you have to come right out and say it, and say it clearly. This is especially true of invitations. Some people pick up on certain signals more easily than others. Close friends might phone and say no more than "What are you doing next Sunday?" and within five minutes they've arranged a picnic. But if you informally invite an interesting colleague to your famous New Year's Eve ball while chatting on the train in October, you'll be ringing in the new year without her. Meaning that the more guests you'll have and the more important the party is to you, the clearer you'll have to make the invitation. Clear means making it early enough so guests have time to decide and straightforward enough so they know what it's about—and formal enough so they know they need to respond!

So what's early enough? A week or less only if you mean it to be a spontaneous invitation, for instance to celebrate a promotion. Two weeks for a loosely organized meal, for example when Eric's passing through on his way to Toronto. If there's a special occasion for a larger celebration (birthday), it's better to ask three to four weeks ahead of time. And if the occasion is very, very special and the party equally as special ("We're emigrating!"), six to eight weeks ahead. For the biggest event of the year ("We're getting married!"), two to three months. For the event of a lifetime ("The hundred-year anniversary of my Web page!"), three to six months.

## Stand-up Receptions

These types of parties call for good food, but the primary focus is the conversation. Small hors d'oeuvres are typically served to be eaten mostly with fingers, and sometimes dishes requiring forks and spoons (no knives!) as well. These hors d'oeuvres can either be carried around on trays or distributed on tables. Since stand-up receptions often bring together a large number of people in a small space for a short period of time, it's important that everyone get something to eat without having to wait, ask, search or fight for it. A sufficient number of circulating trays or strategically placed appetizers can help. So can some decent cocktails. Not good: "Would you mind holding my plate while I twirl my spaghetti?"

## Word of Mouth? E-Mail? Form Letter?

For spontaneous or loosely organized parties that will be taking place within two weeks, spoken invitations are best, whether in person or over the phone, or you can even send an e-mail or mail an invitation. The only thing about these last two is that you don't know exactly when it will be received and it'll take you longer to find out who's coming. Faxes and e-mails are at least written down and invitations by mail are a sure thing. These are best when the event is more than two weeks away and you have more than ten people on your list. For less than ten, a formal written invitation might seem pretentious.

Have we forgotten anything? Oh yes, what should be written on the invitation? Above all, the answers to the questions we asked above: the reason for the party, who is invited (especially important for official events and when good friends are bringing partners you haven't yet met), what will happen, when (include the date and day of the week and a starting time 30–45 minutes before the meal, depending on the guests and the party) and where. Also, don't forget to include how guests are to RSVP.

## The Formal Dinner Party Menu

This is the fine art of dining at a table with courses served on plates, at least two courses and often three to four but seldom more than six. A formal dinner party is more work and more impressive than ordinary dining and cooking—which is also why more is expected—interesting cuisine, interesting conversation and an interesting time. It's best to invite a varied group of 6–8 people so it won't get too lonely at the table when the hosts are in the kitchen, although hopefully they won't be gone long. Serving more than three courses to 12 people is only for professionals. Not good: "What's all that yelling coming from the kitchen?"

For high profile parties, upscale invitations typically name the host first, then the hostess, and finally the guests, type of invitation (with the occasion, if appropriate) and time and place. "He and she request the presence of him and her at a who-knows-what at such and such a time, at such and such a place." Use classy paper, nice cards, or be highly creative. Leave room for something personal, even if only your signature.

## The Buffet

Allowing people to serve themselves at parties can help relieve the hosts. But it's acceptable only if the hosts aren't being lazy but truly want more time for socializing with guests—or for watching slides from Monica's latest trip to France. Buffets work well for a large number of guests and when the celebration takes precedence over the food. Arranging bowls and platters on a round table (with cutlery separate) or on several tables prevents long lines from forming. Arrange everything in an orderly fashion: start with a stack of plates, then the appetizers, main courses, etc. It's important to show that there's enough to go around, otherwise your guests will snap everything up like it's the first day of the after Christmas sale. Not good: "Now that my plate is finally full, there's no place to sit down!"

## The Potluck

The important element here is cooperation—a full-course meal with guests responsible for each course or a buffet with each person assigned to bring something. Or, try a wok cooking party: each guest brings a bowl of cut up vegetables to put on the buffet—everyone fills their bowls with a variety of these plus meat provided by the host and a wok master cooks it up! Because they're interactive, potlucks work when guests know some of the people and want to get to know others. Not good: "Oh no, you made tamarind chicken from the Party Basics cookbook, too!"

## The Family-Style Meal

What was once the privilege of nobility is now an everyday event: bowls and platters scattered over the table and guests passing them around to fill their own plates. This works great with a giant bowl of spaghetti alla marinara. For Sunday dinner, try a platter of roasted meat and several bowls with side-dishes. Or on a weekend night, try a table full of tapas for that multicultural feel. It's as appropriate for an average family as for a group of up to 12. Not good: "Can somebody please pass me the gravy? There isn't any more? Damn!"

# Making
## room

A good kitchen is always an asset for a party. But having the party IN the kitchen is not such a good idea.

No, no, please don't go to so much trouble, really. Naturally, when everything looks perfect, people feel intimidated. And the kitchen really is the most comfortable place to be in, which is why that's where even the best of parties naturally end up. Except that your front door doesn't open into the kitchen, and you don't have a bathroom in the kitchen (which is fine!), and the table is in the living room, and there's only room for three people between the stove and the window. Not enough room for a real party, wouldn't you agree?

So forget about the friendly, spontaneous kitchen party as a basic party for all occasions, because it's too much like the large, happy family you see in magazines but know are extremely rare in real life. But since you want to party in real life, why not prepare your entire apartment for your guests from start to finish, from a place to put their coats, to places to sit, dance, eat, talk and rest? And prepare the kitchen as well. This all sounds great, but what if you don't have a lot of room?

### The "Make the Best of It" Formula

Even the President is only a human being and it's not hard to imagine him having a barbecue on his lanai with his closest friend, or even his worst enemy, if they could arrive at a plan for saving the world. And maybe the two of them could even come up with this plan while dining at your house if you served them the world's best steaks. Which goes to show that if one single, focal element of a party is the best of the best, the rest doesn't have to be quite as perfect. This also follows: you can have a great party even in a studio apartment if you make the best of it. For example, if you have an open house party from 10 a.m. to 8 p.m., everybody can be free to come and go when they want— and hopefully they'll bring something to eat to share. Even 40 guests won't be too many when they're coming in stages.

The "make the best of it" formula is simple: if there's too little of one thing, provide more of something else. Make up for your tiny living room by having a longer open house. Or, if an important celebrity is visiting your humble abode, keep the party simple, for instance a two to three course dinner for four to six people (so you can focus on the food being of quality). If there's a lot of room for celebrating and dancing, finger food will be enough. But there are limits. Clearing out a two-car garage and putting out chips and beer cans is too tacky even for a 12-year-old. And if the President really does show up, it's extremely risky to try to make the world's best steak in an under-equipped kitchenette.

### 20 People in a tiny apartment: The Basic Party

Imagine the following basic party: you are entertaining 20 guests in a two-room-plus-kitchenette-bathroom apartment that has a large entryway and a small balcony. You can forget about serving a meal with everyone seated around the table. Instead, offer something hot on the stove that people can ladle into bowls, a buffet in the living room and a lot of places to sit down in between. These don't all have to be chairs— remember that sofas and benches are made for scrunching together.

So we've established that people can eat and drink more easily when sitting down. But also keep in mind that not everybody has to have a table, but you at least should provide a cleared surface within reach, at a convenient height. TV trays work great. Or, put barstools next to a wide windowsill, upside-down crates covered with fabric next the sofa, or use pillows as seats around a coffee table. With a little imagination, you can make a two-room apartment into a nightclub with cozy nooks and crannies where guests can circulate as though attending a ball, moving from the Windowsill Bar to the Sofa Lounge, and back to the Chill-out Pillow Den.

You can make these oases even cozier by adding lamps, creating new "walls" by moving furniture or making fabric corridors, lowering the ceiling in one room by suspending fabric from it, or by putting an extra rug on the floor. When reworking a room, don't just think in terms of how furniture is typically positioned. Put the sofa in the middle of the living room and move the TV, for example into the bedroom (but leave the coffee table by the sofa). Which brings us to the other rooms.

## Where Do We Put Our Coats?

If the weather is chilly on the day or eve of your party, the first thing your guests will need is a place to throw their coats (preferably the bedroom) or to hang them up (if you don't like the idea of rummaging through the pile when they leave). If you don't want people to go into your bedroom, you'll have to play the part of maid or butler—you can be the one to retrieve their coats, which is convenient in any case when it's time to say goodbye. But even then, the chances of someone wandering in there are great, whether to make a quick phone call in a quiet spot, lay a sleeping child down on the bed or hide from an irritating ex. So it's a good idea to put away any personal or potentially embarrassing items, including that pile of dirty laundry.

It's also not a bad idea to straighten up before your guests arrive. Even your laid-back friends who scatter crumbs all around them and colleagues whose desks could be declared disaster areas want, as guests, to take refuge in the True, the Beautiful and the Uncluttered, so they will take notice if they find the same sloppy piles in your corners that they have at home. Do yourself and your guests a big favor and clear out all that junk, at least until next time. And yes, unfortunately, straightening up also means cleaning.

Naturally, the cleaning rule applies most of all to the primary mandatory room, the bathroom. If the bathtub and toilet are in the same room, you won't be able to make it look as clinically impersonal as a hotel bathroom at check-in, but there's still an important lesson to be learned from hotels. Get rid of all traces of the previous occupant. This means that you surrender the bathroom to the party. Clear out your used towels and ragged toothbrushes along with all the other junk on the sink and put out fresh soap and towels. And then you do a cleaning job worthy of the finest hotel maid.

## Extra touches

Once you have mastered cleaning, add something special. Fresh flowers in a small vase or scented candles are just the right thing. If not using scented candles in the bathroom, leave some room spray out where guests can see it.

## Lighting

Lighting can set the mood for the party. But lights that are too dim like those in nightclubs or wine cellars are less likely to encourage intimate coziness than irresistible "doziness," especially if you can't see the food or the person sitting across from you. Conversely, just because the electrician put the very bright light fixture in the middle of the ceiling doesn't mean it has to be the only source of light to illuminate every corner. Who wants to feel like they're partying in a public hallway of a community center? It's better to place small lamps in strategic places, even bedroom lamps or floor lamps borrowed from the neighbors. Then you can light candles and even turn on the ceiling light, but maybe with a lower-wattage bulb than usual.

## Air

Have you ever felt like a fish at a party? Packed in like sardines (crowded!)? And a little like smoked salmon (smoky!)? Of course there's a simple solution—air the rooms continuously or frequently and put smokers out on the balcony. Don't let things get to the sardine-salmon stage in the first place. But even 8 well-rested non-smokers seated at the table will quickly start yawning in a closed room, so bring in a little fresh air. If it's cold out, you can either air the place for a quick five minutes every 30 to 45 minutes or leave a window open in an adjacent room.

## Smokers

Smokers are guests too, but hopefully they won't need to light up until after the main course or, even better, till coffee is served. If they're considerate, they'll smoke in the area designated by the also considerate hosts. But you're being inconsiderate if you condemn your guests to smoking in the street when the party is on the 4th floor. It's better to offer them an open window. That said, if you have a balcony, you have the perfect spot.

## Music

Music choice is up to you but we will say, as with food, your taste won't always match that of your guests. Music during a meal can remind people of department stores and elevators and interfere with their enjoyment. Music before a meal, provided that it's light, not too loud and the host isn't constantly occupied with the CD player, can relax your guests and fill in awkward pauses in the small talk. As for music after a meal, it's OK if it's a little more intense, as long as it doesn't reach the level of clearing people out—for instance, because you've started competing with the neighbors who are trying to drown you out, or Jessica wants to demonstrate the very first songs she's learned to play on the clarinet, or Carl just discovered some death-punk records behind the bookcase.

# The Dish on Dishes

## Dining with a capital D is possible in any household if the size is right

Stretching out on the sofa with a pizza box flipped open and not a care in the world is a wonderful way to party alone. Even if there are two of you, it still works great, especially for taking a friendly break. As of three or more, however, the couch + pizza style is no longer festive. You'd be better off organizing a spontaneous party. "Come by tomorrow night for some pasta" means the table will already be set, the red wine will be breathing and comfortable partying can begin.

A carefully set table forms the basis for Dining with a capital D, not only with regard to the food itself but also with extras such as drinks, conversation, hospitality and the "I'm glad we're us" feeling. A well-set table shows guests someone thought of them and went to the trouble to produce something special. It loosens everybody up and heightens anticipation, including that of the host's. It also gives hosts more time to think about what they're doing, instead of: Spoons? "Don't forget the garnish for the soup!" What about wine glasses? "I hope she likes red." Wait a minute, the tablecloth! "Shouldn't that have come first?" Once we get all this squared away, everything else should work out fine.

## Be Basic, Not Perfect— Sizes S to XL

The good thing about celebrating at home is that you can "make yourself at home." In other words, you don't have to parallel park the cutlery beside plates with matching coasters and a crumb catcher. When setting the table for basic dining, let your motto be "Be basic, not perfect." Do only what you can do, what you want to do and what fits the size of your household. If you only want to invite a handful of people now and then for stew at the table, the standard (S) size will fit the bill and will also serve all your own needs: small plates for everything small, large for what's large, and bowls for anything requiring a spoon. Serving bowls? That's what pots are for. Salad utensils? That's for size M people, M for "More going on." These are the people who invite guests more often and want to offer them more than a stew, perhaps even wine and dessert. Or do you want to go straight to the large, full-course meal? Then you need size L, as in Luxurious, with cloth napkins, fish knives and forks and white wine glasses. Genuine fanatics belong in the "bread and butter plate" class—size XL, as in eXtra Luxurious.

If you think S types are stingy and XL types are pretentious, think again. For example, consider two S types who move in together and want to establish an M- to L-sized household. If the result is a little haphazard, all the better. But to ensure that the appearance of their table before a party isn't the way it will look after a party, something is needed to tie all the elements together. For example: six plates of the same size can offset the six pasta plates from another set of dishes and six mismatched dessert plates. This works especially well when the tie-everything-together dishes are plain white and thus don't clash with other colors, patterns, shapes and materials. Even these can be mixed as long as some element remains stable, for example a consistent color scheme that unifies polka dots and checks, or a striped pattern that combines all the colors of the rainbow. Add to this individual pieces such as salad bowls made of coconut palm wood and you begin to achieve something of the eXtra luxurious. That's how quickly an S type can turn into an XL type.

## S for "Standard"

### Dishes
* Small plates—for breakfast, snacks, bread, salad, appetizers, desserts
* Flat plates—for all main dishes
* Wide, shallow soup bowls—for soup, pasta
* Rice bowls or cereal bowls—very versatile: rice, cereal, soup, salad, dessert, café au lait
* Mugs—for all hot drinks

### Cutlery
* Knives, forks, big spoons—for everything from breakfast to late-night soup (Big spoons double as serving spoons)
* Teaspoons—for dessert and for stirring

### Glasses
* Drinking glasses—for water, juice, beer, milk, mixed drinks, parfait desserts
* Wine glasses with stems—for white wine, red wine, sparkling wines

### Plus
* Paper napkins, place mats
* Coffeemaker and carafe for service and to keep coffee warm
* Saucepans and mixing bowls—can double as serving bowls and soup tureens

## The Basic Dinner Party

Let's move on to a basic sit-down dinner scenario: A young couple, size M to L, invites six people to a 4-course dinner including appetizer, soup, main course and dessert plus champagne, wine and water. The table is set with a tablecloth and 6 place settings. If the table is small (anything smaller than 3' x 5' is too small for six), it's best to fill the plates in the kitchen and serve them on chargers (a large bottom plate) at the table.

And now for the cutlery. For one course meals, the knife and fork can both be placed to the right of the plate. But for this 4-course meal, the fork is on the left and the knife on the right. If you have a knife and fork for the appetizer, they belong to the left and right and outside the first set so guests can start from the outside and work their way in. A soup spoon belongs to the right side of the knife, or between the main course knife and the appetizer knife, or crosswise above the plate with the handle to the right like the dessert spoon below it. Anything more will be even more confusing.

Place glasses above the plate and to the right. The glass for the first drink is the furthest right, followed by the glass for the next drink. The water glass is placed above the plate in the center or to the left. Between these and the edge of the table you can still place salad plates and bread and butter plates, and arrange the napkin to the left or on the plate. Why isn't it artistically folded? A swan shape is cute, but guests may not appreciate others fiddling with their napkin first. It's better to spend time polishing the cutlery or making your wine glasses spotless. Now take one last look. Is everything organized and ready? If this is starting to sound like the military, don't worry. The guests will be here soon along with a healthy dose of disorder.

## M for "More going on"
* Size S plus the following—

### Dishes
* Cups to fit the saucers—matching the small plates
* Salad bowl—china, also for pasta
* Casserole—nice looking for oven-to-table service
* Serving platters, bowls for side dishes
* Peppermill, salt shaker (preferably decorative)
* Teapot, coffee pot, sugar bowl, creamer

### Cutlery
* Salad utensils, parmesan grater
* Serving forks & spoons, cake server

### Glasses
* Champagne glasses, wine glasses, beer glasses
* Cocktail glasses

### Plus
* Tablecloths—at least one in white
* Bread basket
* Candlesticks

## L for "Luxurious"
* Size M plus the following—

### Dishes
* Charger plates, salad plates, special dessert plates
* Small soup bowls or cups—especially for clear soups
* Tiny bowls for sauces on the side
* Soup tureen, gravy boat
* Carving board, cheese board
* Espresso cups, pretty tea pot, cake plates

### Cutlery
* Appetizer cutlery, fish knives, steak knives
* Carving set, cheese knife, serving cutlery

### Glasses
* Separate glasses for white and red wine
* Beer glasses appropriate to brew type
* Glasses for aperitifs and digestifs

### Plus
* Cloth napkins, table pad
* Wine bucket, can double as an ice bucket when no wine is served
* Vinegar and oil cruets
* 2nd or 3rd set of dishes, cutlery, glasses used only for parties

## XL for "Extra Luxurious"
* Size L plus the following—

### Dishes
* Finger bowls
* Bread and butter plates
* Candy dishes

### Cutlery
* Gravy ladle, small bread knives, knife rests
* Specialized cutlery and serving pieces, for serving lobster to snails
* Sugar tongs, espresso spoons

### Glasses
* Wine glasses for specific types of wine (e.g. Bordeaux glasses)
* Demitasse cups
* Glass carafes, punch bowl set

### Plus
* Champagne bucket
* Chafing dishes
* Fruit bowls
* Napkin rings
* Anything else you need, from fondue to sushi sets—even a crumb catcher is allowed

## How Much for What Type of Party?

Even a hospitable S household should have 6 place settings consisting of plates, cutlery and glasses so they can serve a traditional group at the table. This is enough for 1 or 2 courses but as of 3, it's a good idea to have a second set of dishes, which can also be different from the first set. More ambitious hosts should purchase a full dozen of one set so they have the option to invite more people to dine. Otherwise, two different sets of coordinated place settings can be alternated on the table. For a family-style meal of 6–8 people, you need own only 1 serving platter, 2 serving bowls and 1 gravy boat. For each additional 4–6 people, you'll need another serving set (platter, bowls, gravy boat). For a self-service buffet, 2 place settings per guest will insure you against having to run around gathering up and washing dishes. At stand-up receptions, provide 3 glasses per person.

17 Things
that
Make Your
Party
Sparkle

# Color

Color gives your decorating its direction, though too many colors can be over stimulating. If you place pastels next to a Turkish carpet, you're asking for a major visual collision. So first determine the tones of your floors, walls, curtains, furniture and pictures. Then you can match your decorations accordingly, tone for tone (for example, light turquoise with dark or bright colors with subdued), in contrasts (such as turquoise with red-orange), or neighboring colors in the spectrum (turquoise with green or blue). It might help you to know that red, orange, yellow and gold warm; blue, white and silver refresh; green and purple warm or cool depending on the shade. Also: red stimulates, yellow cheers, orange evokes hunger, blue awakens and violet casts a spell.

# Clothing

If you're wearing something nice, your whole party will look better. A bright, summery t-shirt that fits in with the pool theme will help you feel like a star—it gives you that relaxed yet excited party feeling. (Just remember that it's your guests who are the true stars of the party!) If you know your guests and they know what to expect, there's no problem. But if you want to invite people to a Hollywood pool party and receive them in an evening gown, you have to prepare them ahead of time; otherwise it is just plain weird. Another taboo would be soiled or ripped clothing—not the message you want to send. But what's really bad is receiving guests in your stocking feet and calling out, "Take off your shoes!" (What if some of them have holey socks?)

# Theme

A theme makes partying and decorating easier. On the one hand, there are obvious themes like "Everything's Coming up Roses" with raspberry mousse and sparkling rosé on a salmon-colored tablecloth, plus red rose petals and homemade pink confetti. Obviously, this type of theme can mean a lot of work. You might be better off with something like a "Greek Wine Festival." Most of us already have white walls, so drape a few sea-blue sails from the ceiling and over the table, wear a white shirt, light the candles and you're done! Even simpler is a "Welcome Spring" party. Open the windows, put tulips all around, play a CD of nature sounds such as birds chirping and wear something pretty, bright and new.

# Windows

Windows let in light during the day, which is great as long as it doesn't blind your guests with too much brightness. In the evening, however, windows can have the appearance of black holes. Though closing the curtains helps, it can also cause feelings of claustrophobia. Solve the problem by hanging transparent fabric from curtain rods or by attaching pretty objects such as flowers to your curtains to liven up the party. Depending on the size and location of the windows, you can use a windowsill as a bar, buffet, counter, seat or smoking area, in which case you'll need to clear it off; then set it up so everyone will understand how to use the space.

# Walls

Everybody has the right to decorate their own four walls however they see fit, but that doesn't mean that people want to look at your baby pictures or appointment calendar during a party. A host who takes down the eight photos of sunsets from previous vacations and replaces them with eight posters of bullfights lets you know that this tapas party is destined to be really special. For an even stronger effect, you can disguise your walls with colorful fabric, plastic or paper. If you suspend fabric from nails or on cords, you can also hide a few pieces of furniture behind them. The illusion is complete when you create new walls, hallways and rooms—but only if your apartment or house is large enough to do this.

# Ceiling

Once people run out of things to say and start gazing off toward the ceiling, your party is doomed. Experienced entertainers never let it get that far. They put up a sort of "false ceiling" for whenever conversation threatens to die down. Transform your high-ceilinged, neon-lighted entryway into a cozy corner with a swatch of fabric. Or, when you hang fabric from two broom handles suspended from the ceiling using hooks, your combination kitchen-dinner table becomes a prince's banquet table under a canopy. More trouble but fascinating—lots of colorful, glittery, funny touches like homemade banners or flypaper with sequins suspended from the ceiling—but not directly above the table (so it doesn't get in the food).

# Table

The best table is one that's big enough. Each person's space should be at least 2' wide, plus an extra half foot for meals that include bread and butter or salad plates and a number of glasses. They'll also need about $1\frac{1}{2}'$ from the edge of the table to the center and a gap of about $1\frac{1}{2}'$ between their setting and the area of the person across from them. For soup bowls or bread baskets, the middle zone has to be at least twice as wide. This means, for example, that a table for six must be at least 3'x 5' if not 3.5'x 6'. The best is often a round table, which makes it easy for everyone to join in the conversation, and with a diameter of 4.5' it'll provide plenty of room for eight.

# Candles

Even the dullest small-town pizza joint looks more charming in candlelight, so make sure to capitalize on this for your evening dinner party. Just make sure the candles don't flicker at eye level. To prevent this, use tall candlestick holders and taper candles. Don't set candles on a slanted surface or near a draft or the wax will drip. Tea lights and small candles are cute, but make sure they're in a fireproof candle-holder. Also, they're not good on the dinner table because of people reaching across them. Candles should only augment, not replace, electrical lighting (so people can see). But the cardinal rule is: NEVER burn scented candles during the meal!

# Fabric

A beautiful piece of fabric can turn two sawhorse and a sheet of plywood into a table fit for a king if you let it hang 2' over the edges. It looks even better if you use two pieces of fabric, one brightly colored and patterned hanging to the floor and a quieter, plain piece of fabric on top serving as a tablecloth. This second piece could stop at the edges, hang to the floor at each end, serve as a narrow runner or even be two bands of cloth that cross in the middle. If using a makeshift table, place a large piece of felt or thick cloth underneath to soften the hard, rickety impression of the board itself. This is even more important if you cover it with only one cloth. If you have a nice wooden table already, maybe all that's needed are some thick, attractive cloth placements.

## Invitations

Even people with whom you have a near-telepathic relationship appreciate a good, old-fashioned, written invitation. It's even nicer if it's unique. There's nothing original about e-mails or faxes, which is why they tend to look like announcements for an ordering-out-for-pizza office party. Black ink on heavy white parchment makes people think of black cocktail dresses and starched white shirts. Colored inks on kraft paper give a more casual feeling. Although the invitation should be creative, don't go too far or it loses its purpose (invite and inform). Enigmatic can work as long as it heightens anticipation and doesn't obscure the facts, which are: who is celebrating, what, how, where, exactly when, who can come and where they can get in touch with you ahead of time.

## Menu

"What's to eat?" "You'll see." That's not very nice, nor does it inspire confidence or sound particularly promising. If you prepared something wonderful for the party, write it out so guests have something to look forward to—plus, it's a conversation piece. It doesn't have to be on paper—you can also write menus on cardboard boxes, palm leaves, felt pennants, disposable tablecloths, or inexpensive dish towels. You'll need one menu for every four people. For a large number of guests or a simple meal, write everything on a chalkboard in bistro fashion, or with soap or lipstick on a mirror or window. But always limit it to the essentials—you don't want to give *everything* away!

## Place Cards

If you're serving spaghetti for two, you don't need place cards. For a four-course dinner for 12 people who barely know each other, however, they lessen confusion and add to the pleasure. If guests know each another fairly well, first names are enough or cards may even seem strange and you'd be better off without them. If guests are not yet acquainted, the cards should include first and last names in large lettering. Never use titles. "Mr." and "Ms." are only used in a group of strangers. Make sure you use the same form of address for everyone. And then there are the portable place cards in the form of name tags for walk-around-and-mingle parties.

## Doors

Isn't it great when the party mood is already established at the door? When, instead of "Johnson", the doorbell is labeled with a snazzy "Brick House" to invite guests to a seventies disco party on the top floor. Or when a different colored light bulb shines on every landing and the glow makes the climb all the more beautiful. Or when a handsome doorman waits at the top and gladly ushers guests through a door hung with glamour graffiti posters, granting entrance to Studio 54. Or when all the doors inside (except the bathroom door) have been taken off their hinges and used as buffet tables, and curtains of flashing, glittery foil strips hang in the doorways. Or when a silvery sprig of mistletoe hangs over the doorway that says, "Plant one on me."

# 17 Things that Make Your Party Sparkle

## Chairs

A throw pillow can turn an ordinary chair into a comfy armchair and a crate with cushions into a Bedouin throne. A bench can serve the purpose of four chairs. A board on two crates makes a bench and when you cover it with cushions and cloth, it can even become a sofa. The sofa that you had to move when you extended the dining table can transform your entryway into a salon or the kitchen into a coffee-house. Patio chairs make your living room into an exotic island; cushions instead of chairs make it into a cave. Wide chairs make tables seem narrower. A bring-your-own-chair party can be fun. No fun at all: not enough chairs.

## Nature

A good meal can transform natural elements into civilized dishes. Leaves become salad, potatoes become croquettes and apples form the basis for a cake. This also applies to décor: grass mats can be used as charger plates, a pumpkin becomes a centerpiece and river gravel sits in for chopstick holders. Dried cornstalks at the apartment building's entrance are an excellent indicator of the Thanksgiving feast on the 3rd floor; a couple of kumquats, limes and chiles scattered across the tablecloth are an apt centerpiece for an Asian party. But always be sure to keep inedible nature items separate from the food, and decorate only with objects that won't be missed if you take them away from their natural surroundings.

## Garnish

Whatever is put on a plate is to be eaten, regardless of where you place it. If you really want to lick up minced parsley, then go ahead and scatter them around the edges of the plate. If you happen to like nibbling on thyme sprigs and never eat your fish without raw bell pepper strips, feel free to use them as garnish. But when you invite guests, consider something more like the following: add whole parsley leaves at the last minute to fish fillets browned in thyme butter with sautéed diced red and yellow bell peppers. Pile it up on a deep plate, trickle juice from the frying pan over it and top it off with a small dollop of sour cream—then hands off! Put it right on the table. Wanna bet that the plate will come back clean?

## Outdoors

There's nothing like fresh air and sunshine for decorations at a dinner party. When you have them, even a tiny balcony seems superior to the ballroom of a grand hotel—most guests prefer a babbling brook to a cascading champagne glass pyramid. Of course it's even better to have the champagne AND a babbling brook because that little bit of civilization can enhance your love of nature, as does the picnic blanket that protects you from bugs or is suspended as an awning. Kerosene lanterns can help brighten darkness, gloomy weather and even illuminate mosquitoes (now get a citronella candle to make them go away!). A wicker chair in the grass can make you feel like the lord of all you survey.

# Throwing a Party

"I can't wait!" For what? "To try your cheese skewers!!" That reminds me of something...

The last days and hours before a party are always the most frantic. Writing a grocery list for your favorite produce market, estimating beer consumption, purchasing wine, informing the neighbors, clearing out the refrigerator and answering the phone: "Oh, hi Peter. No, there's no problem if you get here a little late on Saturday, but we're having cheese skewers as an appetizer."

Then you curse your favorite produce market for the hard mangos, start preparing the ratatouille, wonder if Barb and Carl are going to fight again, get mom's elderberry syrup out of the cellar—you deserve a drink.

Finally, "Oh, Peter, so you're here already! That's right, the last shall be first. My cheese skewers?" Ummm...

# Planning
## the Drinks

You can survive for quite a while without food, but you can't entertain without drinks because drinks are what jump start the party. Fortunately, the vintners and brewers have done most of your work for you already. All you have to do is bring home the bottles, although...

Party drinking is different from everyday drinking. You have more people in the house with different preferences, lots of energy, things to eat, a certain kind of weather, a particular time of day, the party itself—sparkling water alone just won't do. Is it starting to sound expensive? You can simplify it. Once again, be basic. Make the most important decisions about drinks before you go shopping, including whether your guests are of a legal age to make their own decisions. And then don't give them too many choices—but make the choices good ones. It's like a stellar web page: If you know what you'll find there after only a few clicks, you feel relieved and comfortable. And if the contents are right, you're happy to stay.

Back to the party—there has to be both alcoholic and non-alcoholic drinks. "Alcoholic" includes wine and beer, certainly. For wine, you should have a red and a white. For beer, offer one or two kinds such as an import and maybe something from a local micro-brewery. "Non-alcoholic" means first of all water and sparkling water, plus sparkling juices and soft drinks. That's all you need as far as the wine, beer and soft drink drinks are concerned. Then there's plenty of room for extras—something bubbly for openers, liquor and liqueurs for later, the basics for cocktails, coffee and tea. To estimate how much of each, refer to the front inside flap of this book.

## One Good Wine for All Instead of a Little Something for Everyone

If you're smart, you will shop early and leave your last day open for cooking. But what's not so smart is placing a something-for-everyone assortment of wines on the buffet. It gives the impression that you're trying to clean out your cabinet and even if you include a few good bottles with the rest, people may be disappointed because these will be emptied first. It's better to pick out a wine you like and buy multiple bottles. You can't go wrong with a wine that's pleasant to drink, neither bone dry nor headachy sweet, nothing to die for but nothing to make you grimace either. For wines, try to shoot for $10 and above and for champagnes, $20 and above (that said, if you know of a great wine that's less expensive, go for it). Research wine magazines and books for ratings if you're feeling anxious.

## Chill!

As the party approaches, you'll need to make the drinks drinkable, especially those that foam, fizz or bubble. This means one day of chill-time. But what if your refrigerator is full of party food? Invite your nice neighbors in exchange for the use of their refrigerator or bug your friends. (A second refrigerator from a rummage sale would come in handy at this point.) You can put bottles in the freezer 1–2 hours before the party starts and then move them to the emptied refrigerator 30 minutes beforehand (set a timer!). Or make giant ice cubes in square containers and, 1 hour before the party, fill a tub with cold water about a hand's width deep, stand the bottles in it and put the ice in between. For wine, refrigerator temperature is too cold for drinking. Take young, dry wines and full-bodied, smooth wines out of the refrigerator $1/2$ hour before serving. Remove full-bodied dry, semidry, rosé and light, fresh red wines

1 hour ahead of time. Open full-bodied reds 1 hour before drinking. (Red wines should be served at a temperature of around 65 degrees—the temperature of old-fashioned cellars.)

# Drinking at a Basic Party

Scorpio birthday, 20-person basic party in a tiny apartment with a small balcony at 40°F. The refrigerator contains self-service beer as well as water and white wine for later. On the kitchen counter, a white and a red wine are open and will soon be ready for serving, plus water, juice, 20 wine glasses and 20 drinking glasses. Twenty coffee cups and glasses are stacked behind the cupboard door for later. The kitchen table stands next to the kitchen door and holds a terracotta pot (chills well) full of salted ice cubes (chills even better) containing bottles of alcoholic French cider, sparkling juices and waters. Next to this stand another 20 wine glasses and the elderberry syrup await for making the aperitif. The balcony is also used for chilling beverages.

The party starts and some aperitif glasses have been filled—a Kir Normand made from the French cider and syrup, and Elderberry Spritzers (sparkling water and syrup) for the designated drivers. Nobody asks for anything else just yet but if they do, they are given instructions on how to serve themselves. Also: jockey from the balcony to the refrigerator to the kitchen

table/counter to the glasses, keep glasses ready for guests (sometimes means washing and drying) and provide coffee and after-dinner drinks. This is a lot to keep track of so it's a good idea to enlist the aid of an assistant.

# Drinking at a Basic Dinner Party

Cousins visiting from Europe, six-person 4-course basic dinner party in a small apartment with a balcony. For the aperitif, you don't need a home cocktail bar but you can offer a number of choices. Something bubbly as a standard opener (or save the bubbly for dessert), a light white wine, a spritzer or other non-alcoholic option. Or be Provençal and try Pastis mixed with water or a chilled small glass of Muscat de Beaumes de Venise. Drinking then continues at the table with wine—the general rule is to serve white before red, light before hearty, young before aged and sparkling before full-bodied. For a basic dinner party, this means one white for lip-smacking and one red for swooning—then match your food accordingly. You can serve wine in restaurant style, pouring from the right glass to the left, one wine at a time. Remove the white wine glasses when you serve the red (provided the guest wants red).

Or, consider placing both bottles on the table and letting guests serve themselves—a more relaxing way. Letting the guests decide which wine to drink with which course is fine if both wines fit the menu. The color of the wine and food is less important than the cooking style. Full-bodied, aged wines go with full-bodied, slow-cooked dishes such as stews. Buttery, mellow wines go with creamy dishes. Young, sparkling wines or light dry wines go with rapidly stir-fried foods. In the case of acidic, fruity or sweet foods, you're better off with beer or water. The meal is followed by coffee and after-dinner drinks to stimulate and satisfy, which means they should be of the highest quality: strong espresso, a refreshing fruit brandy, a masculine whiskey, a soothing cognac.

# Preparing the Food

Now the waiter becomes the chef. The food is being prepared—lovingly, carefully and tastefully, of course, but above all intelligently because without intelligence, all the cooking in the world can't help. And without food, there's no party!

## The Well-Styled Menu: No Repetitions

If your guests rejoice over the first course, ask the name of the second, stare out the window with the third and fall asleep over their coffee, what do you suppose is missing? A little menu planning, that's what, as well as more variety, more time spent with the guests instead of in the kitchen and something less heavy on the plates. Learn from the great chefs. They know that their food is only part of the celebration—the part that livens up the rest.

Four courses is a good average for a dinner party at home—cold appetizer, soup or a warm appetizer, main course and dessert. Family-style meals and buffets follow a similar pattern. For a wonderful evening from start to finish, follow the "no repetitions" rule of menu planning. In other words, don't serve more than one dish with the same main ingredients such as poultry, zucchini or

potatoes, even if you deep-fry them in one and purée them in another. For instance, don't follow up a creamy soup with meat sautéed in a cream sauce and don't serve blue cheese pizza before a camembert soufflé.

Which brings us to preparation styles. The same rule applies: serve only one course that is baked, boiled, braised, fried, stir-fried, grilled, deep-fried, bruléed, marinated or raw. That's not difficult if there are only three or four courses. For a buffet, the rule isn't as strictly applied. Even a Mediterranean menu is more interesting if everything isn't covered in olive oil and garlic. What you need is a unifying theme that binds together a large number of individual parts in one perfect meal. For instance, base your menu on a region or even a season—rejuvenation in spring, refreshment in summer, fortification in the fall or warmth in winter. Or build the dinner around a particular style—rustic or sophisticated, ethereal or down-to-earth. Keep away from extremes such as all rich, all substantial, all spicy. Everything should go well together on a single plate. If you've ever eaten pasta (starch, cooked) with pesto (herbs, raw) and celery-root chips (vegetable, fried), you know what we mean. (It's good.)

## Taking Time Earlier Saves Time Later

Another rule known to the pros: don't try to achieve the impossible. Six servings of rare saddle of venison with a cranberry hollandaise sauce not only tastes as bad as it sounds but stresses out even the professional chef. The recipes in Party Basics are an antidote to this problem, in particular because we give you suggestions such as "Preparation: the night before." Foods that need to be prepared just before the party include any that are supposed to be crispy or airy, are sensitive or fragile, can become watery or soggy, contain raw onions or raw eggs, or don't do well in the refrigerator.

If you know the menu, you can write out a complete shopping list sufficiently ahead of time. Buying every-

thing the day before is about as intelligent and relaxing as doing all your Christmas shopping on Christmas Eve. What if your favorite produce market fails you and the mangos for your tart are as hard as rocks? Do you make apricot tart? You won't have to if you buy the mangos far enough ahead of time. Anything on the supermarket shelves—whatever doesn't need refrigerating and can't dry out—can be bought a week or more ahead of time. You can purchase hardy vegetables and fruits such as carrots and apples 3–4 days ahead, and supermarket bread (not artisan loaves) and refrigerated goods such as roasted meats, tender vegetables, lettuce, herbs, cheese and other dairy products 2–3 days ahead. Sensitive items such as fish, sliced meat, and poultry should be purchased no more than 1 day ahead and don't pick up the ground meat, fresh French bread and rolls until the very day. Then you'll be free to start cooking and more relaxed for hosting.

# Preparing Food for a Basic Buffet

To eat: Buffet full of skewers, dips, breads, various appetizers, stuffed foods, marinated foods, substantial salads such as a pasta variety, cheeses, cold roasted meats

The day before: Marinate and bake what you can; prepare fillings, creams and dips; prepare items to be chilled; make dessert

Earlier on the party day: Marinate tender items; bake or deep-fry crispy items; cut up cold foods; fill and garnish bowls for buffet

During the last hour: Remove cheese, butter and spreads from refrigerator; prepare cold platters (keep some in reserve!); place bowls of food on buffet (keep some in reserve!)

Just before starting: Put remaining dishes on buffet; slice bread and add to buffet

When the party starts: Open the buffet; help guests; refill bowls and platters

# Preparing Food for a Basic Dinner Party

The multi-course menu: Terrine (or other appetizer) and salad; soup; main course: roast with side dish of pasta and vegetables; dessert.

The day before: Make terrine; clean lettuce; prepare any sauces, stocks and hearty soup bases (transfer to refrigerator in container); cut up firm vegetables—briefly parboil then rinse in cold water; marinate the roast; make dessert.

Earlier on the party day: Remove terrine from mold; make salad dressing; prepare ingredients to be added to soup; do any remaining chopping; put roast in the oven.

During the last hour: Cook pasta used as a side dish until al dente, rinse under cold water, sprinkle with oil and cover with plastic.

Just before starting: Slice terrine and if you can, transfer to individual plates, cover and refrigerate; do the same with the dessert. Group prepared ingredients by courses; Heat soup, heat sauce(s) and also bring a large pot of water to a boil (for later use, to warm up a colander full of pasta or vegetables); arrange all utensils from wire whisks to tablespoons so they're accessible.

When the party starts: When the doorbell rings, remove terrine plates from the refrigerator. For the first course, dress salad—then serve with terrine (meanwhile, heat up soup). 2nd course: Serve soup (remove roast from oven and let stand). 3rd course: Place pasta and/or vegetables in a colander and immerse in hot water, drain, toss with butter, salt and pepper and other herbs and seasonings. Slice roast. Serve sliced meat with pasta and vegetables, along with sauce(s). Dessert course: garnish and serve.

# Let's
# Party

It's all rehearsal until the curtain goes up, both in theater and at parties. The show must go on. So put away your makeup mirror, crib notes and stage fright. Turn on the spotlight and let the performance begin. It's great to have you all here because I, too, am now HERE.

## I'm Here

Do whatever you have to do in the moment to be present, focused on your guests. In other words, be well prepared and then let go of your worries when the party starts.

This includes scheduling at least a 15-minute break well before the party starts. Even better, make it last a half an hour or more. Banish all thoughts of "But I still have to…" Look around to make sure the most important tasks are done, including getting dressed. Then take a break. Be with yourself. If you're calm, your guests will be calm. You say you can't do it? Then go over the list of guests in your head while you sit—play the party through in your mind and make a note of possible tricky moments. And make yourself a drink. Test out the house cocktail or sip espresso and walk around and think of the good parts, like your favorite guests. Does it sound too good to be true? Trust us, you'll be so cheerful when you greet your guests that everything will take care of itself.

## It's Great to Have You Here

Now the doorbell rings and the hosts open the door. Greet your guests and use the aperitif as bait to lure them away from the door (if it's chilly, take their coats to the designated spot). It's great if more than one person is answering the door and handling coats, offering drinks, and such.

If you don't recognize the person at the door (guest of a co-host? friend of another guest?) and nobody tells you who they are, introduce yourself. If the party is small enough, always introduce the guests to one another as well. For etiquette on polite introductions, refer to the back inside flap under "Greeting." There you'll also learn that it's easier to make introductions one at a time. In addition to names, it's also good to provide a few basic details such as how you two know each other, or the person's career or hobbies. It flatters the one introduced and hooks the interest of the other person— you'll also give them both some ideas for small talk.

## Have You Already Met?

Large parties soon get out of hand because the hosts have so much to attend to. Just be sure to keep the door in sight so you'll spot any new arrivals. If anyone gets by you, say hello as soon as you see them. One way or another, make sure they find their way to drinks, food, the bathroom and the ultimate goal: "Have you met…?"

And pretty soon these new guests will begin greeting the next new guests, will quickly discover what they have in common, and everyone will be thinking, "It's really nice to be here."

Bringing together a group of people who have a good time together is the host's greatest joy. So when making out a guest list, think about who would get along with whom and why. If you invite people over often, you can allow yourself a change in the lineup and leave out the usual invitees. A pleasant side-effect of having frequent parties is that it's the best way to train for winning the title of "Host of the Season." In addition to good housekeeping, this prize is also awarded on the basis of superior knowledge (for instance, knowing that outgoing Cora comes from the same town as shy Alfred, that Ernie and Eugene are both football fans but of opposing teams, that handsome Henry is a software engineer and Nancy is just dying to learn more about technology and that a movie opened yesterday that all the newspapers are raving about). If you know your guests and know what they know, you can provide the most important fuel for any party—conversation.

## Let's Have Some Good Conversation

A party will be long remembered when its conversation moves from greetings to small talk to dialog then finally to deeper discussions. As will the party (unfortunately)

where the hosts, once again, spent the whole time talking only about themselves. So let's not do that. Instead, give your attention to the people who don't say very much, those you don't often get a chance to talk to, or those you're talking to for the first time. Let your closest friends wait. If they really are good friends, they'll take part in the general conversation and seek to include others. They'll also help you if the topic of conversation becomes uncomfortable and needs to be changed. In general, if you aren't able to change a dangerous topic, your only choice is to declare a clear "halt." It's better to offend one or two guests than to ruin the whole party.

The purpose of seating arrangements is to bring people together for more focused conversation. With six people, this can be as simple as saying "Please sit next to me"; for a 12-person table, use place cards. Again, try to keep it simple: seat people together who have common interests but don't generally spend time together. Try not to seat old colleagues or close relatives next to each other. As hosts, set the example for your guests so no one will have reason to complain. Keep in mind that when the guest count hits 8, smaller conversation groupings form—it's nice when the host can keep these from being "clique" oriented.

## Take It Easy, See You Later

Does the party end when the last guests decide to leave or when the first guests start yawning? It's best if the hosts take charge and set a time limit beforehand. Keep the dinner itself within a certain time frame and allow the guests enough time to leave in a state of satisfaction. If it starts droning on, you'll have to put an end to it yourself. Don't make it too abrupt; be sure to let your guests know that you're really glad they came and that now it's time to go. Don't let them wash dishes or straighten up; just say "Let us take care of that. Go home and get some rest—this was our treat." If anyone is just starting to warm up or has something they absolutely have to discuss right this minute, say, "Sorry, too late." If anyone thinks you ought to get together again soon, say "Great! Let's talk about it tomorrow." If anyone says we ought to do this more often, say "We'd love to! We'll look forward to your invitation. See you at the next party!"

# 16
## Dinner Parties
### from around the
## World

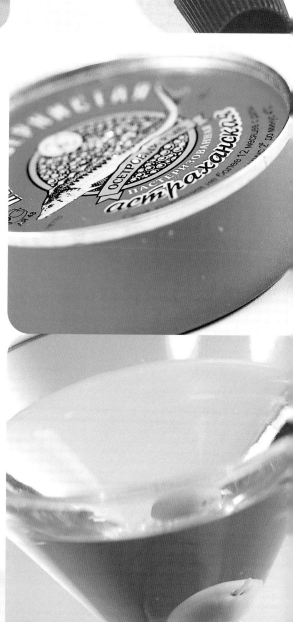

## Germany
### Coffee

Drinking coffee is a German family tradition that comes halfway between the pleasant post-lunch stupor and the period of satisfied contentment felt just before the smaller evening meal. The reason people feel satisfied before dinner is that coffee in Germany is almost always accompanied by cake, especially in villages where the farmwife treats the cake table as a sort of catwalk on which she may parade a Black Forest cake, a marble cake or a Bee Sting cake for each guest. Standard fare in southern Germany is coffee with sugar and milk followed by Schnapps. A special exception exists in northern Germany in the form of its most famous coffee drink, the Pharisee—a shot of rum in coffee beneath a hood of whipped cream.

## Italy
### Lunch

Even though in Rome more and more people are expected to live on tramezzini at noon during the work week, the holidays still belong to the "pranzo," the extended Italian lunch. After the aperitivo come a few antipasti or insalata, followed by the pasta (or risotto, polenta, etc.) or maybe only soup, rarely both and more frequently the two in one (pasta in broth). Then it's time for the main course, a piece of fish or meat with side dishes that may also be served afterwards or not at all (you've already had pasta and salad). Then cheese or dessert or fruit and finally caffé and perhaps a little drink—mamma mia, it's already dark out!

## Australia
### Barbecue

Since the weather down under is nicer than in England, Australians were able to expand the picnic culture of the British immigrants and hold barbecues on the lawn. Today barbecues usually stand in backyards or are permanently installed at favorite locations such as beaches and children's playgrounds. If Australians want to arrange a quick dinner or if it's Christmas time, they say "Let's have a barbie" (a "man thing", traditionally with a beer bottle in one hand) and "Bring a plate" (a "woman thing" meaning, will you make a salad?). Traditionally, barbies are for grilling beef and lamb as well as sausages and onions, but more recently seafood and Asian-style marinated poultry have begun to make an appearance.

## Thailand
### Banquet

As was once the case in Europe, royal Thailand prefers to exhibit its treasures at banquets (known in America as family-style meals). Since there aren't any courses, all the riches of Thai cuisine converge on the table at once. There may be smaller, cold items to start, such as stuffed salad rolls, which can then be followed by satay skewers and peanut sauce, fish cakes or all kinds of shrimp soups and a variety of spices, accompanied by stir-fry from the wok, sweet and sour spareribs or curries made with coconut milk, all of which give flavor to the steamed rice. Fried noodles, salads and sweets such as sticky rice in banana leaves and exotic fruits round out the feast fit for a king and queen.

## Japan
### Chado

Being invited to a tea ceremony is a real honor because it means you're being shown a great deal of respect. Chado isn't just about tea, it's about the "Way of Tea." It starts with the guests crawling through the entrance to the tearoom (kai = respect) where they examine the flowers, utensils and their fellow drinkers in a set ritual (wa = harmony) before following the established route to the tea master (sei = purity). He then whisks the green tea made of macha powder using ritual movements and utensils until the tea is foamy and serves it. Once the guests have also partaken of the tea in accordance with the rules, the way is clear for jaku (tranquility).

## France
### Menu

Like the "restaurant," the "menu" was invented by the French and has come to be associated with fine dining throughout the world. In the 19th century, it replaced the overflowing jumble of bowls and platters on the banquet table with single dishes ordered a la carte. Equality for all! But what an equality—trout confit as an "amuse gueule" (appetizer), brioche salad with duck liver as an entrée, then a loup de mer fillet (sea bass) followed by leg of lamb au gratin, Roquefort accompanied by a shot of dessert wine and crème brulée with ginger. In other words, esprit, bistro, bourgeoisie, nouvelle cuisine, haute cuisine, ooh la la! (Ideal for formal dinners as well as Sunday dinners "en famille".)

## England
### Picnic

Is it any wonder that the country with the least number of sunny days makes eating outdoors into a party? The British picnic is an institution that shows England and its cuisine in its best light. British picnics are tastefully uncomplicated (on a checked blanket on the lawn, even the Earl of Somewhere-or-Other appears much more laid back), sociably organized (originally, a picnic was simply a gathering to which guests each brought food), and delicious (as the picnic classics—sandwiches, pies and pickles—testify). Australians go one step further with a sporting "chicken & champagne" at the races (chicken eaten with your fingers while drinking champagne).

## Israel
### Purim Pastries

Although Purim originated in Persia, it's celebrated by Jewish people all over the world in a manner similar to the European Carnival, with masks, playacting, a lot of drinking and sweet pastries. These pastries may resemble a doughnut but are more typically filled pastry "pockets." In Israel, their filling is as colorfully varied as the inhabitants. There they have "Hamantaschen," whose fillings of plum jelly, cheese, walnuts, almonds or poppy seeds reflect their Eastern European background. But Turkish böreks, Indian samosas and even ravioli have also been served at Purim. According to the tradition, food (preferably something sweet such as pastries and candy) is shared with relatives, friends and the poor.

## Turkey
### Raki Table

For a traditional Turkish dinner party, you must have lots of time and lots of food – and drink (R is the Turkish national alcohol—anise-flavored "Mez(z)es x menu + raki = raki table" is the formula for this celebration. The result can be (1) cold mezes such as marinated beans, cucumb with yogurt, tomato salad with mint, sweet car with nuts, dips; (2) warm mezes such as stuffe vegetables, filled pastries and rolls, spicy pancak (3) various main courses with fish, meat, poult (4) side dishes with vegetables, noodles, rice; soup to aid digestion; (6) something (very) swe (7) fruit; (8) Turk Kahvesi (Turkish coffee with pulized coffee and sugar brewed together in a co pot)—and raki with water before, during and a

# 16
# Dinner Parties
## from around the
# World

## Spain
### Tapas

Although, today, Spain's contribution to finger food is more commonly eaten in the evening at home, tapas supposedly originated as a Sunday lunch. As the story goes, Sundays after church the women immediately retreated to their kitchens and the men to the bars, the former to cook Sunday dinner and the latter to tide themselves over with wine and a few small plates. Since then, interests in churches, cooking and bars have changed but tapas continue to be the prelude to something special. Another thing that has remained the same is the focus on "cosas de picar" (finger food, like olives), "pinchos" (skewers and bite-sized fork food) and "cazuelas" (for spooning or dipping, often warm bite-sized chunks with sauce in an earthenware pot).

## Scandinavia
### Brød

In the far north, bread is called Brød. That's nice, but what does it have to do with a dinner party? We need only say Smørrebrød, Smørbrød and Smørgåsbord, the Danish, Norwegian and Swedish equivalents of "feast until you're satisfied." Especially in Norway and Denmark, heavy bread spread with delicious butter is the basis for many sandwiches that often include fish and frequently a little sugar. The Swedes take it even further and add platefuls of small, elegant, cold appetizers to the Smørgåsbord, a word that, all over the world, has come to mean "cold buffet." And this is exactly how it's served, sometimes as open-faced sandwiches already made and sometimes with plates of ingredients for people to make their own.

## Middle East
### Mezze

The Middle East stretches across three seas and two continents, with its two poles of Arabic-Mediterranean cuisine located in Morocco and Lebanon. What the entire region has in common is "Mezzes," which are not only appetizers, but a party in themselves. A table filled with mezzes shows that the hosts went to a great deal of trouble in the kitchen. This is a special honor for guests, who gladly dip their flatbread into hummus (tahini dip) or a spicy lentil mixture, spread bread slices with tabbouleh (bulgur salad) and pop falafel (tiny garbanzo bean balls) into their mouths, preferably with their fingers and always using the clean right hand.

## Russia
### Zakuska

We sail across the tundra as the sleigh runners throw up a spray of snow crystals in the late afternoon light and the shadows of the birches slowly lengthen. Ah, there it is, the Dacha of Doctor Ivanigor. Lights twinkle behind the window panes—is it possible? Yes! In the middle of the hall stands the large table with the doctor's steaming samovar surrounded by pitchers full of marinated mushrooms, sweet and sour herring, caviar by the spoonful, bowls of pirogi, platters of cold, roasted meast—a genuine zakuska table. And since we aren't interested in getting warm, Ivanigor fetches his home-distilled vodka from the natural refrigerator in the garden. Now the party can begin!

## China
### Dim Sum

Whenever there's a celebration in China's streets, or on Sundays when families want to start the day in a festive mood, Dim Sum is offered at refreshment stands or Yum Cha restaurants. In the latter, customers are seated at large round tables and surrounded by trays full of steamed delicacies covered in pastry from which they can take whatever they like—fine ground pork with mushrooms and shrimp in a transparent wrapping, grilled meat with sesame rolled in a rice noodle pastry, sweet lotus paste buns. Besides these Dim Sum prepared in a steamer, other specialties are also available, such as pot stickers or braised chicken feet. And don't forget the tea!

## Mexico
### Pan de Muertos

What sounds so classy in Spanish is actually "Day of the Dead bread" in English and goes with one of the most colorful celebrations in Mexico, the "Días de los Muertos," the equivalent of All Saints' or All Souls' Days, or even Halloween. All over Mexico, people prepare the favorite foods of their dead and take them to the cemetery, where public festivals often add an aroma of grills and the lively clamor of bands. The family then holds a quiet picnic on the grave, heartily inviting the souls visiting on this day to join them. A main attraction is the "pan de muertos," a sweet loaf of yeast bread decorated with dough shaped like bones or meringue. ¡Vivan los muertos!

## USA
### Happy hour

Let's get this straight. We're not talking about late afternoons where sophisticated ladies and gentlemen stand around in salons with champagne flutes and canapés. We mean the "real thing" that resulted when immigrants to the New World took the tradition of five o'clock tea from the Old World and turned it upside-down, mixing hard liquor from all over the world into strong colorful cocktails and then "let themselves go" for just a little while. The happy hour was born. Happy hour involves hearty finger food (as spicy and substantial as possible)—but not always great for the waistline!

# The Recipes

# Finge

Welcome to the World of Self-Indulgence...

# r Food

A mom is trying to feed her kid oatmeal by a spoon. "By myself!" the near-toddler cries as she plunges her little hands straight into the bowl, resulting in a gooey mess. Some parents would shudder and react, "Yuck, stop that!" But the best of parents don't mind one bit, knowing their child is having a good time eating. They cherish the thought.

For us bigger kids, "By myself!" means finger food. That's why parties make us feel like we're back home visiting mom, who always has food waiting, eager to thrust something delicious into our hands. The best hosts are like good parents: they put their worries aside and make sure everyone's happy. They know what friends want and when they want it. So what is it party guests want? Food and fun! With skewers and wraps, chips and dips, and meatballs and finger sandwiches, how can you go wrong?

# Finger art

Finger food means a buffet-style party where everybody's hands are full of food and drink. This is fine for a group of good friends, even if it's hard to find a place to set down a wine glass or greasy meatball plate. But it's not so good when you want to shake hands with the Secretary of State and the meatballs get in your way or when you go to wave to the camera and then end up appearing in all the newspapers sloshing red wine in the Vice President's face.

Never fear—there's a solution: the "One-Handed, Five-Finger Stance." It allows you to hold your plate and stemmed glass in one hand while leaving your other hand free for greeting people or drawing your weapon (also works with martinis). Here's how: hold out your hand with the palm-side up and all five fingers extended. Clamp the stem of the glass between your little and ring fingers, holding it steady. Set the plate on your index and middle fingers and clamp down on it from above with your thumb. To drink, remove the glass from the finger holder, take a sip and put it back. Then you can either greet or fire.

## S.O.S.

### "And you are…?"

Dear Advice Columnist,
Recently I sent out invitations to a witch's gathering and Grizelda showed up with her boyfriend, dressed as Harry Potter no less. "I didn't know it was women only," she says and besides, she thinks that's a dumb idea. Isn't that the ultimate in rude?
Esmerelda from L.A.

### Dear Esmeralda:

You tried to perform the greatest magic trick of all: Hold a unisex party where you separate couples. You won't get that using wishy-washy incantations—you have to say it straight out: "Witches only; warlocks stay home and mind the cave." If all you do is invite friends and relatives, you have to expect them to bring their "other half;" in fact, it would be rude if they didn't. If you don't happen to like someone's partner, let them know over a cup of herbal tea instead. It also works the other way around: If you're invited to a party and have a problem with the invitation, clear it up beforehand. Ask whether you can bring your sister who's in town for the weekend. (Normally that should be OK, unless it's a bridge party or a "family council.") And you should also let your host know if there's someone new in your life.

As for Harry the gatecrasher, should you throw him out? You still have to consider your friend Grizelda. But then there are the feelings of the others who were planning on spending some quality time together. Some of your other options:
1) Sentence Harry to bartender duty,
2) Cast a spell and turn him into a DJ, or
3) Banish him to the children's table. If Grizelda complains, send her back to her cave and keep Harry for the rabbit-out-of-a-hat trick.

# "Hello"

Hello, Ciao, Hola…in any language, just make sure you greet your guests.

| | |
|---|---|
| English | Hello, Hi |
| German | Hallo |
| French | Salut |
| Italian | Ciao, Salve |
| Spanish | Hola |
| Dutch | Hoi |
| Scandinavian | Hei, Hey |
| Portuguese | Olá |
| Hungarian | Szia |
| Turkish | Merhaba |
| Slovenian | Zdravo |
| Hebrew | Shalom |
| Polish | Czesc |
| Swiss | Grüezi |
| Austrian | Habedere |
| Japanese | Konnichiwa |
| But not | My, how you've grown! |

# Lime Fizz

A surefire way to start a successful party is with this homemade drink. This recipe makes enough for 12 partiers. But one note: start on this the night before, or you won't be able to satisfy the thirst.

Rinse 4 limes. For each lime: remove a thin layer of the peel (the zest) without any of the white part; cut in half and squeeze out the juice. Peel a walnut-sized piece of ginger, cut into thin slices and place in a small bowl with the lime zest. Bring 1 cup water to a boil and pour just enough into the bowl to cover the contents. Let steep overnight. To the remaining water, add 1 cup + 2 tablespoons sugar and simmer till it dissolves to create a syrupy liquid; cool. Stir lime juice into the cooled syrup.

The next day, strain the lime-ginger water into the syrup. Mix with about 3 quarts of sparkling water and pour into glasses over ice. Garnish with a slice of lime and drink. Or: Fill a glass with crushed ice, 2 tablespoons of the lime syrup and 2 tablespoons vodka or rum. Add a sprig of mint and fill up with sparkling water (similar to a Mojito). Or: Pour 1 tablespoon lime syrup and 2 tablespoons gin over ice cubes with tonic water. And finally, a lemon fizz: Follow the recipe for lime fizz but use 2–3 lemons instead and leave out the ginger.

# Gimme Five
# for
# Munching

Avoid having your friends say "Don't you have any munchies?" by being prepared. For last minute parties, chips, pretzels and nuts are essentials. But if you don't want your life-long memories to be out of a bag, here are five ideas for homemade snacks that make a statement (enough for four people each):

### Dukkah
For this North African nut-seed mix, brown 1¼ cups sesame seeds, ⅓ cup coriander seeds and ⅓ cup cumin seeds in an ungreased pan until they become aromatic and the sesame seeds turn lightly golden. Remove from pan. Brown about 50 hazelnuts until you can rub off the skins with a cloth. Combine all these ingredients with 1 teaspoon coarse sea salt and ½ teaspoon fresh ground black pepper in a blender or food processor and chop for 5 seconds to achieve a coarse mixture, but don't turn it into a paste. Distribute on small plates along with small dishes of olive oil. Dip pieces of flatbread or baguette first in the oil, then in the dukkah and bite!

### Spicy macadamia nuts
Finely chop or crush 1 dried red chile; work with gloves, omit seeds, and don't touch your eyes! Grind chile with 1 tablespoon fennel seeds. Set aside. In a pan, combine 1 tablespoon ground coriander, 1 tablespoon paprika, 2 tablespoons brown sugar and 2 tablespoons oil. Add a pound of unsalted macadamia nuts or unsalted cashews. Cook over low heat for 5 minutes while stirring until the nuts are coated with the spice mixture. Sprinkle chile-fennel powder on nuts (stirring to evenly coat) until hotness suits your taste.

### Wonton chips
Take 20 (6" square) egg roll wrappers and pat dry; separate dough wrappers, cut into eighths and deep fry in 350°F oil (use a slotted metal utensil when working with oil) taking care not to overcrowd. Mix 2 tablespoons curry powder with 1 teaspoon salt. Drain fried chips on paper towels and sprinkle with the curry powder-salt mixture to taste. Provide lime wedges and soy sauce for sprinkling on top, sweet-and-sour sauce for dipping (add a few drops of hot chili oil if desired), and place all on the table.

### Welsh Crispbread
Grate 5 ounces cheddar cheese. Melt 3 tablespoons butter and let cool. Mix these ingredients with 1 tablespoon spicy mustard, 1 teaspoon Worcestershire sauce, 1 teaspoon horseradish and 1 egg to form a smooth mixture. Flake apart 3 ounces of canned tuna (preferably olive oil-packed variety). Rinse 8 chive spears; shake dry and chop; mix with tuna. Spread cheese mixture on 8 Wasa crispbread crackers and brown until slightly bubbly under the broiler. Top with a bit of the fish-chive mixture. Sprinkle with a little salt; cut crispbread pieces in half and munch immediately.

### Homemade buttered popcorn
In a pan, heat 3 tablespoons oil. Add 1 kernel unpopped popcorn. As soon as it pops, add ¼ cup popcorn; cover and shake pan every 10 seconds until it really gets going. Then shake constantly until you don't hear any more popping. Remove pan from heat and wait a little to make sure it's really done and that all the kernels have finished popping. Pour popcorn into a bowl. Melt ¼ cup butter; mix with popped corn and add salt to taste. Also tasty with herb or garlic butter and flavored salts.

# Frittata Cubes
No cash?
Have fun anyway!

**Preparation:** Make frittata in the afternoon, 1 or 2 hours before party time; don't skewer with toothpicks until 1 hour before serving
**Storage:** At room temperature covered loosely with plastic wrap if for a short time; best when prepared close to serving time.
**Serve with:** Tomato dip, stuffed mushrooms, marinated vegetables

Makes enough for 4:

1 onion

1 1/4 lb. potatoes (about 3)

3 tablespoons olive oil

6 eggs

Salt, freshly ground black pepper

For skewering with the frittata cubes (and for garnish): sun-dried tomatoes marinated in oil, cherry tomatoes, green or black olives

**1** Peel onion and chop finely. Rinse and peel potatoes, and cut into thin slices; put in salted water to prevent them from turning brown. Pour onto a clean dish towel and pat dry.

**2** In a medium non-stick frypan, heat oil. Add potatoes and onions and brown 6–8 minutes over medium heat, stirring occasionally.

**3** In the meantime, combine eggs with salt and pepper and whisk with a fork until foamy. Redistribute potatoes and onions evenly in the frypan, add a bit of salt and pour eggs over the potatoes. Switch to low heat, cover and cook about 10–15 minutes or until the potatoes are tender. Test by piercing with a knife.

**4** Carefully slide frittata from the pan onto a plate and let cool. Cut into 3/4" cubes and skewer a sun-dried tomato piece, fresh cherry tomato, or pitted olive onto each cube. Arrange on a platter.

Prep time: 40 minutes
Calories per serving: 290

# Chicken Saltimbocca
## Italian for "jumps right into your mouth"

**Preparation:** Fry the night before. Before the party, assemble with other ingredients on toothpicks.
**Storage:** Loosely covered in the refrigerator
**Serve with:** Stuffed tomatoes, vegetable crostini with almonds, calamari salad

Makes enough for 4 (about 40 skewers):

4 chicken breast fillets

10–20 slices prosciutto (or about 7 oz.)

20 fresh sage leaves

Salt, freshly ground black pepper

1 tablespoon butter

1 tablespoon olive oil

For garnish: About 40 cherry tomatoes (smaller the better), marinated chile peppers (such as hot Italian type or pepperoncini), or sun-dried tomatoes in oil

**1** Slice chicken fillets diagonally into slices about 1/4" thick. Cut each slice of prosciutto into 2–4 pieces. Rinse sage and pat dry. Season each slice of chicken with salt and pepper and top with 1 sage leaf. Fold strip of chicken with the sage inside, and wrap in 1 piece of prosciutto.

**2** In a pan, heat butter and oil. Add chicken-prosciutto (saltimbocca) rolls and fry about 5 minutes over medium heat. Turn and brown about another 5 minutes or until chicken is opaque. Remove from pan and let cool. Rinse tomatoes or drain other ingredients and skewer with the saltimbocca rolls on a toothpick.

Prep time: 30 minutes
Calories per serving: 285

# Cheese Skewers
## Not at all skewed

**Preparation:** Morning
**Storage:** In the refrigerator covered loosely with plastic wrap
**Serve with:** Stuffed tomatoes and frittata cubes from previous page

When our parents gave a party, it was considered especially chic to chat while nibbling on Emmenthal cheese and a grape on a plastic toothpick. And if we're honest, we have to admit that we still love it today. It's just a fantastic combo. But try some of the other ideas, too!

Makes enough for 4 (20–30 toothpicks):

About 12 oz. cheese

20–30 pieces of vegetable or fruit

(such as grapes) for skewering on top
**Great pairings:**

Mozzarella bocconcini, cherry tomato and basil leaf

Roquefort or gorgonzola on a quarter of a fig or a piece of melon

Feta cube with an olive or marinated Italian hot chile pepper (from a jar)

Brie or camembert with radishes

Provolone or aged pecorino with sun-dried tomatoes (oil packed type, drained and patted dry)

## A little more work…

…but really good: Heat vegetable or peanut oil to 350°F (use an oil thermometer). Cut about 12 oz. feta cheese into 3/4" cubes. Whisk 2 eggs. First roll feta cubes in 2 tablespoons flour with a dusting of cayenne pepper, then dip in egg to coat. Deep fry in hot oil till golden, remove with a slotted metal spoon, and drain on paper towels. Skewer on toothpicks with grapes, olives or 1 small pepperoncini.

# Vegetable Skewers
## Crudité kebabs!

**Preparation:** No earlier than that morning
**Storage:** Covered in the refrigerator
**Serve with:** Cucumber raita, shrimp dip

Makes enough for 4:

2 tablespoons honey

3 tablespoons grapeseed oil

1 teaspoon sesame oil

1/2 teaspoon chile oil (or to taste)

3 tablespoons soy sauce

8 small radishes or section of daikon radish

1 zucchini

2 large carrots

**1** Combine honey with grapeseed oil, sesame oil, chile oil and soy sauce and mix thoroughly.

**2** Rinse or peel vegetables, clean and slice lengthwise into paper-thin slices. Mix each type in separate bowls with some of the marinade and let stand at least 1 hour. Then pierce and thread on long skewers in alternating colors. Sprinkle with salt and serve.

Prep time: 10 minutes
(+ 1 hour marinating time)
Calories per serving: 145

## Greek Potato Purée
Unbelievably thrifty!

**Preparation:** The night before or in the morning
**Storage:** In a covered bowl in the refrigerator
**Serve with:** Marinated vegetables, cheese rolls, tomato soup

Makes enough for 4:

2 small potatoes (about 10 oz.), 2 cloves garlic

6 pitted black olives, preferably kalamata

$\frac{1}{2}$ cup fresh parsley sprigs

2 tablespoons fresh lemon juice

3 tablespoons olive oil

Salt, freshly ground black pepper

**1** Rinse potatoes and boil skin-on until tender. Let cool briefly, peel and mash finely (with a fork or an electric mixer).

**2** Peel garlic, squeeze through a press and add to potatoes. Chop olives finely (remove any pits first). Rinse parsley and chop finely. Add to mashed potatoes along with $\frac{1}{3}$ cup hot water, lemon juice and oil. Season with salt and pepper. Serve at room temperature or chilled.

Prep time: 40 minutes, half of which you're actually busy
Goes with: Spears of celery root or fennel bulb, breadsticks
Calories per serving: 125

42

## Moroccan Cream Cheese Dip
It's made for crackers

**Preparation:** No more than 2 days ahead
**Storage:** In a covered bowl in the refrigerator
**Serve with:** Beet dip, meatballs, rice salad with pomegranates

Makes enough for 4:

8 oz. cream cheese, room temperature

$\frac{1}{3}$ cup milk

Zest of $\frac{1}{2}$ lemon

About 6 pitted green olives

$\frac{1}{2}$ teaspoon curry powder

Salt, freshly ground black pepper

**1** Mix room temperature cream cheese and milk until creamy. Rinse lemon and dry. Grate off a thin layer of zest of half a lemon. Chop olives very finely.

**2** Stir lemon zest and olives into cream cheese and season with curry powder, salt and pepper.

Prep time: 15 minutes
Goes with: Bell peppers, kohlrabi sticks or slices, crackers
Calories per serving: 150

## Roquefort-Crème Fraiche Dip
Perfect with celery root

**Preparation:** No more than 2 days ahead; don't top with pistachios until you serve
**Storage:** In a covered bowl in the refrigerator
**Serve with:** Stuffed tomatoes, bacon rolls, potato vegetable Niçoise salad

Makes enough for 4:

$3\frac{1}{2}$ oz. Roquefort (blue cheese)

$\frac{1}{2}$ cup crème fraiche or sour cream

2 tablespoons milk or cream

2–3 tablespoons mayonnaise

Salt, freshly ground black pepper

1 tablespoon pistachios

**1** Crumble Roquefort finely with your fingers into a small bowl. Stir in crème fraiche (or sour cream), milk and mayonnaise. Season carefully to taste with salt and pepper.

**2** Chop pistachios finely and sprinkle on top.

Prep time: 10 minutes
Goes with: Raw vegetables, baguette
Calories per serving: 170

# Tahini Dip (Hummus)
Always welcome!

**Preparation:** Best if made fresh
**Storage:** Only briefly in the refrigerator, covered
**Serve with:** Meatballs, eggplant caviar, carrot salad with grapes, falafel

Makes enough for 4:

1 (15 oz.) can cooked garbanzo beans

¼ cup tahini (sesame paste)

Juice from 1 large lemon

2 tablespoons olive oil, Salt

½ to 1 teaspoon harissa (spicy Middle Eastern/North African paste)

2 teaspoons parsley leaves

**1** Drain garbanzo beans and puree finely with 3½ tablespoons water using a hand blender or food processor. Add tahini, lemon juice and oil.

**2** Season dip to taste with salt and harissa and distribute in bowls. Rinse parsley, chop and sprinkle on top.

Prep time: 10 minutes
Goes with: Warmed pita, tortilla chips, vegetables, grilled chicken, grapes
Calories per serving: 270

# Spicy Shrimp Sauce
Liven up your vegetables

**Preparation:** No more than 1 day ahead
**Storage:** Covered in the refrigerator
**Serve with:** Chinese herb rolls, duck curry, miso soup

Makes enough for 4:

1 fresh red chile pepper, 4 cloves garlic

4 small onions, 1 tablespoon peanut oil

¾ lb. cooked, peeled and deveined shrimp

3 tablespoons fish sauce (nam pla)

3 tablespoons lemon juice, Salt

**1** Rinse chile and mince with seeds (wear gloves and don't touch your eyes!). For less spiciness, omit seeds and ribs. Peel garlic and onions and mince.

**2** Heat oil, add chopped ingredients and brown 5–10 minutes while stirring constantly. Place ingredients in a food processor along with cooked shrimp, 3 tablespoons water, fish sauce, lemon juice and salt. Pulse until well-mixed.

Prep time: 35 minutes
Goes with: Daikon or icicle radishes, white cabbage strips, carrots, cucumbers
Calories per serving: 105

# Ginger Dip
Quick

**Preparation:** No more than 3 days ahead
**Storage:** In a covered bowl in the refrigerator
**Serve with:** Fishcakes, dim sum, Japanese noodle soup

Makes enough for 4:

1 piece fresh ginger (about ¾" long)

2 cloves garlic

½ cup cilantro sprigs

1 fresh red chile pepper

¼ cup fish sauce (nam pla)

½ cup soy sauce

**1** Peel ginger and garlic and mince. Rinse cilantro, shake dry, remove any tough stems and discard; chop rest. Rinse chile and cut into very thinly-sliced rings. (Wear gloves and don't touch your eyes.)

**2** Combine fish and soy sauces and mix together with all chopped ingredients.

Prep time: 15 minutes
Goes with: Best with cooked shrimp but also with meatballs or fried tofu
Calories per serving: 30

43

# Avocado Dip
## Chip fixer-upper

**Preparation:** No more than 1 hour ahead
**Storage:** Covered in refrigerator with avocado pits added
**Serve with:** Tamarind chicken, rice salad with pomegranates, chili con pollo

Makes enough for 4:

1 onion

1 jalapeño

1/2 cup cilantro sprigs

2 ripe avocados

2–3 tablespoons fresh lemon juice

Salt, freshly ground black pepper

**1** Peel onion and mince finely. Rinse chile and chop finely with the seeds (for less spice, omit seeds and ribs). Rinse cilantro, shake dry and remove any tough stems. Set aside a couple leaves for garnish and chop the rest finely.

**2** Cut avocados lengthwise to the pit, rotate halves in opposite directions and remove pits. Spoon out flesh and mash finely. Mix with lemon juice and all chopped ingredients; season with salt and pepper.

Prep time: 15 minutes
Goes with: Tortilla chips
Calories per serving: 230

# Cucumber Raita
## Refreshes fading party-goers

**Preparation:** Several hours ahead of time
**Storage:** Covered in the refrigerator
**Serve with:** Cheese rolls, marinated vegetables, bread salad

Makes enough for 4:

1 medium cucumber

About 12 fresh mint leaves

1 1/4 cup yogurt

1/2 teaspoon ground cumin

1/2 teaspoon ground coriander, Salt

**1** Peel cucumber and cut lengthwise. Remove seeds from center with a spoon and finely dice what remains. Rinse mint, shake dry, remove leaves and chop finely.

**2** Stir together cucumber, mint and yogurt and season with cumin, coriander and salt to taste.

Prep time: 15 minutes
Goes with: Flat bread such as pita, tortilla chips
Calories per serving: 55

# Herb Relish
## Summer fling

**Preparation:** Several hours ahead
**Storage:** Covered in the refrigerator
**Serve with:** Stuffed mild banana peppers, jambalaya, falafel

Makes enough for 4:

1 cup Italian flat-leaf parsley
(leaves and tender stems)

1 small bunch arugula, 12 fresh mint leaves

4–6 green onions

2 nectarines

1/4 cup fresh lemon juice

Salt, freshly ground black pepper

1/4 cup olive oil

2 teaspoons capers

**1** Rinse parsley, arugula, and mint; shake dry. Remove leaves and chop. Remove roots and wilted parts from green onions. Rinse and cut into rings.

**2** Rinse nectarines; cut in half, remove pits, and dice finely. Combine with lemon juice, salt, pepper and oil. Mix together nectarines, herbs, onions and capers.

Prep time: 35 minutes
Goes with: Toasted flatbread or baguette rounds, grilled meats or fish, tomatoes or cucumbers
Calories per serving: 145

# Tomato Dip
## Rivals ketchup

**Preparation:** No more than 4 days ahead
**Storage:** Sealed in the refrigerator
**Serve with:** Meatballs, cucumber raita

Makes enough for 4:

1 14 oz. can peeled tomatoes, 1 onion

2 cloves garlic, 1 tablespoon vegetable oil

Juice of 1 lime

Salt, chili powder, 1 pinch sugar

**1** Drain tomatoes and dice (set aside). Peel onion and garlic, chop and sauté briefly in oil. Add tomatoes and simmer 10 minutes.

**2** Purée tomato mixture in a blender or food processor, and season to taste with lime juice, salt, chili powder and sugar. Let cool.

Prep time: 15 minutes
Goes with: Tortilla chips
Calories per serving: 35

## Another dip, this time in pink:

Peel 1 clove garlic and 1 piece ginger root about 3/4" in length. Puree with 1 cup canned, diced beets (drained, and not the pickled variety). Stir in 1/2 cup crème fraîche and 1/4 cup yogurt; season with cumin, salt and pepper.

# Deviled Eggs with Mango Chutney
1950s hit with a new twist

**Preparation:** Hard-boil eggs in the morning; prepare rest of recipe no more than 4 hours before the party
**Storage:** Covered with plastic wrap in the refrigerator. Remove shortly before serving, especially in summer.
**Serve with:** Carrot salad with grapes, tomato soup, tahini dip

Makes enough for 4 (16 deviled eggs):

8 eggs

½ cup basil leaves

1 tablespoon mango chutney (from a jar)

1 tablespoon mayonnaise

1 teaspoon curry powder

Salt, freshly ground black pepper

**1** Place eggs in a pot, cover with water and heat. After water comes to a boil, let boil about 6 minutes. Plunge eggs into cold water and let cool. Remove basil leaves from stems and mince. Chop chutney finely.

**2** Peel eggs and halve lengthwise. Remove yolks with a spoon, mash with a fork and stir in mayonnaise.

**3** Add basil and chutney to yolk mixture and season to taste with curry powder, salt and pepper. Use a teaspoon to fill egg halves with the mixture. If you want to do it absolutely perfectly, use a pastry bag. You can make one of these yourself: put the mixture in a freezer bag, snip off a small corner and squeeze the contents from the bag into the egg halves.

Prep time: 40 minutes
Calories per serving: 190

## Variations:

• Finely chop 1 tablespoon canned tuna and 1 teaspoon capers. Add ½ teaspoon of tomato paste stirred into the hard-boiled egg yolks along with the mayonnaise.

• Chop 1 dill pickle and a little dill very finely. Add to hard-boiled egg yolks along with 1 tablespoon sour cream.

• Chop a couple olives, 1 clove garlic and 2 green onions very finely. Combine with hard-boiled egg yolks along with 1 tablespoon sherry and a little orange zest. Season to taste with a little lemon zest and cayenne pepper.

• Chop 8 chive spears and add to hard-boiled egg yolks along with 1 tablespoon crème fraiche (or sour cream) and 1–2 teaspoons spicy mustard. Season with salt and ground caraway seeds.

# Stuffed Tomatoes
That's amoré!

**Preparation:** Prepare filling in the morning; stuff tomatoes 1–2 hours ahead
**Storage:** In a refrigerator covered with plastic wrap
**Serve with:** Meatballs, potato-vegetable Niçoise salad, rosemary onion soup

Makes enough for 4 (about 16 tomatoes):

About 1 lb. cherry tomatoes (not too small—with a diameter of about 1½")

1 tablespoon pitted black olives, preferably kalamata

1 clove garlic, ½ cup parsley, ¼ cup ricotta

2 tablespoons freshly grated parmesan

Salt, freshly ground black pepper

**1** Rinse tomatoes and cut ¼ of tomato off tops. Finely chop about 1 tablespoon of the tomato tops; discard rest of tops. Carefully remove contents of tomatoes with a small spoon; discard.

**2** Remove olive pits, peel garlic and remove leaves from parsley. Chop all three ingredients finely and combine with chopped tomato, ricotta and parmesan. Season with salt and pepper, fill tomatoes and serve.

Prep time: 15 minutes
Calories per serving: 80

# Stuffed Mushrooms
## Right on the button

**Preparation:** Cook filling on previous day or in the morning. Stuff and bake no more than 2–3 hours ahead
**Storage:** Covered in the refrigerator
**Serve with:** Ham carpaccio, lentil salad, cheese rolls

Makes enough for 4 (16 mushrooms):

1 pound chorizo or spicy Hungarian sausage

16 relatively large mushrooms (white button or brown cremini)

1 onion, 2 cloves garlic

3/4 cup parsley, 1 tablespoon olive oil

2 tablespoons dry sherry

1 tablespoon breadcrumbs

1 tablespoon grated mozzarella cheese

Salt, 1/2 teaspoon paprika

**1** Slit the skin on the chorizo with a knife and pull it off. Cut 16 thin slices of the skinned sausage link and finely dice remaining sausage.

**2** Wipe off mushrooms with a damp paper towel. Clean and remove stems. Chop stems finely. Peel onion and garlic and mince. Rinse

parsley under cold water, shake dry, remove leaves and chop.

**3** Preheat oven to 375°F and place mushroom tops in a baking dish. Heat oil in a pan and first sauté the sliced chorizo until fully cooked; remove and drain on paper towels. Next in the same oil, sauté mushroom stems, onion and garlic for about 5 minutes. Add parsley and diced chorizo. Add sherry and let boil away.

**4** Mix all these ingredients with breadcrumbs and cheese. Season with salt and paprika and stuff the mushroom tops. Place in the oven for about 10 minutes. If the filling turns too brown, cover loosely. Let cool. Place each mushroom on 1 cooked chorizo slice and skewer with a toothpick.

Prep time: 30 minutes
Calories per serving: 590

# Stuffed Mild Banana Peppers
## A slice of life

**Preparation:** No more than 2 days ahead
**Storage:** Covered with plastic wrap in the refrigerator
**Serve with:** Provençal potato soup, tomato dip, eggplant caviar

Makes enough for 4–6 (about thirty pieces):

3 1/2 oz. feta, 2/3 cup low-fat sour cream

1 teaspoon capers, 1/2 teaspoon caraway seeds

6 tablespoons softened butter

1 teaspoon anchovy paste

1 teaspoon dijon mustard

1 tablespoon paprika, Salt, Pepper

4–6 largish anaheim peppers

(or mild banana peppers)

**1** Crumble feta with a fork. Chop capers and grind caraway seeds. Mix together feta, sour cream, butter, capers, caraway, anchovy paste, mustard and paprika thoroughly; season with salt and pepper.

**2** Rinse peppers, cut out stems and pull out seeds and ribs. Use a small spoon to stuff peppers with cheese mixture. Refrigerate overnight. Cut into 1/2" slices.

Prep time: 35 minutes (+ refrigeration time)
Calories per serving (6 servings): 340

# Danish "Smorgasbord"
## Open-faced sandwiches from Scandinavia, 3 ways

**Preparation:** Prepare toppings a couple hours ahead, don't spread on bread or crispbread until just before serving
**Storage:** On plates loosely covered with plastic wrap
**Serve with:** Salad greens, radishes, cucumber slices, etc.

Makes enough for 4:

**With smoked fish:**

1 large egg

7 oz. smoked salmon, trout, or halibut

1 cup parsley leaves and tender stems

½ cup sour cream

1 teaspoon curry powder

Salt to taste

1 tablespoon butter (optional, for spreading on crispbread)

4 slices mixed-grain bread or 8 pieces Wasa crispbread

**With shrimp omelet:**

½ cup dill fronds

1 tablespoon butter

4 eggs

¼ cup milk

Salt, freshly ground pepper

⅓ lb. cooked shrimp, peeled and deveined

1 tablespoon butter

4 slices white or mixed-grain bread

**With ham:**

1 carrot

1 (2"x2") piece celery root

½ apple

2 white cabbage leaves

1 pickle (or 8 cornichons)

2 tablespoons mayonnaise

Salt and pepper

1 teaspoon fresh lemon juice

4 slices bread (mixed-grain or dark rye)

1 tablespoon butter

4 slices cooked ham

**1** For the smoked fish type, hard boil the egg (see p. 46 for instructions) and run cold water over it; peel and chop. Shred smoked fish with two forks (removing any bones, skin, etc.). Rinse parsley and chop finely. Mix all these ingredients with sour cream and curry powder; season with salt and spread on buttered (or plain) Wasa crispbread. Cut topped crispbreads in half.

**2** For shrimp omelet, rinse dill and chop finely. Melt butter in a pan. Gently whisk eggs and milk, season with salt and pepper and pour in with the butter. Cook over medium heat until the egg solidifies; don't scramble, and don't let dry out. Remove from pan and let omelet cool; cut into pieces. Place on buttered, toasted bread topped with cooked shrimp and dill.

**3** For the ham open-face sandwich, peel carrots, celery root and apple; grate finely. Rinse cabbage leaves and cut into very fine strips; then chop. Dice pickle very finely. Mix all these ingredients with mayonnaise and season with salt, pepper and lemon juice. Butter and toast the bread; top with ham then vegetable salad and cut into fourths.

Prep time: About 20 minutes each
Calories per serving: With smoked fish—215; with shrimp omelet—200; with ham—225

## Here are some other ways the Danish do it:

• Place tomato slices on buttered bread or crispbread, sprinkle with finely diced red onion and season with salt and pepper.

• Spread butter and horse-radish on bread, top with cheese and dot with cranberry preserves.

• Dice pickles and hard-boiled eggs, mix with sour cream and spread on small pieces of bread. Sprinkle a little caviar on top.

• Top bread with smoked salmon. Finely chop a couple radishes and mix them with a small amount of oil and vinegar. Sprinkle on top.

# Salmon Tramezzini
Very ritzy finger sandwiches

**Preparation:** Midday prior to a party
**Storage:** In the refrigerator covered with plastic wrap
**Serve with:** Marinated vegetables, potato terrine with goat's cheese, stuffed tomatoes

Makes enough for 4:

7 oz. smoked salmon, 1 small, young zucchini

½ cup dill fronds

⅓ cup ricotta or cream cheese

3 tablespoons mayonnaise

Salt, freshly ground black pepper

4 lettuce leaves, 8 slices sandwich bread

**1** Finely dice salmon. Rinse zucchini and dice finely. Remove dill leaves and cut finely.

**2** Mix ricotta and mayonnaise. Add salmon, zucchini and dill and season with salt and pepper. Rinse lettuce leaves and pat dry. Cut out thick ribs.

**3** Cover half the bread slices with lettuce and spread salmon mixture on top. Place remaining slices on top and press down gently. Using a sharp knife, cut into 1" squares (trim crusts).

Prep time: 25 minutes
Calories per serving: 350

# Rye bread with mushroom caviar
Caviar for the poor? No, for gourmets!

**Preparation:** Make mushroom caviar no more than 2 days ahead
**Storage:** In a covered bowl in the refrigerator
**Serve with:** Hungarian paprika soup

Makes enough for 4:

¾ lb. mushrooms (your favorite varieties)

1 onion, 2 tablespoons butter

½ cup parsley sprigs

½ teaspoon fresh marjoram leaves (optional)

⅓ cup sour cream

3 tablespoons cream cheese

Salt, Paprika

4–6 thin slices of rye bread

**1** Wipe off mushrooms with a paper towel, cut off ends of stems and chop mushrooms finely. Peel onion and mince.

**2** Melt butter in a pan. Add mushrooms and onions, toss with butter quickly, and then sauté for about 10 minutes over medium heat, stirring diligently! Set aside to cool.

**3** Rinse parsley and shake dry. Remove leaves and chop finely. Chop marjoram leaves.

**4** Stir together sour cream and cream cheese. Stir in cooled mushroom mixture, marjoram, and parsley and season with salt and dashes of paprika. Spread a thick layer of mushroom caviar on bread, top with another slice, cut into pieces and arrange on a platter.

Prep time: 30 minutes
Calories per serving: 190

# Canapés with Potato-Cheese Cream
Lay it on thick!

**Preparation:** Prepare potato mixture no more than 1 day ahead; don't spread on bread until just before the party
**Storage:** Covered in the refrigerator
**Serve with:** Creamy mushroom soup, colombo, cheese skewers

Makes enough for 4:

½ lb. potatoes, 1 egg, 1 onion

2 anchovy fillets packed in oil (optional)

1 pickle, 8 chive spears

4½ tablespoons softened butter

1 teaspoon spicy mustard

2–3 tablespoons sour cream

Salt, Paprika

8 slices sandwich bread

**1** Boil potatoes until tender (about 25 minutes). Hard boil egg (see p. 46), plunge both into cold water and let cool.

**2** Peel onion and chop finely along with anchovies and pickle. Rinse chives and chop.

**3** Peel egg, remove yolk and chop egg white finely. In a medium bowl, mash yolk and combine with butter and mustard. Peel potatoes and mash finely (with potato ricer, electric mixer, or fork); combine with chopped ingredients and sour cream and stir into yolk-butter mixture. Season to taste with salt and paprika. Spread potato-cheese cream on 4 slices of bread, cover with the remaining slices, press together and cut each sandwich into 4 sections (trim crusts).

Prep time: 40 minutes
Calories per serving: 255

# Cucumber Sandwiches
Very British!

**Preparation:** Rinse lettuce in the morning, prepare cheese, but don't assemble until the last minute
**Storage:** Refrigerate cheese mixture
**Serve with:** Cheese skewers, meatballs, eggplant caviar

Makes enough for 4:

½ cucumber, 1 avocado

2 tablespoons fresh lemon juice, Salt

4 leaves of head lettuce

⅔ cup cream cheese, room temperature

1 tablespoon grated horseradish (from a jar)

8 slices sandwich bread

1 handful radish sprouts, alfalfa sprouts

or cress

Curry powder

**1** Peel cucumber and cut diagonally into ¼" slices. Cut avocado in half, remove pit, peel, mash with a fork with the lemon juice and season with salt.

**2** Rinse lettuce, dry and cut out center ribs. Combine cream cheese with horseradish and spread on all the bread slices. Top half the bread slices with cucumbers and spread avocado cream on the other half.

**3** Sprinkle sprouts over the cucumbers and season with salt and curry powder. Top with lettuce leaves, then the other bread slice with the avocado side down.

**4** Easy and thrifty: Cut each sandwich lengthwise into three pieces (rectangular strips). British-style: Cut off crusts and cut each sandwich into two pieces. In any case: Serve immediately.

Prep time: 30 minutes
Calories per serving: 320

# Cheesy Crackers
Going, going, gone

**Preparation:** Cheese balls without mint, 1–2 days ahead. Roll in mint a short time before serving.
**Storage:** Covered in the refrigerator
**Serve with:** Bacon rolls, peanut soup with carrots, chili con pollo

Makes enough for 4:

2 green onions

6–8 oz. goat cheese

½ teaspoon cumin powder

½ teaspoon chili powder, Salt

About 12 fresh mint leaves or

other favorite herb

About 20 crackers

**1** Remove roots and dark-green parts from green onions, rinse and chop finely. Mix goat cheese together with green onions, cumin, chili powder and salt. Wet your hands and take teaspoonfuls of the misture; roll into balls.

**2** Rinse mint, shake dry and chop very finely. Roll cheese balls in mint. Refrigerate for 1 hour. Cut each ball in half and place one cheese ball half on each cracker.

Prep time:
25 minutes (+ 1 hour refrigeration time)
Calories per serving: 285

# Mini Cabernet Cream Puffs
## Festive and fancy

**Preparation:** After baking cream puffs, freeze immediately. Before the party, heat up for 5 minutes (375°F, see page 162). Prepare filling no more than 1 day ahead of time. Fill cream puffs just before the party.
**Storage:** Refrigerate cream
**Serve with:** Potato vegetable salad Niçoise, Ratatouille with cheese baguette

Makes enough for 6 (about 30 cream puffs):

¼ cup butter

Salt

1 cup + 2 tablespoons flour

4 eggs

Vegetable oil and flour for baking sheet

½ cup dry red wine (e.g. Cabernet Sauvignon)

1 tablespoon honey

1 handful walnuts

6 oz. cream cheese (about ⅔ cup)

3½ oz. blue cheese

Freshly ground pepper

**1** Starting with the dough: Bring 1 cup water, butter and salt to a boil. Remove from heat, pour in flour and stir quickly.

**2** Return to heat and cook until the dough becomes a ball and a film covers the bottom of the pan. Place the dough in a bowl and immediately beat in 1 egg (OK to use an electric mixer), mixing until smooth. Repeat with remaining 3 eggs, one at a time.

**3** Heat oven to 375°F (or convection oven to 350°F). Grease two baking sheets and sprinkle with flour (or use baking parchment). With two small spoons, make dollops of dough and place on a baking sheet with about 2 inches between them. Bake each sheet about 15–20 minutes in the oven or until balls are golden on top.

**4** In the meantime, pour red wine and honey into a pan and reduce until 1–2 tablespoons remain. Crumble the walnuts with your fingers. Mash cream cheese and blue cheese together with a fork. Add red wine (cooled!) and walnuts and season with pepper—mix.

**5** Remove mini cream puffs from the oven and cool slightly; cut off the tops. Distribute filling on the bottom halves; place the other halves on top.

Prep time: 1¼ hours
Calories per serving: 260

A faster way: Spread cheese mixture on lightly toasted bread triangles.

# Vegetable Crostini with Almonds
## A quick fix

**Preparation:** Prepare spread on previous day
**Storage:** Covered in the refrigerator; spread just before the party
**Serve with:** Pasta salad with radicchio, Greek potato pureé, meatballs

Makes enough for 4:

1 tomato, 1 clove garlic

1 yellow or red bell pepper, ¼ cucumber

2 tablespoons almonds, A couple basil leaves

¼ cup olive oil, Salt, Pepper

Baguette slices

**1** Rinse tomato and peel garlic. Rinse bell pepper and remove seeds and core. Rinse the ¼ cucumber. In a blender or food processor, chop all these ingredients together with the almonds but not too finely. Cut basil into strips or mince and mix with vegetables along with the oil. Season with salt and pepper.

**2** Heat oven to 475°F (or convection oven to 450°F). Arrange baguette slices on a baking sheet and heat in the oven for about 5 minutes. Put the vegetables on top and eat!

Prep time: 25 minutes
Calories per serving: 235

# Polenta Crostini with Pesto
Finger food
alla Italiana

**Preparation:** Prepare polenta and pesto cream the day before
**Storage:** Covered in the refrigerator. Just before the party, brown polenta and spread pesto cream on top.
**Serve with:** Marinated vegetables, rosemary onion soup, lentils with pancetta

Makes enough for 4:

Salt

3/4 cup dry polenta

3 tablespoons olive oil

1 bunch basil

1 tomato

3 pitted black olives, preferably kalamata

1 tablespoon pesto (best homemade:
see Basic Italian cookbook, p. 61; or
buy readymade)

2 tablespoons crème fraiche

Freshly ground black pepper

**1** Pour 1 2/3 cups water into a pot and salt generously. Place on the stove and bring to a boil. Stir in polenta with a wire whisk. Turn heat down low (very important); cover and cook polenta for 10 minutes.

**2** Grease a square pan with 1 tablespoon oil; pour in polenta and brush it smooth on top. Let cool.

**3** Remove basil leaves from stems and chop finely. Rinse tomato. Remove pits from olives and dice tomato and olives very finely. Combine pesto and crème fraîche and stir in tomato, basil and olives. Season with salt and pepper.

**4** Turn on the broiler or heat the oven to 475°F. Cut polenta into 3/4" wide strips and then cut those strips in two (you can also cut in 1" squares). Grease a baking sheet, arrange polenta slices on it and brush oil on top. Heat in the oven about 10 minutes until golden brown. Spread pesto cream on top of each one and serve warm or cold.

Prep time: 50 minutes (+ refrigeration time)
Calories per serving: 220

# Ham Canapés
What could be quicker?

**Preparation:** Prepare the ham spread the day before
**Storage:** Covered in the refrigerator
**Serve with:** Roquefort crème fraiche dip, herb dip, duck pâté

Makes enough for 4:

8 chive spears, 5 oz. cooked ham

7 tablespoons butter

1 tablespoon coarse mustard

2 tablespoons cream

2 tablespoons cognac or chicken broth

(or beef broth)

1–2 teaspoons fresh lemon juice

8 slices sandwich bread, crackers

and/or cucumber slices

**1** Rinse chives and chop coarsely. Tear ham into pieces and purée along with chives, butter, mustard, cream and cognac (with a blender, hand blender, or food processor). Season to taste with lemon juice.

**2** Toast bread, spread on ham mixture and cut into eighths (trim crusts first). Or spread on crackers or cucumber slices.

Prep time: 15 minutes
Calories per serving with toast: 400

# That's a Wrap

Actually, the fun is just beginning. Leave your forks in the drawer and tell your guests to check their pretense at the door. It's time to wrap 'n' roll.

## Creating the Right Atmosphere

Think sun, desert, white walls, dark heavy wood. Picture chili red, corn yellow, lime green, pacific blue. Send out gaudy napkins as invitations and forget the silverware. Hang garlic braids, decorate with brilliant sunflowers and flickering lanterns. Set out thick, colorful glasses and heavy ceramic bowls. Pin notes to tiny cactuses that tell what's in each bowl. Stick posters on the wall showing how to make a wrap. Play lively guitar music—Mexican mariachi or samba style, ZZ Top or Red Hot Chili Peppers — it makes no difference as long as everybody can sing along.

When your home is filled with close friends, your best bet is to let them roll tortillas into wraps—Tex-Mex-Californian combos with a little Asian and Mediterranean thrown in. Wraps are ideal for spicing up spur-of-the-moment parties because there's always something in your cupboards that can be used. They also guarantee the sort of relaxed confusion where strangers become the best of friends—and they leave you with almost no cleanup. Plus, your guests make their own food!

## What You Need

Another incentive for spontaneity: The basic equipment for wraps—a pan and two hands—can be found in any household. Add to this a couple of bowls and dishes to set out the fillings, and spoons for spreading and sprinkling.

For serving you only need napkins, a lot of multicolored ones. But lest your more sophisticated friends turn up their noses, keep a few plates and some silverware handy—discreetly hidden in the background, of course, so your other more down-to-earth guests will be encouraged to use their hands.

Drink beer straight from the bottle in Tex-Mex fashion (with a wedge of lime in the bottleneck to keep out the desert flies). What else? A glass pitcher of lime-infused water and glasses that can also be used for mixed drinks. What about the spots on them from guests' messy fingers? Either put up with them or deal with them as the Russians do—smash them against the nearest wall. Just kidding!

Don't be afraid to bring out the wine and some wine glasses, too.

## How to Wrap

Simple: The host or hostess heats an ungreased pan, throws in a tortilla and browns it half a minute on each side. If this host is really on top of things, he or she will meanwhile explain how it's done (having an assistant comes in handy).

When the tortilla is hot, take it out of the pan and lay it on top of a napkin held by one of your guests (plates for snobs only). They can now add their own thin layer of a spread and then heap on the herbs and other fillings. Vegetables, legumes, marinated delicacies, seafood, meat, cheese and nuts give the wrap substance. Everything should be distributed (not too thickly!) to within half an inch of the edges so that it can easily be wrapped up, which is best done on a table or board.

There are two ways to do this, either by rolling up the tortilla on an angle like an ice-cream cone or the professional way: Fold up an inch of the tortilla along the bottom and then roll it up so tightly from one side to the other so that nothing falls out. Now wrap it up in the napkin so the bottom is "drip safe." The best way to eat is standing up because the wrap may be messy and because guzzling beer out of the bottle comes more naturally when standing.

Hopefully you don't have white carpet!

# Here's What You Need:

**In any case:** Tortillas

**For spreading:** Ketchup, BBQ sauce, chile sauce, mayonnaise, cream cheese, everything from yogurt to crème fraiche, guacamole (see Basic Cooking, page 89), peanut butter, pesto, mustard (but not all on the same wrap please!)

**For sprinkling:** Chopped basil, cilantro, chives, parsley; coarsely chopped iceberg lettuce, romaine, arugula, radicchio; nuts, seeds, crumbled chips, croutons; grated cheese from cheddar to parmesan; marinated foods such as chile peppers, capers, olives, bell peppers, anchovies, sun-dried tomatoes

**For filling:** Thinly sliced raw vegetables such as mushrooms, carrots, bell peppers, celery, tomatoes, and avocado; canned corn and beans (such as kidney); diced hard-boiled eggs, feta cheese, mozzarella; shrimp, canned tuna, smoked fish; strips of ham, salami, roast meat; fried bacon, stir-fried or grilled meat or chicken strips

**For drinking:** Ice water with slices of lime; alcoholic and/or non-alcoholic fruit drinks; beer (Mexican or U.S.); hearty red wine (Spanish); tequila—straight or mixed (for those who dare)

**For before:** Sherry onions (page 64), cheese skewers (page 41), avocado dip (page 44))

**For after:** Oranges in honey (page 150), coconut flan (page 147), fruit balls (page 156)

55

# Cheese Rolls
## Highly addictive

**Preparation:** No more than 1 day ahead, heat up briefly before the party (page 162)
**Storage**: Uncovered in the refrigerator
**Serve with:** Cucumber raita, eggplant caviar, stuffed mushrooms

Makes enough for 4 (approx. 40 rolls):

½ cup dill fronds

1 cup parsley

Several mint leaves

2 marinated Italian hot chile peppers (green) or pepperoncini

1 lb. feta cheese

2 eggs

Freshly ground black pepper

Paprika

Salt, if necessary

9 sheets filo dough (carefully remove sheets from package and cover with a cloth; freeze rest of package immediately)

About 1 quart vegetable or peanut oil, for deep frying

**1** Rinse herbs under cold water and shake thoroughly dry. Snip off thick stems and finely chop the rest. Finely chop chile peppers. Drain feta and crumble finely. Combine with herbs, chile peppers and eggs and season with pepper and paprika. You need salt only if the cheese is very mild, which it almost never is.

**2** Stack 3 sheets of filo dough and cut into eight squares. Cut each eighth diagonally into two triangles. Distribute a little cheese filling in the shape of a small log along the long edge of each triangle; fold the two end corners inward and roll the triangle from the long edge to the point edge. Use a bit of water on your fingers to seal.

**3** When you've rolled them all, heat the oil to 350–375°F. Test it by inserting a wooden spoon. The oil is hot enough when a lot of tiny bubbles rise to the top (or, use an oil thermometer). Add a few of the rolls (no more than 6 at a time) and deep fry for 2–3 minutes or until golden. Cover a plate with a double layer of paper towels. Drain the rolls on the paper towels.

Prep time: 1 hour
Calories per serving: 370

# Variation: Spring Rolls

Finely chop 7 oz. cooked shrimp or raw fish, ½ pound bean sprouts and 1 handful spinach. Fry in 1 tablespoon oil with a little ginger. Finely chop 1 oz. of softened cellophane noodles and combine with 2 tablespoons chopped chives, soy sauce and 1 teaspoon toasted sesame oil. Use to top one side of spring roll pastry (from frozen-food section of an Asian market), tuck in the ends, roll up and deep fry.

# Bacon Rolls
## A natural with beer or wine

**Preparation:** On the day before
**Storage:** Uncovered in the refrigerator
**Serve with:** Moroccan cream cheese dip, carrot salad with grapes, bread salad

Makes enough for 4 (16 rolls):

1 dried chile pepper

2 juniper berries (specialty store)

2 tablespoons fresh lemon juice

16 dried apricots, 8–16 thin slices of bacon

Freshly ground black pepper

**1** Crush chile pepper (omit seeds and ribs for less heat) and juniper berries in a mortar and pestle. Combine with ½ cup hot water and lemon juice. Pour over the apricots and soak for 2 hours.

**2** Spread out bacon on a board, cutting larger slices in two. Roll 1 apricot in each bacon length and season with pepper.

**3** Heat a pan (preferably non-stick). Fry rolls on all sides for about 5 minutes total and let cool. Skewer with toothpicks and serve.

Prep time: 20 minutes
(not including soaking time)
Calories per serving: 310

# Chinese Herb Rolls
## Absolutely delicious!

**Preparation:** 2–3 days ahead
**Storage:** Covered in the refrigerator
**Serve with:** Miso soup, ginger dip, fish cakes

Makes enough for 4 (16 rolls):

1 head white cabbage (you won't use it all)

Salt

1 red bell pepper

1 bunch green onions (5–6)

1 fresh red chile pepper

1 piece fresh ginger

3 tablespoons oil

2 tablespoons sugar

4 tablespoons rice vinegar

**1** Remove wilted leaves from cabbage. Remove the core from the cabbage head by cutting it out in a wedge. Bring a large amount of salted water to a boil. Add cabbage head and simmer for about 8 minutes. Place cooked cabbage in a colander and drain. Carefully detach about 16 small leaves (or 8 large ones and then cut in half). And then remove another 4 leaves.

**2** Rinse bell pepper and green onions and cut into fine strips along with the 4 cabbage leaves. Spread out the rest of the cabbage leaves on a board, top with several vegetable strips and fold the sides together. Roll tightly and place the rolls in a bowl.

**3** Rinse chile pepper and cut into rings (wear gloves and don't touch your eyes). Peel ginger and slice into rounds. Boil ½ cup water with chile pepper rings, ginger, oil, sugar, salt and vinegar. Pour over rolls and marinate 1–3 days.

Prep time: 25 minutes (+ marinating time)
Calories per serving: 135

# Meatballs
## Practically Middle-Eastern

**Preparation:** No more than 1 day ahead
**Storage:** Covered in the refrigerator
**Serve with:** Tomato dip, cucumber raita, potato-vegetable Niçoise salad

Makes enough for 4 (about 30 meatballs):

1 tablespoon raisins, 2 tablespoons pine nuts

Several fresh sprigs of mint, 1 large onion

2–3 tablespoons clarified butter or Ghee

1 lb. ground lamb

(order from butcher ahead of time)

A couple threads saffron

$^1/_2$ teaspoon chili powder

$^1/_2$ teaspoon cumin powder

$^1/_2$ teaspoon cinnamon

Salt, freshly ground black pepper

1 egg, 3 tablespoons breadcrumbs

**1** Place raisins in a bowl, pour hot water over the top and soak. Place pine nuts in a pan and toast on the stove while stirring constantly until they're slightly golden-yellow. Remove from the pan and chop.

**2** Rinse and dry mint leaves and chop finely. Peel and chop onion and cook for about 5 minutes in 1 tablespoon of the clarified butter.

**3** Drain raisins and chop coarsely. Combine with mint, pine nut, onion, ground meat, spices, egg and breadcrumbs and mix together well. Shape into balls.

**4** In a large frying pan, heat remaining clarified butter. Fry meatballs until nice and brown on all sides, a total of about 8 minutes or until cooked through. Let cool.

Prep time: 35 minutes
Calories per serving: 620

# More Meatballs
## This time in miniature

**Preparation:** Prepare meat and dip in the morning—then you can either bake them right away or just before the party
**Storage:** Covered in the refrigerator
**Serve with:** Ham canapes, cheesy crackers

Makes enough for 4:

### For about 40 mini-meatballs:

1 handful chervil, 1 onion

2 anchovies packed in oil (optional)

1 tablespoon oil

1$^1/_3$ lbs. ground veal (ask your butcher)

$^1/_4$ cup breadcrumbs, 2 tablespoons brandy

1 teaspoon Worcestershire sauce

Salt, freshly ground pepper

### For the dip:

$^1/_2$ cup mayonnaise, $^3/_4$ cup sour cream

1 tablespoon capers, Worcestershire sauce

$^1/_2$ teaspoon fresh lemon juice

Salt, freshly ground pepper

**1** Rinse chervil, snip off thick stems and chop leaves. Peel onion and dice. Drain anchovies and chop. In a pan, heat oil and brown onions with anchovies. Add chervil, stir briefly and let cool.

**2** Preheat oven to 375°F (or convection oven to 350°F). Lightly grease a baking sheet. Combine onion mixture with other meatball ingredients (including some salt and pepper) and chop thoroughly in a food processor or with a hand blender. Bit by bit, mix into a smooth mass. Wet your hands and form into walnut-sized balls. Place on the baking sheet and bake about 15 minutes.

**3** In the meantime, chop capers and stir together with mayonnaise and sour cream. Season to taste with Worcestershire sauce, lemon juice, salt and pepper.

**4** Let meatballs cool, then arrange on a plate. Pierce with toothpicks so that guests can each take one and dip it in the sauce.

Prep time: 1 hour
Calories per serving: 340

# Fishcakes
## Trendy Thai

**Preparation:** Fry in the morning and heat up before the party (page 162)
**Storage:** Covered in the refrigerator
**Serve with:** Leek tofu salad with peanut dressing, carrot salad with grapes, ginger dip

Makes enough for 4–6 (about 45 cakes):

2¼ lb. fish fillets (use white fish)

Salt, ½ lb. green beans

1 (6") section of lemon grass

1 cup cilantro leaves and tender stems

1–2 tablespoons curry paste

(Asian market or specialty store)

1 egg, 2 teaspoons brown sugar, ¾ cup flour

1 quart oil for frying

**1** Cover fish fillet in ¼ cup salted water and simmer over medium heat for about 5 minutes or until opaque. Drain and let cool. Rinse beans; snip off ends and simmer 5 minutes in some salted water. Rinse under cold water and drain.

**2** Chop beans finely. Rinse lemon grass, peel off the tough outer layer, and finely chop the tender part remaining. Chop cilantro. Finely mash fish with a fork and stir in curry paste, beans, lemon grass, cilantro, egg, sugar, flour and salt. Refrigerate for 1 hour.

**3** Form mixture into small balls and flatten slightly. Heat oil to 350–375°F (use an oil thermometer) and deep fry fishcakes a few at a time for 4 minutes or until golden-yellow. Drain and place on paper towels to soak up excess oil.

Prep time: 1 hour (+ refrigeration time)
Calories per serving (6 servings): 290

# Falafel
## So simple, yet so good

**Preparation:** 1–2 days ahead, but no more
**Storage:** On a plate in the refrigerator, heat up before party (page 162)
**Serve with:** Avocado dip, turkey with Cajun sauce, tamarind chicken

Makes enough for 4:

**For about 40 falafel:**

½ pound dried garbanzo beans

1 onion, 1 clove garlic

1 cup parsley leaves and tender stems

½ teaspoon ground coriander

½ teaspoon paprika, ½ teaspoon cumin

1 tablespoon fresh lemon juice

Salt, generous to taste

About 1 quart oil for frying

**For the sauce:**

6 seedless grapes, ⅓ cup yogurt

1 tablespoon lemon juice

1 tablespoon sesame paste, Salt

Harissa sauce, if desired

(we recommend 1 teaspoon)

**1** Pour garbanzo beans into a bowl; pour water over the top and soak overnight.

**2** The next day, peel onion and garlic and chop coarsely. Rinse parsley and snip off thick stems; chop coarsely. Drain garbanzo beans and mix with the chopped ingredients and spices. In two batches, puree in a heavy duty food processor as finely as possible. Add a tablespoon of water and pulse briefly. Season to taste with spices, lemon juice and salt and form into balls or disks—squeezing them together with your hands. They will only hold together loosely, but once you drop them in the hot oil, they'll be fine.

**3** Deep fry falafel balls in 350–375°F oil (use an oil thermometer) for 2–4 minutes or until golden brown. Drain well and place on paper towels to soak up excess oil.

**4** For the sauce, rinse grapes and mince. Stir together yogurt, lemon juice and sesame paste, add grapes and season to taste with salt and harissa. Dip the falafel in the sauce.

Variation: Serve with Tahini dip.
Prep time: 40 minutes (+ soaking time)
Calories per serving: 34

# Fork

They who wield the fork and chopsticks rule...

# Food

While the ancients were primitively pulling pork shanks out of the fire with their hands, the Greeks and Romans had already fitted the roasting skewer with tines for retrieving fish from pots and eggplant from platters. The European nobility were the first to insert the fork in their mouths, an action deplored by the Church which considered the trident a symbol of the devil. (Even though the French introduced eating with a fork to the court, they first had to learn it from the Italians!)

If you're beyond fingers but haven't quite mastered the knife, you only need to wield the fork to demonstrate the grace of an elegant fencer among fist-fighters and spear-throwers. You'll give the impression of living only from the finest seafood cocktails and French rabbit pâté, but also of nibbling on the occasional pasta salad if it's exotic enough. And when "wokking," you'll stand out as one who knows how to conduct with chopsticks. You're a leader, a warrior, a ruler if you will.

# Fun with Forks

Do you still like it? Did you ever like it? Did you ever not like it? Most importantly, have you never done it? OK, for all of you who are still trying to figure out what to make of that chemistry set left under the kitchen sink by the previous renter, it is in fact a fondue set, meant for cooking and for partying. That thing that looks like a Bunsen burner gets filled with a little sterno and lit on fire. And that crucible-like pot goes on top and gets filled three-quarters full with oil or broth (generally 1 to 2 quarts, but it depends on the size of the pot).

For a chicken or beef stock fondue, heat up the stock and simmer over the flame. In it you can cook meat, fish or vegetables (see "Firepot" Fondue, Basic Cooking, page 78). For an oil fondue, fill the pot with $2/3$ to $3/4$ full with vegetable or peanut oil. This works for quickly frying tender meats such as lamb, duck, beef and fish, as well as sliced vegetables (usually battered). Heat the oil on the stove first. Test it by inserting a wooden spoon. If tiny bubbles immediately start rising up (like champagne bubbles), it's reached the right temperature (or use an oil thermometer and heat to 350–375 degrees). If it smokes, it's too hot (take it off the heat). Transfer pot to fondue burner. Then experiment with how long it takes to cook a piece of meat to a rare state or to a well-done state, according to your preference. Finally, the culinary magic occurs when you dip the cooked item into a dreamy sauce. It just has to be good, if only because you've gone to so much trouble! (If you're nostalgic for cheese fondue, don't despair: see page 87.)

## Drink of the Day
# Tankini Martini

The martini has evolved since the late 1800s and today, great liberties are taken with the drink—you can almost put together any mixed drink and call it a martini. But whatever it's supposed to be, this version is delicious. Rinse 8 lemons, cut in half, and squeeze juice into a 2-quart pitcher. Add 1 cup sugar and stir. Add ice cubes and then fill almost to the top with cold water. Rinse one lemon, slice into rounds and add rounds to the pitcher. (Adjust fresh lemon juice and sugar to taste.) Refrigerate until chilled through. This fresh-squeezed lemonade (which can be enjoyed "as is" by friends who aren't drinking alcohol) is what you'll use to make your tankini martinis.

A day ahead of time, put a bottle of vodka in the freezer. On the day of, for each guest, have a martini glass ready. Rub the inside of each martini glass with fresh mint leaves and then discard the mint. Put a few drops of vermouth into each glass. Make sure lemonade is ice cold; pour about $1/4$ cup of fresh-squeezed lemonade and 3 Tablespoons vodka into each glass. These are stirred and not shaken. Garnish with a piece of lemon if desired.

62

small talk

## "How are you?"

This is a standard question asked the world over, either immediately following or instead of a greeting. The accepted response goes something like "Fine, thanks, and you?" If you attempt to give an even halfway intelligent or personal answer, you come off as a clueless idiot who can't even understand the simplest warm-up rituals. And who would ever want to risk an intelligent or personal conversation with someone like that?

| | |
|---|---|
| German | Wie geht's? |
| French | Ça va? |
| Italian | Come va? |
| Spanish | ¿Cómo está? |
| Dutch | Hoe gaat het ermee? |
| Norwegian | Hvorden har du det? |
| Swedish | Hur star det till? |
| Hungarian | Hogy vagy? |
| Polish | Jak sie masz? |
| Slovenic | Kakosi? |
| Finnish | Mitä Kuuluu? |
| Hessian | Ei gude wie? |
| But not | How are you really? |

# S.O.S.

## "Help, I Forgot the Food!"

Dear Advice Columnist, Whenever I invite people over, I can't get anything done because I'm paralyzed with stage fright. When the doorbell rings, the wine is still warm, the soup is still unmade and the dessert is still at the store. Even if I excuse myself a thousand times, nothing ever goes right until we get to the after-dinner coffee. Why not sooner?
Patrick from Little Rock

Dear Patrick:

Just imagine you're going out to eat. The waiter starts off by telling you that everything is going wrong today. He tells you that the chef made something fantastic but it's not on the menu and anyway, it just fell into the sink. Would you like coffee or milk? Sorry, we're out of milk. Wouldn't that be an unforgettable experience? And now, what do you imagine your friends are thinking when you invite them over—"You've got to be kidding?" Then why do they come? They're probably as nice as you are so instead, they're asking themselves, "Why does he put himself through it?" And nothing is more uncomfortable for guests than to feel like a burden. So in the future, do it like this:

1. Write it all down: the menu, the shopping list and the timetable. Don't make the lists too long or you'll be overwhelmed by them. After each party, make a note of what went wrong so you'll remember for next time.
2. Ask for help. Have a talented friend show up before everyone else, even if his only talent is remembering things. Have a reliable guest call you just before she leaves home so she can pick up anything you might have forgotten.
3. Let it go. If the party is just about to start and you remember that you wanted to make a bombe glacée, just let it go. Instead, make sure everything else is OK, including yourself.
4. Be resourceful. Make the salad into the appetizer if the roast is taking more time than expected.
5. Make it easy on yourself. Limit yourself to making coq au vin and do it a day ahead of time. Then you'll already have wine and won't have to chill it at the last minute.
6. If something still goes wrong, play it up big. Excuse yourself once and for all. Does everything still go wrong? Then invite your friends to join you at a bar for drinks or stop inviting people altogether. Sometimes that can make friends happier than anything else you try to do.

# Fondue times five

"The nice thing about fondue is that there's so little work involved." Oh yeah, dear guest? And what about the whole day I just spent cutting up meat, chopping vegetables, mixing sauces—do you call that nothing? "Yes, but we're doing part of the work now. And besides, you can buy the sauces already made." Is that the kind of sauce you like? "Well, no." OK then, these sauces here are nice and quick. And feed four:

## Sauce Phil
Peel and chop 1 clove garlic and grate 1 piece ginger (½" chunk) for its juice. Peel a small mango and dice. Puree these ingredients together with ½ cup tomato ketchup, 1 tablespoon honey and 1 tablespoon balsamic

vinegar. Salt and pepper to taste. Best with meats cooked in an oil fondue.

## Sauce Carlita
Mix ¼ cup spicy mustard with ½ cup mayonnaise, 1 teaspoon harissa, salt and pepper. Thin with some cream and stir. Adjust salt and add freshly ground black pepper to taste.

## Sauce Pierre
Cut 1 green onion into rings and sauté briefly in 2 tablespoons butter. Add 1 cup frozen peas and ½ cup vegetable stock and simmer for 5 minutes. Stir in ⅓ cup crème fraiche,

1 tablespoon spicy mustard, ½ teaspoon Worcestershire sauce and a couple drops of fresh lemon juice. Let cool and transfer to a blender or food processor; puree. Salt and pepper to taste. Good with fish, veal or poultry cooked in stock fondue.

## Sauce Madame Wong
Lightly toast 1¼ cups sesame seeds in a dry frying pan over medium heat. Pour in ¼ cup soy sauce, ¼ cup rice vinegar and ½ cup stock. Add 1 tablespoon brown sugar and simmer until the sugar dissolves. Let cool. Best with a stock fondue.

## Sauce Estrellita
Reduce ¼ cup sherry vinegar and ½ cup sugar. Briefly simmer 1 cup raisins in this mixture and let cool. In a food processor or blender, puree mixture with 2 peeled garlic cloves, 1–2 jalapeño peppers (ribs and seeds discarded for less heat) and the zest and juice of 1 lime. Salt and pepper to taste. Good with vegetables, meat and poultry cooked in an oil fondue.

# Marinated Vegetables
## Trendy tapas

**Preparation:** No more than 2 days ahead
**Storage:** Covered with plastic wrap in the refrigerator
**Serve with:** Goes with anything

Makes enough for 4:

**For the sherry onions:**

4 cups pearl onions or small shallots

2 tablespoons olive oil

$\frac{1}{4}$ cup dry sherry

$3\frac{1}{2}$ tablespoons white wine vinegar

1 dried chile pepper

Salt, 2 teaspoons sugar

**For the zucchini:**

1 pound zucchini (about $2\frac{2}{3}$ cups)

$\frac{1}{3}$ cup olive oil

Salt, freshly ground black pepper

4 sprigs fresh thyme

$\frac{1}{2}$ lemon, 2 garlic cloves

Capers for sprinkling (optional)

**For the bell peppers:**

1 large or 2 small red bell peppers

1 large or 2 small yellow bell peppers

1 fresh red chile pepper

1 tablespoon fresh lemon juice

2 tablespoons olive oil, Salt

$\frac{1}{2}$ cup fresh parsley sprigs

**1** Onions: Peel well and brown whole in oil in a pot. Pour in sherry and vinegar. Chop chile pepper and add (for less spice, don't chop). Add $\frac{1}{2}$ cup water, salt and sugar. Simmer 20 minutes. Let cool.

**2** Zucchini: Preheat oven to 450°F. Rinse and clean zucchini, cut lengthwise into slices

¼" thick and cut slices in half. Grease baking sheet with 2 tablespoons of the oil, place the zucchini on it and season with salt and pepper.

3 Rinse thyme, strip leaves off stems and sprinkle over zucchini. Then sprinkle with 2 tablespoons of the oil, place in oven (center shelf) and bake about 10 minutes until zucchini is brown. Turn slices over halfway through.

4 In the meantime, rinse lemon, remove zest and squeeze out juice. Peel garlic and mince. Place zucchini in a bowl. Mix garlic around in the baking juice left on the baking sheet; add lemon juice, zest and remaining oil and pour over the zucchini. Marinate at least 4 hours. If you want, you can sprinkle capers over the top.

5 Bell peppers: Take advantage of the hot oven. Rinse bell and chile peppers. Cut bell peppers in half and remove the interior. Place chile and bell peppers on a baking sheet. Bake for about 20 minutes in the hot oven until their peels turn brown. Let cool briefly and remove peels (use gloves when working with spicy peppers).

6 Cut bell peppers into lengthwise strips and chile pepper into ½" rounds. Combine both with lemon juice, oil and salt and marinate for 4 hours. Before the party, rinse parsley, chop finely and sprinkle over the top.

Prep time: Onions—20 minutes (+ 20 minutes for simmering); zucchini—20 minutes; peppers—35 minutes
Calories per serving: Sherry onions—130; zucchini—130; peppers—55

# Calamari Salad
## Has a Mediterranean flavor

**Preparation:** The day before
**Storage:** Covered serving bowl in the refrigerator
**Serve with:** Greek potato puree, pasta salad with radicchio, eggplant caviar

Makes enough for 4:

1 lb. uncooked calamari fillets or rings

4 red wine corks

2 cloves garlic

⅓ cup parsley sprigs

2 tablespoons fresh lemon juice

¼ cup extra virgin olive oil

Salt, freshly ground black pepper

1 Rinse calamari well in cold water; if fillets, cut into rings. Place rings in a pot and pour water over the top. Add the corks (the tannins make the squid nice and tender) and heat to a gentle boil. Reduce heat and simmer the squid for about 30 minutes with the lid halfway off (stir once during the process). Leave it in the water to cool.

2 Peel garlic and mince. Rinse parsley, shake dry and mince. Combine both with lemon juice and olive oil.

3 Remove squid from the water, rinse, then add to the marinade and stir; season with salt and pepper and marinate at least 4 hours.

Prep time: 40 minutes
(+ 4 hours marinating time)
Calories per serving: 220

# Ham Carpaccio
## It doesn't always have to be beef

**Preparation:** Mix vinaigrette 1–2 hours ahead and pour over prosciutto at the last minute
**Storage:** Briefly in refrigerator
**Serve with:** Frittata cubes, stuffed tomatoes, creamy mushroom soup

Makes enough for 4:

½ pound honeydew melon (about 1½ cups)

½ lemon

½ teaspoon green peppercorns

Salt

¾ cup arugula leaves

1 tablespoon pine nuts

8 slices prosciutto

(or serrano or other cured ham)

2 tablespoons extra virgin olive oil

1 Peel melon, scoop out seeds and dice melon finely. Zest lemon and squeeze out juice into a cup. Chop peppercorns coarsely or grind briefly in a grinder (or mortar and pestle). Combine melon with pepper, lemon zest and 2–3 teaspoons of the lemon juice. Salt lightly.

2 Rinse arugula, shake dry and cut off tough stems. Tear coarsely. Toast pine nuts in a dry frying pan over medium heat.

3 Cut prosciutto into large bite-sized pieces and arrange on small plates with the arugula. Top with diced melon mixture and pine nuts. Sprinkle with the olive oil.

Prep time: 20 minutes
Calories per serving: 205

# Eggplant Caviar
## Fresh and fruity

**Preparation:** No more than 3 days ahead
**Storage:** Covered in the refrigerator
**Serve with:** Chicken saltimbocca, Greek potato purée, stuffed tomatoes

Makes enough for 4:

2 medium-sized eggplants (a little over 1 lb.)

1 medium onion

2 cloves garlic

1 small red bell pepper

1 small yellow bell pepper

2 small tomatoes

1/4 cup olive oil

1 tablespoon fresh lemon juice

1 pinch sugar

Salt, freshly ground black pepper

Parsley leaves for garnish

1 First preheat the oven to 400°F. Place eggplants whole on a baking sheet and place in oven. Bake about 30 minutes until tender.

2 In the meantime, peel onions and garlic and mince both finely. Rinse bell peppers; remove tops, remove contents and dice rest finely.

3 Remove stems from tomatoes. Pour boiling water over the top and let stand briefly. Pour off water and remove peels. Seed tomatoes and dice finely.

4 In a large pan, heat 2 tablespoons of the oil, add onions and brown briefly. Add bell peppers and let cook for about 5 minutes, stirring occasionally. Add garlic.

5 Halve eggplants lengthwise. Scrape tender flesh away from peel with a spoon and mash it with a fork. Add to peppers along with tomatoes and remaining oil.

6 Cover and simmer vegetable puree over low heat for about 1 hour, stirring occasionally. If liquid still remains in the purée at the end of this time, simmer uncovered. Season eggplant puree with lemon juice, sugar, salt and pepper; pour into a bowl, cover and refrigerate for at least 1 day. Garnish with parsley leaves.

Prep time: 40 minutes (+ 1 hour cooking time and 1 day refrigeration time)
Goes with: Fresh flatbread or baguette, chicken, lamb
Calories per serving: 125

# Chopped Asian Chicken Salad
## For impromptu weeknight gatherings

**Preparation:** Right before serving
**Storage:** Not recommended
**Serve with:** Tamago maki, Won ton chips, Chinese herb rolls

Makes enough for 4:

6 oz. grilled cubed chicken (purchased)

16 leaves romaine lettuce

4 mandarin oranges, 1 red bell pepper

1/4 red onion, 1/2 cup peanuts

1 cup crispy chow mein noodles

3 tablespoons fresh lemon juice

1/4 cup canola or peanut oil

1 teaspoon sesame oil

1 1/2 tablespoons sugar

1/2 teaspoon grated ginger

Salt, freshly ground pepper

1 Cut cooked chicken into 1/4–1/2" cubes. Rinse romaine leaves, cut off tough ends and pat dry. Cut mandarins in half, remove visible seeds, and remove peels; separate the halved segments. Rinse and chop bell pepper, minus ribs and seeds, into 1/4–1/2" pieces. Chop red onion. Cut romaine into bite-sized pieces.

**2** Toss everything you just chopped with peanuts and chow mein noodles.

**3** Whisk together lemon juice, sesame oil, grated ginger, sugar, salt, pepper, and oil. Add in small amounts to the chopped salad, tossing, until lettuce pieces are shiny. If desired, add more dressing; salt and pepper to taste.

Prep time: 30 minutes

# Turkey with Cajun Salsa
## Light a fire under the party

**Preparation:** No more than 1 day ahead
**Storage:** Covered in the refrigerator
**Serve with:** Marinated vegetables, frittata cubes, Roquefort-crème fraiche dip

Makes enough for 4:

3 stalks celery, 1 red bell pepper

$1/2$ white onion, $1/2$ cup fresh parsley sprigs

4 sprigs fresh thyme or $1/2$ teaspoon dried

$1/3$ cup peeled and cooked shrimp

1 tablespoon spicy mustard

1 tablespoon white wine vinegar

Worcestershire sauce

A few drops Tabasco, Salt

1 lb. smoked turkey breast (thinly sliced)

1 cup sour cream

**1** Rinse vegetables. Clean celery and cut lengthwise into narrow strips, then dice. Dice bell pepper finely. Peel onion and mince. Rinse thyme and parsley, remove leaves and chop.

**2** Chop shrimp and combine with chopped vegetables, mustard and vinegar; season to taste with Worcestershire sauce, Tabasco and salt. Refrigerate Cajun salsa for at least 1 hour.

**3** Roll up turkey slices. Serve with Cajun salsa and sour cream on the side or arrange all three on small plates.

Prep time: 30 minutes
(+ 1 hour marinating time)
Calories per serving: 320

# Tamago Maki
## Imitates sushi

**Preparation:** 2 days ahead
**Storage:** Covered with plastic wrap in the refrigerator
**Serve with:** Shrimp dip, tamarind chicken, Chinese herb rolls

Makes enough for 4:

$6 1/2$ cups fresh spinach

3 tablespoons soy sauce

2 tablespoons rice wine (sake or mirin)

4 eggs, 1 tablespoon sugar

3 tablespoons fish stock (dashi) (specialty store)

2–3 tablespoons oil for frying

**1** In a large pot, heat a large amount of water. Rinse spinach thoroughly, removing any wilted leaves and cutting off thick and long stems. Toss the spinach into the boiling water for 1 minute. Pour into a colander, rinse under cold water and let cool. Squeeze out as much moisture as possible and mix with 1 tablespoon of the soy sauce, plus 1 tablespoon of the rice wine.

**2** Briefly whisk together eggs, remaining soy sauce, sugar, fish stock and remaining rice wine but stop before it gets foamy. Heat a pan and spread a little oil in it. Pour in $1/4$ of the egg mixture and cook over medium heat until it becomes firm. It should still be slightly moist on top. Slide eggs from the pan onto a board. Fry the remaining egg mixture in the same way in 3 more portions.

**3** Divide the pile of spinach into 4 portions. Shape each spinach portion into a long cylinder as you lay it on top of one of the omelets. Roll up the omelets, wrap in plastic wrap and chill thoroughly. Cut into rounds and serve on the buffet with a side of soy sauce.

Prep time: 30 minutes (+ refrigeration time)
Calories per serving: 175

# Potato Terrine with Goat Cheese
Combo for discerning tastes

**Preparation:** 1–2 days ahead
**Storage:** Covered in the refrigerator
**Serve with:** Tomato soup, herb relish, rye bread with mushroom caviar

Not worth it for less than 8:

1⅛ lbs. potatoes (about 2¼ cups; about 2 potatoes depending on size)

1 cup pine nuts

1 cup basil leaves

⅔ cup goat cheese

⅓ cup freshly grated Parmesan

3½ tablespoons softened butter

¾ cup cream

Salt, freshly ground white pepper

1¼ teaspoons agar powder (or 1½ teaspoons gelatin powder)

Butter for the terrine

1 Rinse potatoes and place in a pot. Pour in enough water to cover them halfway, cover and cook until tender (about 25 minutes).

2 This will leave you enough time to toast the pine nuts—in a dry pan over medium heat while constantly stirring. Finely chop one-third of the nuts. Remove leaves from basil and chop finely.

3 Mix goat cheese together with Parmesan and butter. Pour water off potatoes, slip off skins, and mash immediately using a potato masher, electric mixer, or fork.

4 Beat half of the cream until stiff. Combine potatoes, cheese mixture, chopped pine nuts and basil and season generously with salt and pepper. Fold in whipped cream. Combine remaining cream with agar and simmer 1–2 minutes. Let cool slightly and add to potato mixture. Butter a long, narrow terrine pan (about 1 quart volume); or use several small narrow loaf pans. Sprinkle in the pine nuts, distributing them evenly. Pour in potato mixture. Refrigerate for at least 2 hours, then carefully detach the sides from the terrine with a knife, reverse onto a plate and cut into thin slices.

Prep time: 1 hour (+ refrigeration time)
Calories per serving: 365

# Shrimp Terrine Canapés
Truly upscale

**Preparation:** 1-2 days ahead
**Storage:** Covered in the refrigerator
**Serve with:** Herb relish, cauliflower salad with capers, marinated vegetables

Not worth it for less than 8:

1⅓ lbs. fish fillets (perch, trout, salmon or pike)

1 tablespoon fresh lemon juice

1 tablespoon Grappa liquor (or other high alcohol % liquor)

Salt, freshly ground white pepper

¾ cup cream

7 oz. or ⅔ cup uncooked shrimp (peeled and deveined)

1 tablespoon butter for the terrine

¾ cup dill fronds

Crackers or small toasts

1 Dice fish fillets very finely. Combine with lemon juice, Grappa, about a teaspoon of salt and a ½ teaspoon white pepper and place in the freezer for 20 minutes.

2 Then purée finely with a hand blender or in a food processor while gradually adding

the cream. Pour into a bowl, season again with a little salt and pepper and fold in shrimp.

**3** Preheat the oven to 300°F. Thoroughly butter the longest and narrowest terrine pan or casserole dish you can find (about 1 quart volume). Rinse dill and reserve some for garnishing; chop rest, sprinkling it in the terrine. Slowly and carefully spread the fish mixture in the terrine. Seal with aluminum foil.

**4** In a larger baking dish, pour some water and lower terrine dish down into the "water bath"—the water should come about halfway up the sides of the terrine baking dish. Place dish in the oven (bottom shelf) and bake for about 50 minutes. Remove the terrine from the water bath and let cool. Then tightly cover with plastic wrap and refrigerate for 1–2 days. Before the party, carefully reverse onto a plate and slice. If liquid has formed, carefully pour it off ahead of time.

**5** Take small slices of the terrine and place on top of water crackers or small pieces of toast. (For making the toasts, trim edges of white bread, cut into fourths diagonally, brush tops with butter and bake in a 350 degree oven until lightly golden.) Garnish with dill!

Prep time: At least 1½ hours, 30 minutes of which you're actually busy. (+ 1 day or more refrigeration time)
Calories per serving: 215

# Duck Pâté
## Very fancy and time consuming

**Preparation:** 2–3 days ahead; remove from terrine pan after baking
**Storage:** Covered in the refrigerator
**Serve with:** Fresh salads

Not worth it for less than 14:

5½ tablespoons butter, 3 cups flour

1 egg white (reserve egg yolk), Salt

1 duck (about 4 to 5 lbs.)

½ lb. boneless-skinless chicken breast fillets

1 tablespoon ground coriander

2 teaspoons freshly ground black pepper

3 tablespoons Calvados (apple brandy)

6 fresh thyme sprigs

2 eggs, ¾ cup cream

2 tablespoons chopped pistachios

For brushing on: 1 egg yolk (that you reserved), 1 tablespoon milk

**1** First the crust: Cut butter into bits and combine with flour, egg white and 1 teaspoon salt in a bowl—use a pastry cutter, two forks, or your hands to mix. Add ⅓ to ½ cup cold water and knead with a dough hook on an electric mixer or your hands until dough is smooth. Refrigerate covered 1 hour or more.

**2** Remove skin from the duck; cut meat off bones and chop into pieces. Mix chopped duck meat with coriander, pepper and Calvados and place in the freezer for 30 minutes. Chop chicken breast into pieces (refrigerate).

**3** Then puree duck-mixture in a food processor or with a hand blender. Rinse thyme, remove leaves and combine with eggs, cream and pistachios. Then add diced chicken breast meat and season generously with about 1 teaspoon salt or a little more. Refrigerate.

**4** Now you need a pâté, terrine or narrow bread pan (about a foot long). The dough will need to cover it completely on bottom, sides, and on top of the filling. Roll out the dough to about ⅛–¼" thick and cut into large pieces, using the pan as a template. Don't forget the top. Place the dough pieces for the bottom and sides in the pan. Gradually spread in the filling, periodically tapping the pan onto the table to release any trapped air bubbles. Cut a few holes in the dough piece for the top and set it on the filling. Make decorations from the remaining dough and arrange them on top.

**5** Preheat oven to 450°F. Place pâté on center shelf and bake for 20 minutes. Then brush with egg yolk and milk, reduce heat to 350°F and bake it about another 35 minutes. Perform a doneness test: pierce the top with a long wooden skewer. Wait till juice runs out and the juice is clear. Let pâté cool in the pan.

Prep time: 2½ hours (+55 minutes baking time)
Calories per serving: 530

# Tamarind Chicken
### Are you craving fruit and spices?

**Preparation:** Prepare chicken no more than 1–2 days ahead, make salad up fresh
**Storage:** Covered in the refrigerator
**Serve with:** Tomato dip, Indian potato salad, colombo

Makes enough for 4:

1 tablespoon tamarind pulp (from a jar) or

prepared tamarind paste

4 cloves garlic

1 piece fresh ginger (about 3/4" long)

1–2 teaspoons sambal oelek (Indian, Asian, or specialty market)

1 teaspoon ground cumin

Salt

4 chicken breast fillets (about 1 to 1 1/2 pounds)

2 tablespoons vegetable oil

1 mango

1 small cucumber

1 tomato

3 tablespoons fresh lemon juice

1/3 cup coconut milk (from a can)

1 Place tamarind pulp in a bowl, pour 1/3 cup hot water over the top and steep briefly. Or stir paste into 1/4 cup water.

2 Peel garlic and ginger, squeeze through a press and place in another bowl. Add sambal oelek and cumin. Stir tamarind pulp in its steeping water, press through a strainer and add liquid to garlic mixture. Season with salt. Mix with chicken breasts and marinate for at least 2 hours, turning them over occasionally.

3 Then remove them from the marinade. Heat oil in a pan, add the chicken breast fillets and sauté over medium heat for about 5 minutes on each side. Pour marinade in pan and let boil down; turning fillets occasionally. Let cool.

4 Peel mango. Cut fruit away from pit and slice into thin 1"-long strips. Peel cucumber, halve lengthwise, remove seeds with a spoon and slice into half rounds on the diagonal. Rinse tomato and dice. Cut chicken into thin 1"-wide strips or bite-sized pieces. Combine lemon juice and coconut milk and season with salt. Mix all the salad ingredients with this dressing. Adjust spices to taste and serve.

Prep time: 40 minutes
(not including marinating time)
Calories per serving: 310

# Variation: Turkey Grapefruit Salad

Cook about a pound of turkey breast meat in chicken stock (or broth) covered, over medium heat, for about 20 minutes. Let cool and dice. Cut peeling off 1 pink grapefruit, cut out sections, and dice. Drain 1 small can pineapple chunks. Combine 2 tablespoons pineapple juice with 2/3 cup yogurt and 1 teaspoon curry powder and season with salt. Combine all salad ingredients and add dressing. Place oakleaf lettuce, iceberg lettuce or curly endive leaves in glasses and fill with turkey salad.

# Tangy Marinated Cheese and Vegetables
You won't be sorry

**Preparation:** No more than 6–8 hours ahead
**Storage:** Covered in the refrigerator
**Serve with:** Dutch Stamppott stew, deviled eggs, rye bread with mushroom caviar

Makes enough for 4–6:

8 radishes

8 chive spears

1 firm tomato

½ red onion

1 lb. cheese (gouda, fresh mozzarella,

or any white semi-firm cheese—

even feta or ricotta would work)

2–3 tablespoons vinegar

2 teaspoons spicy mustard

Salt, freshly ground black pepper

¼ cup vegetable oil

1 cup arugula leaves

**1** Rinse radishes, chives and tomato. Slice radishes, chop chives and dice tomato finely. Peel onion and mince half.

**2** Dice cheese and add to other chopped ingredients. Combine vinegar, mustard, salt and pepper. Whisk in oil and add dressing to cheese-vegetable mixture. Let marinate covered in refrigerator for at least 30 minutes. Rinse arugula. Place inside glasses and fill with marinated cheese and vegetables.

Prep time: 20 minutes
Calories per serving: 420

# Ham Salad Nouveau
Pretty in pink

**Preparation:** 1–2 days ahead
**Storage:** Covered in the refrigerator
**Serve with:** Eggplant caviar, Hungarian paprika soup, cheesy crackers

Makes enough for 4–6:

1 russet potato (a little less than a cup,

about 7 oz.)

1 teaspoon mustard powder

Half can of diced cooked beets, not

the pickled type (about 7½ oz.)

1 small tart apple (granny smith, etc.)

1 lb. cooked ham, unsliced

1 dill pickle or 8 cornichons

¾ cup sour cream

Salt, freshly ground black pepper

**1** Boil potato skin on until pierces easily with a paring knife (but don't let it get mushy); drain and let cool. You can also use a previously cooked potato. Stir mustard powder into 1 tablespoon warm water and let stand 10 minutes.

**2** Drain beets. Peel apple and remove core. Peel potato. Dice all three ingredients into uniform cubes along with the ham and pickles.

**3** Stir mustard powder mixture into sour cream; season with salt and pepper and mix with diced ingredients. Adjust salt and pepper to taste and it's done!

Prep time: 30 minutes
Calories per serving: 415

# Carrot Salad with Grapes
Middle-Eastern!

**Preparation:** In the morning or afternoon
**Storage:** In the refrigerator covered with plastic wrap
**Serve with:** Falafel, tomato dip, orzo soup with garbanzo beans

Makes enough for 4:

2½ cups seedless grapes (preferably

a mixture of black, red, and green)

1 lb. carrots

2 tablespoons olive oil

Salt, freshly ground black pepper

2 green onions

2 sprigs fresh mint or 4 sprigs parsley

1–2 tablespoons fresh lemon juice

1 pinch ground cumin

1 pinch ground coriander

¼ teaspoon chili powder

**1** Rinse grapes, remove stems and cut in half. Peel carrots, rinse and cut into ¼" round slices.

**2** In a pot, heat 1 tablespoon of the oil. Stir in carrots. Add 2 tablespoons water and season with salt and pepper. Cover and cook over medium heat for about 5 minutes or until they are crisp-tender. Let cool.

**3** Remove roots from green onions and cut off dark green tops. Rinse remaining part and chop finely. Mince mint (or parsley).

**4** Combine carrots, green onions, grapes, herb, lemon juice, salt, pepper, cumin and coriander and add remaining oil. Stir together; place in a bowl and sprinkle chili powder over the top.

Prep time: 25 minutes
Calories per serving: 105

# Cauliflower Salad with Capers
Italian!

**Preparation:** Morning or midday, but don't add basil and capers until just before the party
**Storage:** In the refrigerator covered with plastic wrap
**Serve with:** Chicken saltimbocca, Greek potato purée, cheese rolls

Makes enough for 4:

1 medium-sized cauliflower

(or broccoflower, or green Italian romanesca)

Salt

¼ cup fresh basil leaves (or parsley)

with 4 sprigs for garnish

2 cloves garlic

4 small roma tomatoes

2–3 tablespoons red wine vinegar

¼ cup olive oil

Salt, freshly ground black pepper

2 tablespoons capers

1 Rinse cauliflower and remove leaves and stalk. Cut off the individual florets. In a pot, bring a large amount of salted water to a boil. When it's really rolling, cook the florets in it for about 5 minutes or just until crisp-tender. You don't want them to be mushy.

2 Carefully pour cauliflower into a colander and rinse under cold water. Let cool.

3 Don't rinse the basil; if you have to, wipe it off with a paper towel; chop. Peel garlic and mince finely. Rinse tomatoes, remove stems and dice finely.

4 Combine vinegar, oil, salt and pepper and mix gently with the other ingredients. Just before the party, sprinkle capers over the top. Garnish with herb sprigs.

Prep time: 20 minutes
(not including cooling time)
Calories per serving: 135

# Leek Tofu Salad with Peanut Dressing
Indonesian!

**Preparation:** Blanch leeks and make dressing on the previous day; dress salad before the party
**Storage:** Covered in the refrigerator
**Serve with:** Miso soup, duck curry, vegetable skewers

Makes enough for 4:

2–3 leeks

Salt

$1/2$ head of iceberg lettuce

1 red bell pepper

1 package firm tofu (about 8 oz.)

$2/3$ cup smooth peanut butter

1 cup vegetable stock

$1/2$ teaspoon chile oil or 1 teaspoon Sambal Oelek

1–2 cloves garlic

2 tablespoons soy sauce

1 tablespoon fresh lemon juice

1 Remove roots and darkest leaf tops from leeks. Slit open lengthwise and rinse thoroughly, then cut into strips about $1/4$" wide x 4" long.

2 Bring salted water to a boil. Throw in the leek strips and cook about 2 minutes until they're al dente. Pour into a colander, run cold water over them and drain.

3 Rinse iceberg lettuce and cut into 2" strips. Rinse bell pepper, remove top and pull out interior and discard; then dice rest finely or cut into 2" strips. Place lettuce on a platter and top with peppers and leeks.

4 Cut tofu into cubes and sprinkle over the top. Puree together the peanut butter, vegetable stock and chile oil (using a hand blender). Peel garlic, squeeze through a press and add. Stir in soy sauce and lemon juice and add salt if desired. Drizzle dressing on the salad just before serving.

Prep time: 25 minutes
Calories per serving: 310

# Pasta Salad with Radicchio
## No party should be without it!

**Preparation:** In the morning
**Storage:** In the refrigerator covered with plastic wrap
**Serve with:** Rolled roast pork, stuffed tomatoes, salmon tramezzini

Makes enough for 4:

8 oz. penne pasta (or fusilli,

orrecchiette, or any short type)

Salt

2 stalks celery

1 small head radicchio

3½ oz. prosciutto

¼ cup olive oil

2 tomatoes

2 tablespoons pine nuts

3 tablespoons red wine vinegar

Salt, freshly ground black pepper

1 In a pot, bring at least 3 quarts water to a boil for the pasta. Add salt and pasta and boil for about 8 minutes or until it's al dente. Some types need a little longer so make sure to test a piece. Pour the pasta into a colander, rinse thoroughly under cold water and let drain.

2 Rinse celery and cut off ends. Cut into ¼" slices. Remove the outermost leaves from the radicchio (reserving 4 to 8 attractive leaves); halve the head through the core and cut the halves into narrow strips. Also cut prosciutto into narrow strips.

3 In a pan, heat 1 tablespoon of the olive oil. Add prosciutto strips and fry until nice and crispy while stirring constantly. Remove prosciutto and sauté radicchio and celery in the same oil for about 2 minutes. Set aside on a plate. Sauté pine nuts in the same pan until lightly brown stirring constantly. Set aside to cool.

4 Rinse tomatoes and dice finely.

5 Mix together vinegar, salt, pepper and remaining oil. Combine all the salad ingredients in a bowl and add dressing. Season to taste.

6 Rinse and pat dry reserved radicchio leaves. Serve the salad using the leaves as cups.

Prep time: 30 minutes
Calories per serving: 480

## Even More Pasta: Thai Salad with Mango

Peel and mince 2 cloves garlic. Rinse 1–2 jalapeño peppers, remove seeds and ribs; mince. Mix 2 tablespoons soy sauce with ⅔ lb. ground pork and let stand 15 minutes. Peel and dice 1 mango. Combine with ¼–⅓ cup lime juice, 1–2 tablespoons fish sauce (nam pla) and 2 teaspoons brown sugar. In the wok, heat 2 tablespoons oil. Fry the meat, breaking it up into crumbles. Let cool. Cook 5–6 oz. thin rice noodles (you can also substitute linguine) in salted water according to the directions on the package. Rinse under cold water and let drain. Mix ⅓ cup fresh basil leaves with noodles, cooked ground meat, mango-mixture, garlic, and jalapeños. Marinate for 30 minutes before serving.

# Potato-Vegetable Salad Niçoise
## Pretend like you're on the Riviera

**Preparation:** Prepare potato vegetable salad in the morning, sprinkle on anchovies, tuna and olives just before the party.
**Storage:** Covered in the refrigerator
**Serve with:** Duck pâté, beet dip, rosemary onion soup

Makes enough for 4:

3–4 small potatoes (firm, about 1 lb. or 3 cups once cooked and sliced)

1 lb. green beans

Salt

1 lb. tomatoes

4 anchovy fillets packed in oil

1 can tuna packed in water

¼ cup fresh basil leaves

2–3 tablespoons white wine vinegar

Freshly ground black pepper

¼ cup extra virgin olive oil

2 tablespoons pitted black olives, preferably kalamata or niçoise

**1** Brush off potatoes under the faucet, place in a pot with the skins on and cover with lightly salted water. Bring to a boil, cover and simmer over medium heat until tender enough to pierce with a paring knife. But don't let them get too soft! You'll want them firm enough to slice well. (About 15 minutes)

**2** In the meantime, rinse beans and break off the ends. And if the beans have strings (you'll notice them when you break off the ends), pull them out. Bring salted water to a boil and cook beans for about 3–5 minutes, or until crisp-tender. Pour into a colander and rinse under cold water. Break larger beans in half.

**3** Cut stem end out from the tomatoes; pour boiling water over them and wait briefly. Pour off the water and rinse under cold water; peel, remove seeds with your fingers, and cut into eighths. Drain anchovies and halve. Drain tuna and pull apart into flakes. Tear larger leaves of basil; leave others whole.

**4** Combine vinegar with salt and pepper. Whisk in olive oil. Peel potatoes and slice, then mix with beans, tomatoes, dressing and basil and place in a bowl. Sprinkle with anchovies, tuna and olives when serving.

Prep time: 40 minutes
Calories per serving: 300

# Indian Potato Salad
## Good & spicy

**Preparation:** Prepare potatoes and cauliflower no more than 1 day ahead, chop and mix ingredients in the morning
**Storage:** In a covered bowl in the refrigerator; sprinkle on mint at the last minute
**Serve with:** Meatballs, cucumber raita, eggplant caviar

Makes enough for 4:

1 lb. potatoes (firm type)

1 small head cauliflower

Salt

1 tomato

2 tablespoons fresh mint leaves and 4 sprigs for garnish

1 cup yogurt

½ teaspoon ground cumin

½ teaspoon ground coriander

½ teaspoon chili powder

½ teaspoon turmeric

1 tablespoon fresh lemon juice

1 tablespoon canola oil

1 Brush off potatoes. Boil in water with skin on until tender enough to pierce easily with a paring knife, but not mushy. Let cool.

2 Rinse cauliflower, remove leaves and cut into individual florets. Heat salted water in a large pot. Add cauliflower florets and boil 4–6 minutes until crisp-tender. Immediately pour into a colander and rinse well under cold water, then let drain.

3 Rinse tomato and dice. Mince mint leaves finely into almost a paste. Mix mint with the yogurt, cumin, coriander, chili powder, turmeric, lemon juice and oil. Add salt and pepper to taste.

4 Peel and dice potatoes. Combine with cauliflower and tomatoes and mix with the yogurt dressing. Adjust salt and garnish with mint sprigs.

Prep time: 40 minutes
Calories per serving: 160

# Rice Salad with Pomegranates
Cool & trendy

**Preparation:** Make rice no more than 1 day ahead of time, dress salad 2–3 hours before the party
**Storage:** Covered in the refrigerator
**Serve with:** Frittata cubes, chicken wings, avocado dip

Makes enough for 4:

2 cloves garlic

2 tablespoons oil

1 cup long-grain rice

2 cups vegetable stock

2 large, firm tomatoes

1 pomegranate

1 fresh red chile pepper

½ cup cilantro leaves

(or Italian flat-leaf parsley)

1 green onion

2 tablespoons lime or lemon juice

Salt

1 Peel garlic and mince. In a pot, sauté briefly in oil. Stir in rice, pour in stock and bring to a boil. Cover and switch to low heat. Cook rice 20–30 minutes until al dente and

the grains separate nicely. If there's too much liquid, cook uncovered for a few minutes to boil off.

2 Rinse tomatoes and dice very finely. Classier still: scald, peel, and seed tomatoes first. Cut the pomegranate in half crosswise. Scoop out the red seeds with a spoon. Rinse chile pepper and remove stem (wear gloves). Slit open pepper lengthwise and discard seeds and ribs; then cut crosswise into fine strips. Rinse cilantro under cold water, shake dry and remove leaves. Remove roots and wilted parts from green onion and chop finely.

3 Let rice cool, then combine with tomato, chile pepper, green onion and pomegranate seeds. Stir in lime juice and season with salt. Sprinkle cilantro leaves over the top.

Prep time: 30 minutes
(not including cooling time for rice)
Calories per serving: 170

Also good:
Mix diced avocado or sliced bananas into the rice, or even cooked shrimp. And it looks great arranged on lettuce leaves. Use types such as iceberg, endive, Boston/bibb or romaine that are sturdy and hold their shape.

# Bread Salad
Also tastes great the next day

**Preparation:** Morning or midday
**Storage:** Covered with plastic wrap in the refrigerator
**Serve with:** Marinated vegetables, calamari salad, tomato soup

Makes enough for 4:

4 roma tomatoes

1 medium-sized cucumber

3–4 cloves garlic

2 tablespoons mint leaves

A few green lettuce leaves

1/2 loaf French or Italian bread

3 tablespoons fresh lemon juice

Salt

1 teaspoon chile pepper flakes

(or substitute 1/2–1 teaspoons harissa)

1 teaspoon ground coriander

1/4 cup olive oil

Pitted black olives for garnish

**1** Rinse tomatoes and cucumber and chop. Peel garlic and mince. Rinse mint, shake dry, remove leaves and cut them into strips. Rinse lettuce leaves, dry and chop coarsely.

**2** Cut bread into 1/4" cubes and fry in a pan (preferably nonstick) until it's slightly toasted, stirring constantly.

**3** Mix lemon juice with salt, chile pepper flakes and coriander and stir in olive oil. Combine all the ingredients and marinate at least 2 hours. Just before the party, sprinkle with olives.

Prep time: 20 minutes
(+ 2 hours marinating time)
Calories per serving: 280

## Variation: Bulgur Salad
Instead of bread, combine 1/2 pound bulgur (about 1 cup) with 1 2/3 cups cold water and let soak about 1 hour or until it's soft. The rest is the same, except you can sprinkle feta cheese on top.

# Lentil Salad
Costs next to nothing

**Preparation:** No more than 1 day ahead
**Storage:** Store salad covered in the refrigerator; keep endive separate
**Serve with:** Chicken wings, Moroccan cream cheese dip, ratatouille with cheese baguette

Makes enough for 4:

1 cup black or green lentils

(specialty or health food store)

2 cloves garlic

8 sprigs thyme (4 are for garnish)

1 dried red chile pepper

1 bunch green onions (5–6)

1 tablespoon coarse mustard

2 tablespoons white wine vinegar

Salt, freshly ground black pepper

1/4 cup olive oil

Pinch sugar

1 head endive

**1** Pour lentils into a pot and cover generously with water. Peel garlic, rinse thyme and add garlic and 4 thyme sprigs to the lentils along with the whole chile pepper. Bring to a boil, cover, and cook over medium heat for about 35 minutes until al dente (test them even earlier). Remove chile pepper. Drain and let cool.

**2** Remove roots and dark green parts from the onions; rinse and cut into rings. Mix mustard, vinegar, salt and pepper. Vigorously whisk in oil. Add a pinch or more of sugar to taste.

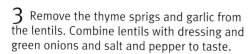

3 Remove the thyme sprigs and garlic from the lentils. Combine lentils with dressing and green onions and salt and pepper to taste.

4 Rinse endive, separate leaves and arrange around the sides of a small bowl. Pour lentil salad in the middle. Garnish with fresh thyme sprigs.

Prep time: 1 hour, about 15 minutes of which you're actually busy
Calories per serving: 270

## Variation: Beans with Pancetta

Rinse ¼ head savoy cabbage (or napa cabbage); clean and cut into narrow strips. Cook about 3–5 minutes in boiling, salted water. Pour into a colander and rinse under cold water. Cut 6 oz. pancetta (or regular bacon) into narrow strips and fry in a pan until crispy (no added oil). Mix both ingredients with 2 cans white beans (rinse and drain them thoroughly first) and 1 handful crumbled walnuts. Mix 3 tablespoons vinegar with ¼ cup olive oil, salt and pepper, and pinches of sugar to taste; add to the rest. Salt and pepper to taste.

# Gnocchi Salad with Almond Dressing
Impressive

**Preparation:** Prepare sauce the day before; cook or chop the rest in the morning. Don't combine gnocchi, sauce, tomatoes and herbs until 1 hour before the party
**Storage:** Covered in the refrigerator
**Serve with:** Ham carpaccio, marinated vegetables, cheese skewers

Makes enough for 4:

3 red bell peppers

1 dried chile pepper

2 cloves garlic

⅓ cup skinless almonds

¼ cup olive oil

1–2 tablespoons fresh lemon juice

Salt

1 lb. potato gnocchi

(from the grocer's refrigerated section)

3 roma tomatoes

½ cup basil leaves

4 green onions

1 First preheat oven to 475°F (or convection oven to 450°F). Rinse bell peppers, cut in

half and remove contents. Place peppers on a baking sheet with the cut side down and bake in the oven for about 20 minutes until the peel forms dark blisters.

2 Remove the peppers from the oven, let them cool until you can hold them in your hand and pull off the peels. If a few pieces of the peel remain, no problem. Dice 1 pepper finely and set aside.

3 Cut rest of the peppers coarsely and throw into the blender along with the chile pepper (rib and seeds removed). Peel garlic and also add to the blender along with almonds and oil. Puree everything finely. Season to taste with lemon juice and salt.

4 For the gnocchi, bring salted water to a boil in a large pot. Cook gnocchi according to the directions on the package, then carefully pour into a colander and rinse under cold water.

5 Rinse tomatoes, seed, and dice very finely. Remove basil leaves and cut into strips. Remove roots and wilted parts from green onions; rinse and cut into fine rings.

6 Loosely mix together gnocchi, almond sauce, tomatoes, basil, and green onions. Season to taste with salt and pepper and place in a bowl, preferably a shallow one.

Prep time: 45 minutes
Calories per serving: 300

# Wok this way!

When it's a large group, when you need some sizzle in your life and when everyone's going to end up in the kitchen anyway.

## Cooking Aromatic Rice

We recommend jasmine rice, which should be prepared somewhat sticky. To serve 12, bring a scant 2 quarts water to a boil. Add 2¼ pounds rice and boil for about 1 minute. Cover, turn the heat to very low and cook rice for 10 minutes. In the bottom of a large pot, bring ½" water to a boil (must be big enough to fit the other pot). Set the pot of partially cooked rice down into this water and cook, covered, for 15 minutes over very low heat. Turn off heat. This will keep it hot and al dente for 1 hour. To reheat rice, bring the bottom pot's water to a boil again and turn off heat (keep covered). Another option: use a rice cooker and follow its manual instructions.

## Creating the Right Atmosphere

Imagine the night market in Phuket, Thailand and the streets of Shanghai, China. Picture lagoon turquoise, palm green, royal purple, neon pink, imperial gold. Send out chopsticks, red placemats and leaves from a jade plant as invitations. Drape colorful banners with golden calligraphy from the ceiling and over the table. Illuminate lanterns and goldfish bowls. Play Bali beat, jungle jive, Singapore swing and Taiwan trance—the main thing is that it be exotic. Just don't play anything for meditating!

You can buy an Asian-style gas burner for tabletop or buffet-top cooking at most Asian markets. Or, cook with the wok on your stove and set up the wok party around it. You are the wok-master, full of "ying." Authentic wok cooking is "yang" – fire, action and creativity. Perfect for when you want an eventful party that mimics Singapore street life, with the kitchen table as a market place and the stove as a food stall. Guests pick what they want to eat and you, the wok-master, sizzle it up and serve it for them on their bowl of rice. Satisfaction guaranteed, with aroma and sound-effects included!

## What You Need

Let's start with the heat source. It should be intense and direct, which means a gas stove is preferable but electric is still acceptable. Depending on the type of heat you use, the wok's bottom is either rounded (gas) or flat (electric) and the wok itself is thin-walled for fast cooking. Here, more are better: buy two woks if you can afford it. Otherwise, a party of 10 or more will lead to traffic jams at your food stall. You can stir with a wok spatula, wooden spoon, or some cooking-style chopsticks!

Place all of the uncooked vegetables, meat, fish and tofu in separate bowls and on plates of various shapes and colors on the buffet area to create the "marketplace." Plus, provide a stack of plates for your guests. Next to the wok, place the rice bowls (1½ to 2 cup capacity). You can buy these in an Asian market but cereal bowls are also fine. And don't forget the chopsticks, plus forks for emergencies. Finally, add some Asian teacups or small teacups and drinking glasses.

## How to Wok

At the buffet guests fill their own plates, keeping each ingredient in a separate pile.

They then proceed to the "food stall" where the wok-master already has the wok extremely hot. Here's how the master proceeds: drops in 1 tablespoon oil and then stir-fries the guest's meat or fish, while stirring constantly. As soon as it no longer looks raw, it is set aside in a bowl. Now 1–2 tablespoons of the garlic-ginger-green onion mixture (next page) are added to the wok along with chiles, lemon peel or lemon grass as desired. That is stir-fried briefly, and then come the vegetables— first the firm ones like eggplant, fennel and carrots—then 30 seconds later the tender ones like bell peppers, mushrooms and zucchini, and 30 seconds after that the leafy vegetables. All vegetables should remain crisp-tender. Stir constantly.

Now for the liquid: For a spicy and crunchy stir fry, you need only 2–3 tablespoons of sauce (cook in sauce for 1 minute). For a saucier and softer texture, cook with stock or coconut milk (no more than ½ cup) for 2–3 minutes. Then add sugar or curry paste if desired. In either case, return the meat and fish to the wok along with any herbs, heat it all up quickly while stirring and put it in the guest's bowl on top of rice (make sure to have an assistant dishing up the rice bowls!). When eating, hold the bowls just below your mouth so it's easier to shovel in the food with chopsticks. No need to excuse yourself—that's the authentic Asian way.

To make sure cooking times and seasoning are done right, your "wokkers" should have a little experience. It's also a good idea to practice with the ingredients before the party. If you're afraid of chaos, forget the buffet. Just give partiers a vegetarian and non-vegetarian option and do the rest yourself: Pick a meat OR fish, a combination of vegetables, and a yummy sauce.

# Wok Party for Twelve

**In any case:** 1 cup vegetable oil; mixture of: 12 cloves chopped garlic, ½ cup grated ginger, 1–2 cups chopped green onion; cooked rice.

**Seasoning (options:** Finely chopped jalapeños and red chiles, lemon grass (tough outer layer removed), lemon zest; basil, cilantro, mint, parsley, shiso leaves, chives; curry powder, curry paste, five-spice powder, salt, sugar; sesame oil, hot chile oil

**Wok veggies (about 6½ pounds):** Eggplant, Napa cabbage, fennel, beans, leeks, green onions, cabbage, carrots, bell peppers, mushrooms, asparagus, zucchini, sugar snap or snow peas; chard and spinach cut into narrow strips; pre-cooked veggies such as cauliflower, broccoli (par-boil briefly in salted water); water chestnuts, bamboo shoots (canned); bean sprouts, tofu

**Wok fish & meat (about 3½ pounds):** Shrimp, fish fillets, mussels; strips of poultry, pork, beef, lamb and veal steak (Hint 1: Japanese grocery stores sell meat already cut to size. Hint 2: meat slices easier when slightly frozen.)

**To top it all off (About 2 cups of various sauces & 1 quart of liquids like stock or coconut milk):** Soy sauce, fish sauce and oyster sauce; garlic-chile sauce; chicken and/or vegetable stock, coconut milk; rice wine (sake or mirin), sherry; rice vinegar, citrus juice; honey

**For drinking:** Green tea, Oolong tea, dry Japanese beer, sake, Sauvignon Blanc

**For before:** Vegetable skewers (page 41), shrimp dip (page 43)

**For after:** Melon in coconut milk (page 151), orange sorbet (page 161)

# Dim Sum Party
## Make it for a large group and it's worth your while

**Preparation:** Up to 1 week ahead
**Storage:** In the freezer
**Serve with:** Chinese herb rolls, fish cakes, ginger dip, shrimp dip

Makes enough for 8–10 (about 4 pieces each):

For the dough:

3 cups flour

1 packet yeast

Oil for brushing on

**Leek filling:**

1 lb. young leeks or tender

inside part of mature leeks

1 piece fresh ginger (1" section)

1 cup oyster mushrooms

1 tablespoon vegetable oil

2 teaspoons soy sauce

1/2 teaspoon toasted sesame oil

Salt

**Shrimp filling:**

1 cup raw, peeled and de-veined shrimp

1 handful bean sprouts (about 1/2 cup)

1 piece fresh ginger (1" section)

1/4 cup cilantro sprigs

1 tablespoon sweet and sour sauce

Drops hot chile oil

**Radish spinach filling:**

About 1/2 cup frozen spinach

2" section daikon or 1/2 cup radishes

2 oz. cooked ham (about 1/3 cup)

1 piece fresh ginger (1" section)

1 tablespoon sugar

1 tablespoon rice vinegar

1 tablespoon soy sauce

1 egg

Also: Baking parchment

**1** (Give some pre-thought to the radish-spinach filling by taking spinach out of freezer to thaw.) For the yeast dough, pour flour in a bowl. Dissolve yeast in 1 cup lukewarm water, add to the flour; mix and knead together until smooth and elastic. Let stand 1 hour, loosely covered with plastic wrap.

**2** Leek filling: Rinse leeks thoroughly (remove and discard tough outer layer) and chop finely. Peel ginger and grate. Brush off mushrooms and dice finely. Brown leeks, ginger, and mushrooms in 1 tablespoon oil. Add soy sauce, sesame oil and salt.

**3** Shrimp filling: Chop shrimp finely. Rinse bean sprouts and chop. Peel ginger and grate. Rinse cilantro under cold water, shake dry, remove tough stems and chop rest. Combine with sweet and sour sauce, chile oil, bean sprouts, and shrimp; mix well.

**4** Radish spinach filling: Squeeze moisture out of thawed spinach and chop finely. Peel daikon radish. First cut into slices, then into sticks. Dice ham finely. Peel ginger and chop finely. Mix all these with sugar, vinegar, soy sauce and egg.

**5** Take walnut-sized pieces of dough and roll into balls. Then roll out into a very thin, round shape on a silpat mat or baking parchment; place a heaping teaspoon of filling on each and seal up by gathering ends and twisting the top. Preheat oven to 475°F. Cut some baking parchment to the size of the broiler rack. Pierce dim sum several times with a toothpick, then brush with oil. Place baking parchment on the broiler rack, set the dim sum on top and cover well with aluminum foil. Pour boiling water into the broiler pan bottom. Place dim sum broiler rack on top of the broiler pan; place in oven and steam for about 8–10 minutes.

Prep time: 2 1/2 hours
Goes with: Besides the dips under "Serve with" above, prepared sweet and sour sauce, soy sauce, and hot chile oil
Calories per serving (10 servings): 270

## Basic Tip

A dim sum party is a unique idea. As a host, you have two options. You can either let your guests help out and fill, twist and steam the little balls immediately, or make all the dim sum one or two weeks ahead of time and freeze them. For the latter, set them out on a board and initially freeze them for 30 minutes (so they won't stick together in the freezer bag). Then pack them up and label the freezer bags by filling type.

For the party, take them out of the freezer and arrange them frozen solid on the broiler rack and pan as described above. They might take 1 minute longer or so to bake. Also, ask around and see if any of your friends have bamboo steamers. Have them bring the steamers to the party—stack a bunch on a couple pots of boiling water and use them to steam the dim sum (8-10 minutes—use parchment cut into circles under the dim sum).

# Spoon

Those who slurp together stay together...

# Food

Forget the old legend of how the world's first recipe was invented when a piece of meat fell into the bonfire. How could a scrap in the coals, without seasoning, be the beginning of the culinary arts? It just seems more humane to believe that all cooking originated from the kettle—from soup, if you will.

Nothing casts a spell over a table like a big pot of soup in the center. Hot soups and stews have a communal way of bonding people together—international leaders should eat soup together when they're in the middle of peace talks! And whether it be broth, stew, curry or jambalaya—you'll find them all easy to prepare.

So it comes as no surprise that the effects of a good soup are only a spoonful away from the effects of a good drink. When you want the original comfort food, look to soup. That's why chicken noodle soup is the old-wives'-tale prescription for colds—because it is emotionally (if not physically) nourishing and will help you feel better.

# Made for Dunking

No matter how good the soup is, it isn't *really* good unless your guests can lay aside their spoons and dunk their bread in it until they've sopped up the last drop. Cheese fondue is a quintessential candidate for this—the bread chunks become the spoon from the very beginning. Guests start off dunking and don't stop until the pot is scraped clean. Have you ever thought of fondue as soup before? It doesn't really matter what you call it 'cuz it's oh so good...

The most important thing is the melting—fondue means "melted." To do this right, make sure the cheese has a high enough fat content (45% or more) and isn't too hard. For good dipping, liquids such as alcohol are added to "bind" with the cheese. To keep it from becoming lumpy or flaky, the mixture also has to have enough acid—this is why certain wines are often added—otherwise, a dash of lemon helps. Adding a little dissolved cornstarch will keep the mixture from "separating." (See actual recipes on next page.)

Now put everything together: Depending on its firmness, dice or grate the cheese. Heat the liquid plus lemon on the stove and gradually add the cheese, stirring gently while it melts. But don't let it boil! In the meantime, whisk the cornstarch into a little wine or other fondue liquid (like schnapps) and stir it into the fondue.

Carefully bring it to a low boil. If it's too thin, add more of the cornstarch mixture. If it's too thick, add liquid. If it's lumpy, there's not enough acid so add lemon. Foolproof method: Combine liquid, lemon and cheese two hours before serving and then melt it all together.

Now rub the inside of a fondue pot with garlic, pour everything into it and place it over the burner on your fondue pot and get a flame going. For dipping, serve white bread or any other baked goods from soft pretzels to tortillas; marinated foods from pickles to olives; tender raw vegetables or firm cooked vegetables. And depending on your tastes you can also dunk cooked seafood, meats, sausage, ham and cheese-compatible fruit such as grapes or dried apricots. It's also good to swirl things around a little while you're at it to keep the cheese smooth!

# S.O.S.

## "Oh! Has the party already started?"

Dear Advice Columnist,
What is it with people who show up too late? Nothing wrong with a couple of minutes but some people always drop in a half an hour late and then are mad because nobody accepts their apology. Am I not being flexible enough?
Laura from Chicago

## Dear Laura:

First of all, congratulations that your friends bother to excuse themselves at all. But even this can get a little old, like having spaghetti on your birthday every year (in which case I would always show up late, too). So you have to do what all good hosts do when something goes wrong – start by considering how you might be contributing to the problem.

What exactly is "too late"? A quarter of an hour never is, not even if you're serving the most fabulous meal imaginable. This is time used as a buffer for greetings, etc. If you have a lot of guests, you can extend this to half an hour: "We're starting at 7:30 and the soufflé will be ready at eight sharp!" Anyone who doesn't make it only has herself to blame—same for the host who doesn't allow for this buffer. But there's one area where you have to be as strict as mom and dad on a Saturday night: If someone is really going

to be late, they have to tell you, always and as soon as possible. Anyone who hasn't called by eight doesn't get dessert. Their washing machine exploded? The phone still works. The taxi driver wouldn't lend them a cell phone? They can stop at a phone booth and use the driver's tip to pay for the call. They've found the love of their life? Oh please.

But never say to repeat offenders, "You'll never change, you party pooper!" Instead say, "Since you're such a flexible guy, you can go get us all some more beer." Next time, make his invitation earlier than the rest and the time after that, make it for so late that everyone will be gone if he shows up any later. And anyone who confirms an invitation and then doesn't show up without contacting you doesn't need to come back at all. But remember: Guests who come too late are preferable to guests who come too early or leave too late.

## Drink of the Day
# Riesling Punch

Punch goes upscale in this cool, breezy tasting recipe. The British actually imported this "punch" idea from sultry India where its five ingredients consisted of water, tea, rum, sugar and lemon. Here we've replaced water with wine and guarantee the results to be perfect for a sophisticated summer evening (yields at least 3½ quarts):

## Times Five
# Cheese Fondue

For over 30 years, cheese has been bubbling at parties world-wide. These five recipes will show you how far the cheese fondue has evolved. Start first on the stove and transfer to fondue pot—each serves 4 (if served as an appetizer, 6-8).

### Heidi Fondue
Coarsely grate 14 oz. Gruyère and 7 oz. Raclette cheeses; mix with 1¼ cups dry white wine and 1 teaspoon lemon juice in a pan. Let rest 2 hours; then melt while stirring constantly over medium-low heat. Whisk 3 teaspoons cornstarch in 2 tablespoons kirsch; stir in and bring to a gentle boil. Rub the inside of the fondue pot with garlic and fill it up. Dip crusty white bread chunks.

### Pippi Longstocking Fondue
Coarsely grate 1 lb. 2 oz. Swiss cheese—Gruyere, Emmenthal, or similar (can use food processor grating attachment). Discard the rind from 3½ oz. Brie or Camembert. Dice 1 onion. Sauté with 1 teaspoon caraway in 1 table-spoon butter until onions soften. Add 1 cup beer and ⅓ cup buttermilk; heat. Melt cheese in this mixture. Whisk 2 teaspoons cornstarch into 2 tablespoons kirsch or brandy; stir well into the cheese mixture and bring to a low boil. Dip rye or pumpernickel bread, soft pretzels, cornichons (mini pickles) and radishes.

Rinse 1 lemon under hot water. Zest it and squeeze out juice. Combine both with 1½ cups sugar and 1 cup rum. Place 5 teaspoons assam black tea leaves and ½ teaspoon aniseed in a pouch made of layered cheese-cloth (cinch up with kitchen string) and add 4 cups boiling water and let steep 3 minutes. Heat 3 bottles of dry riesling wine and combine with the sugar solution and tea (remove cheesecloth pouch); let cool and serve over ice. Looks elegant in Middle Eastern tea glasses with a lemon wedge.

### Fonduta Romeo
Dice 14 oz. Fontina and 3½ oz. Provolone. Grate 3½ oz. Parmesan. Mix cheese with 1 cup whole milk; refrigerate overnight. Heat ⅓ cup white wine. Cut together 1 tablespoon flour and 1 tablespoon butter; stir into wine until paste-like. Add cheese-milk mixture and melt. Bring just to a boil and remove from heat. One at a time, whisk in 3 lukewarm egg yolks and transfer to fondue pot. Dip bread, boiled potatoes and mushrooms.

### Fondue Jacque
Remove rinds and cut cheese into chunks: 14 oz. Roquefort and 7 oz. Butterkäse. Heat a scant ⅔ cup cream and a scant ⅔ cup whole milk; add Roquefort and melt. Stir in 2 tea-spoons lemon juice, then add and melt Butter-käse. Whisk 3 tablespoons white wine with 3 teaspoons cornstarch; stir in and bring to low boil. Dip baguette chunks, pears and celery.

### Fondue Tex
Dice 10½ oz. cheddar and crumble 10½ oz. goat cheese. Brown 2 diced garlic cloves and 2 chopped jalapeños in 1 tablespoon oil. Add ½ cup white wine; bring to a boil. Stir in ⅔ cup whole yogurt and 1 teaspoon lime juice. Melt cheese in this mixture. Whisk 2 tea-spoons cornstarch in 2 tablespoons tequila, stir in and bring to a boil. Dip red bell pepper strips, garlic sausage and tortilla chips.

## small talk
# "Cheers"

No matter who you are or where you are in the world, it's always nice to go where someone knows your name. In any language, raise your glass to toast in celebration with those who know you best. Bottoms up!

| | |
|---|---|
| English | Cheers! |
| German | Prost! |
| French | Santé! |
| Italian | Salute! |
| Spanish | ¡Salud! |
| Swedish, Norwegian | Skål! |
| Dutch | Proost! |
| Finnish | Kippis! |
| Russian | Nazdaravije! |
| Hungarian | Egészségére! |
| Japanese | Kanpai! |
| Polish | Nazdrowie! |
| But not | Down the hatch! |

# Tomato Soup
## ...This time with OJ

A slight problem: You can only get good tomatoes in summer and good oranges in winter. The solution: In winter use the good oranges with tomatoes from a can. In summer use the good tomatoes with orange juice from a carton.

**Preparation:** Make soup on previous day but without yogurt
**Storage:** In a plastic container in the refrigerator—covered. Heat up just before the party in a pot and garnish with yogurt.
**Serve with:** Meatballs, rice salad with pomegranates, avocado dip

Makes enough for 4:

2½ lbs. ripe tomatoes (or 28 oz. can)

1 onion, 2 cloves garlic

1 teaspoon fennel seeds

1 tablespoon oil

3¼ cups vegetable stock

1 cup orange juice (in winter, fresh-squeezed)

Salt, freshly ground black pepper

1 pinch sugar

½ cup whole-milk yogurt

½ cup cilantro sprigs

**1** Remove stems from fresh tomatoes, place in a bowl and pour boiling water over the top. Rinse under cold water; peel, squeeze out seeds and dice.

**2** Peel onion and garlic and dice very finely. Sauté briefly in oil along with fennel seeds. Add tomatoes and stock. Bring to a boil and then simmer about 15 minutes. Mix thoroughly with a hand blender.

**3** Add orange juice, salt, pepper, sugar and heat through. Ladle into bowls with a dollop of yogurt on top. Remove cilantro leaves from stems and sprinkle on top.

Prep time: 30 minutes
Calories per serving: 140

# Creamy Mushroom Soup
## Reminiscent of France

**Preparation:** Make soup in the morning
**Storage:** In a covered plastic container in the refrigerator. Bring to a rolling boil in a pot just before the party.
**Serve with:** Duck pâté, herb relish, stuffed tomatoes

Makes enough for 4:

1 tablespoon dried porcini

(they provide

an intense flavor)

$^1/_2$ pound white button mushrooms

1 small onion

2 tablespoons butter

1 tablespoon flour

$3^1/_4$ cups vegetable stock

Salt, freshly ground black pepper

2–3 teaspoons fresh lemon juice

2 tablespoons crème fraiche

1 small package of daikon sprouts,

or sunflower or pea sprouts

1 Place porcini in a bowl, pour 1 cup hot tap water over the top and let them soak about 30 minutes.

2 In the meantime, wipe off fresh mushrooms with a paper towel, remove ends of stems and discard; dice rest finely. Peel onion and mince. Drain dried mushrooms and chop (reserve liquid). Pour reserved porcini liquid through a coffee filter and set strained liquid aside.

3 Heat butter in a large pot and briefly sauté onion and mushrooms. Sprinkle on flour and stir; cook for about a minute. Pour in stock and mushroom liquid; cover and simmer for 15 minutes.

4 Briefly purée the soup in the pot using a hand blender. You won't be able to get it perfectly smooth. Season to taste with salt, pepper and lemon juice. Stir in crème fraiche (or add a dollop on top). Cut daikon sprout tops off root ends and sprinkle on top.

Prep time: 50 minutes,
20 of which you're actually busy
Calories per serving: 110

# Miso Soup
## Revives tired guests

**Preparation:** Cut up vegetables and tofu
**Storage:** For a couple hours covered in the refrigerator
**Serve with:** Baked dim sum

Makes enough for 4:

1–2 green onions

4 fresh shiitake mushrooms

8 oz. silken tofu (soft tofu)

1 quart dashi stock or 1 quart hot water mixed

with instant dashi powder (Asian grocery)

5 tablespoons miso (Asian grocery has some

intended for soup, otherwise buy mild)

1 Remove roots and wilted parts from green onions; rinse and cut into fine rings. Wipe off shiitakes with a paper towel, remove stems (discard) and slice remainder finely. Cut tofu into $^1/_2$" cubes or a little smaller. Distribute shiitakes, onions, and tofu into soup bowls.

2 Briefly bring dashi stock to a boil and remove from heat. Place miso in a wire strainer and slowly lower it into the hot dashi while gently pushing the miso through the strainer with a wooden mixing spoon.

3 Reheat miso soup and before it comes to a boil, ladle into the soup bowls.

Prep time: 15 minutes
Calories per serving: 115

# Rosemary Onion Soup
## ...à l'italienne

**Preparation:** No more than 1 day ahead; don't add mascarpone until right before serving
**Storage:** In a plastic covered container in the refrigerator.
**Serve with:** Marinated vegetables, salmon tramezzini, roquefort-crème fraiche dip

Makes enough for 4:

1 sprig rosemary, plus more for garnish

1 lb. onions, 2 cloves garlic

2 tablespoons olive oil, 1 quart stock (4 cups)

½ lemon

2 tablespoons pitted black olives,

preferably kalamata

1 tablespoon mascarpone cheese

(or crème fraiche)

Salt, freshly ground black pepper

**1** Rinse rosemary sprig, shake dry, remove needles and chop them finely. Peel onions and garlic and mince.

**2** In a large pot, stir onions into the oil and sauté for about 10 minutes over medium heat. Add garlic and chopped rosemary and sauté briefly. Pour in stock, cover and simmer soup for 10 minutes.

**3** Rinse lemon under hot water and remove zest. Dice pitted olives finely. Add lemon zest, olives and mascarpone to soup. Combine well and season with salt and pepper.

Prep time: 40 minutes
Calories per serving: 130

# Hungarian Paprika Soup
## Roasting is more work but adds aroma

**Preparation:** No more than 2 days ahead, without the sour cream
**Storage:** Covered in a container in the refrigerator
**Serve with:** Rye bread with mushroom caviar, canapés with potato-cheese cream

Makes enough for 4:

3 red bell peppers

1 onion

2 cloves garlic

1 potato (russet or similar variety)

2 tablespoons butter

1 teaspoon chili powder

2 teaspoons paprika

1 cup white wine

3¼ cups stock

Salt, freshly ground black pepper

1 cup sour cream

**1** Preheat oven to 475°F. Rinse bell peppers, cut in half and remove contents. Place peppers on a baking sheet with the cut side down and roast in the oven for about 20 minutes until the peel forms dark blisters. Let cool briefly, peel and dice.

**2** Peel onion and garlic and mince. Peel potato, rinse and grate finely. Keep gratings in salted water until time to use—then strain them and pat dry.

**3** Melt butter in a large pot. Stir in onion and garlic and brown briefly. Sprinkle with chili powder and paprika and again brown briefly.

**4** Add grated potato, white wine and stock, cover and simmer soup for about 10 minutes. Then add diced roasted red pepper, season to taste with salt and pepper and simmer another 10 minutes. Add sour cream, season to taste and that's all!

Prep time: 1 hour, half of which you're actually busy
Calories per serving: 220

# Peanut Soup with Carrots
## Low-budget soup

**Preparation:** No more than 1 day ahead; don't sprinkle watercress on top until after heating up
**Storage:** Covered in the refrigerator
**Serve with:** Spareribs, Moroccan cream cheese dip, frittata cubes

Makes enough for 4:

1 onion, ½ lb. carrots

1 tablespoon oil, 3¼ cups stock

½ cup peanut butter

Salt, freshly ground black pepper

dash Cayenne powder

½ cup watercress leaves

**1** Peel onion and chop finely. Peel carrots and grate.

**2** In a large pot, heat oil. Stir in onion and carrots and sauté briefly. Pour in stock, cover and simmer soup for 20 minutes.

**3** Purée soup in a blender or with a hand blender; add peanut butter and season to taste with salt, pepper and cayenne—combine well. Sprinkle rinsed watercress leaves on top.

Prep time: 35 minutes
Calories per serving: 250

# Borscht
## Makes a statement

**Preparation:** No more than 2 days ahead
**Storage:** Covered in a container in the refrigerator
**Serve with:** Potato terrine with goat cheese, stuffed mild banana peppers, eggplant caviar

Makes enough for 4:

7 oz. high quality cut of lamb, beef or pork

(or you can leave out the meat altogether)

1 onion

1 lb. beets

1 carrot

½ lb. white cabbage

2 tablespoons clarified butter

(or Ghee, or canola oil)

5⅓ cups stock

2 bay leaves

1 teaspoon caraway

4–5 tablespoons red wine vinegar

1 teaspoon sugar

Salt, freshly ground black pepper

½ cup dill fronds

½ cup parsley sprigs

1 cup sour cream

**1** Dice meat finely. Peel onion and dice finely. Peel beets and carrots and dice. Rinse cabbage and cut into strips.

**2** In a large pot, heat clarified butter. Stir in meat and brown. Add all the vegetables and sauté briefly. Pour in stock along with bay leaves and caraway; cover, and simmer soup over medium heat for 30 minutes.

**3** Add vinegar, sugar, salt and pepper and simmer another 30 minutes. Remove bay leaves.

**4** Rinse herbs, shake dry, and chop tops and leaves finely. Mix with sour cream. Serve herb cream on the side, next to the soup pot.

Prep time: 30 minutes chopping, 1 hour cooking
Calories per serving: 460

# Japanese Noodle Soup with Chicken
## Makes for contented guests

**Preparation:** Cook chicken and noodles and thaw spinach the day before
**Storage:** Chicken and cooking liquid together, and noodles and spinach together—covered in the refrigerator. Heat up before the party and place on the buffet with eggs and onion on the side.
**Serve with:** Chinese herb rolls, tamago maki, fish cakes

Makes enough for 4–6:

²/₃ cup frozen spinach

1 piece fresh ginger (about ³/₄" long)

1 clove garlic

²/₃ cup soy sauce

5 tablespoons rice wine or sherry

1 star anise or 10 anise seeds

1 teaspoon sugar

4 chicken breast fillets

2 eggs

12 oz. Japanese ramen or Udon noodles (or thick-style soup noodles)

2 green onions

**1** Remove spinach from the package, place in a colander and thaw. Peel ginger and garlic and slice. Place 2 tablespoons soy sauce in a small bowl and combine the rest with ginger, garlic, rice wine, anise and sugar.

**2** Place chicken breast fillets side by side in a wide pot or deep pan. Pour soy sauce mixture over the top and then enough water to cover the meat. Heat slowly, cover and simmer rather than boil the chicken breasts over low heat for 15 minutes. Let cool in the liquid.

**3** In the meantime, hard-boil eggs (see p. 46) and rinse under cold water. Cook noodles according to the directions on the package; pour into a colander, rinse thoroughly under cold water and drain. Rinse green onions, remove roots and wilted parts and cut into fine rings. Peel eggs and slice. Remove cooked chicken from its cooking liquid temporarily and also slice.

**4** Reheat the cooking liquid. Add chicken slices, spinach and noodles and heat, but only to a simmer. Season to taste with remaining soy sauce and pour into soup bowls. Garnish with eggs and onions.

Prep time: 45 minutes
(not including cooling time)
Calories per serving (6 servings): 370

## Basic Tip

In Japan, rice wine is called "sake" and is made from fermented rice and water. This traditional drink contains about 15% alcohol, can be served cold or hot and is also frequently used for cooking ("mirin" is another cooking type of rice wine). If you want to drink sake with the soup you can heat it up first, which is best done in a double boiler. Or serve chilled.

# Pasta Pesto Soup
Garlicky

**Preparation:** Prepare pesto 2–3 days ahead, make soup fresh
**Storage:** Pesto in a covered container in the refrigerator
**Serve with:** Marinated vegetables, cheese rolls

Makes enough for 4:
About 3–4 cups soup-type vegetables & herbs (such as carrots, celery, leeks and/or parsley)
1 onion, 1 can peeled tomatoes (15 oz.)
1 tablespoon olive oil
3¼ cups stock
About 5 oz. small pasta (fusilli, orecchiette, etc.)
Salt, freshly ground black pepper
**For the pesto:**
4 cloves garlic or more if you dare
¼ cup pine nuts or skinless almonds
¼ cup olive oil
3 tablespoons grated Parmesan
½ to 1 bunch basil (about 1½ packed cups)
Salt
(or 1 tablespoon prepared pesto from a jar per person)

1 Peel onion and then peel or clean vegetables. Dice all finely; chop herbs if using. Drain tomatoes and dice finely (use juice for something else or throw away).

2 In a large pot, heat oil and sauté diced ingredients briefly. Add tomatoes and stock and bring to a boil. Add pasta and simmer over medium heat for 8–10 minutes.

3 For the pesto, puree garlic in a blender or small food processor along with basil, pine nuts (or almonds) and oil. Stir in Parmesan and season with salt.

4 Season soup to taste with salt and pepper, pour into a large bowl and serve pesto on the side. Freeze leftover pesto.

Prep time: 30 minutes
Calories per serving: 490

# Orzo Soup with Garbanzo Beans
Doubly spicy

**Preparation:** No more than 2 days ahead; before the party add a little stock (the noodles absorb liquid) and sprinkle parsley on last minute. Or prepare stock and cook noodles in it when you heat it up.
**Storage:** In a covered container in the refrigerator
**Serve with:** Frittata cubes, avocado dip, tomato dip

Makes enough for 4:
¾ cup fresh parsley sprigs
1 onion, 2 stalks celery
2 tablespoons olive oil, 1 quart stock (4 cups)
1 tablespoon tomato paste
½–1 teaspoon harissa paste, or more (specialty or Middle Eastern market)
½ teaspoon ground coriander
½ teaspoon ground cumin
5–6 ounces dry orzo pasta
1 can cooked garbanzo beans (15 oz.)
1 tablespoon fresh lemon juice
Salt, black pepper

1 Rinse parsley, snip off leaves (reserve) and chop stems finely. Peel and chop onion. Rinse and dice celery.

2 In a large pot, heat oil and brown parsley stems, onion and celery. Pour in stock. Stir in tomato paste and harissa, season with coriander and cumin and bring to a boil. Add dry orzo and rinsed and drained garbanzo beans and simmer for 8–10 minutes.

3 Finely chop parsley leaves. Season soup to taste with additional harissa for spiciness, lemon juice, salt and pepper; sprinkle parsley over the top.

Prep time: 35 minutes
Calories per serving: 520

# Spinach Rice Soup
## Multicultural

**Preparation:** On the day before without yogurt mixture
**Storage:** In a covered container in the refrigerator
**Serve with:** Cheese rolls, carrot salad with grapes, tahini dip

Makes enough for 4:

1 pound frozen spinach

2 cloves garlic

2 cups whole-milk yogurt (optional)

1 teaspoon turmeric (optional)

2 leeks, 2 tablespoons olive oil

½ cup long-grain rice

1 quart vegetable stock (4 cups)

Salt, freshly ground black pepper

1 tablespoon fresh lemon juice

**1** Remove spinach from packaging, place in a colander and thaw. Peel garlic and squeeze through a press. Add garlic to yogurt along with turmeric.

**2** Remove roots and dark green parts from leeks. Slit open lengthwise and rinse thoroughly, then cut crosswise into strips. Squeeze moisture out of spinach and chop.

**3** Heat oil in a pot. Stir in leeks, spinach and rice and sauté briefly. Pour in stock, cover and simmer for about 20 minutes or until rice is tender but not mushy. Season to taste with salt, pepper and lemon juice. Stir in yogurt mixture if desired. Heat until nice and hot but not boiling. (Or, serve yogurt mixture on the side as a condiment.)

Prep time: 35 minutes
Calories per serving: 265

# Provençal potato soup
## Ooo la la!

**Preparation:** Morning or midday
**Storage:** In a covered container in the refrigerator
**Serve with:** Mini Cabernet cream puffs, stuffed mushrooms

Makes enough for 4:

1 lb. potatoes (firm, red or white)

1 medium-sized fennel bulb

2 shallots or small onions

2 cloves garlic

4 fresh thyme sprigs

Pinch fresh lavender florets (optional)

1 tablespoon olive oil

1 teaspoon fennel seeds

3¼ cups stock

A few threads saffron

1 can peeled tomatoes (15 oz.)

1 cup dry white wine

Salt, freshly ground black pepper

**1** Rinse and peel potatoes. Cut in half lengthwise, then cut crosswise into thin half-round slices. Keep in salted water until ready to use (then pat dry). Remove outer layer from fennel bulb, rinse, and cut into quarters and then into narrow strips. Peel and chop shallots and garlic. Rinse thyme and strip off leaves. Chop lavender.

**2** Heat oil in a pot. Stir in shallots, garlic, fennel and potatoes and sauté briefly. Add fennel seeds, thyme, lavender, saffron and stock. Cover and simmer for about 10 minutes until the potatoes are somewhat tender but not mushy.

**3** Drain tomatoes and chop finely, add to soup along with the wine and simmer for another 5–10 minutes. Season to taste with salt and pepper.

Prep time: 35 minutes
Calories per serving: 210

# Soup's on

You invited eight but ten showed up? Pour a little more stock into the soup and make everyone feel welcome. The more the merrier!

## Making the Basic Soup

To serve eight, peel and quarter about 6½ lbs. potatoes (put in salted water). Peel 1 large onion and 4 cloves garlic. Rinse about 6 cups of soup-type vegetables and herbs (carrots, celery, leeks); peel and dice coarsely. Slowly brown these ingredients in ¼ cup oil in large pot. Add potatoes and 4½ quarts vegetable stock and cook for 20–30 minutes until tender. Pour soup liquid through a colander and into another large pot; return potato mixture to the first pot and mash. Press through a strainer or sieve. Mix with liquid, then season soup to taste with salt and nutmeg.

## Creating the Right Atmosphere

Think Halloween or harvest festival. Picture straw yellow, pumpkin orange, sunset red, potato brown, apple green, plum blue. Send out packing paper decorated with ink-stamps as invitations. In the manner of a large family, use the kitchen door as a table and make felt place mats with names on them that guests can take home. Decorate by scattering around fruits and vegetables. Hang corn cobs, light pumpkins, shine lanterns. Play brass band music, Irish drinking songs, country-western, or blues—just make sure you vary music styles.

Now it's time to sit down at the table. You've brought together your closest friends, the ones you can really talk to—sisters and brothers bound in a covenant of soup. Nothing brings you together like dipping a ladle into a common pot and nothing warms your senses like potato soup on the fire. At the same time, each person also adds their own personal touch to the mix and before you know it, you're all reciting your favorite war stories. But don't forget what we said above: If you invited eight but ten showed up, pour a little more stock into the soup pot— You never know who might turn out to be someone you can really talk to.

## What You Need

To allow everyone, including the host, to ladle their soup in peace, two to four fondue sets are ideal for a potato soup party. That way everyone has elbow room. You can use the fondue pots for the soup, small bowls for the ingredients you add to the soup, and plates for various types of garnish such as different herbs or cheeses. Arrange ingredients and garnish strategically and lavishly on the table so no one has to look very far for what they want. You won't need the fondue forks. Instead, provide two ladles that won't disappear into the pot when you let go of them.

It's best to ladle the soup into the biggest soup cups or bowls available but rice or cereal bowls are also OK, even large mugs. Wide shallow soup bowls are not such a good idea because they don't allow the added ingredients to get really hot before the soup cools. Put a flat plate at each place setting (under the bowl), just because it looks cool. Next to it, put a soup spoon and fork for emergencies. Then add basic drinking glasses that look right with beer and are just fine with water, too. Chunky wine glasses are also good.

## How It Works

When everybody's sitting down, fill the fondue pots three-quarters full of the basic potato soup (recipe at left) and place them on the burners over a very low flame. Now everyone puts a selection of vegetables, cooked meat and fish in their own bowls, but no more than about ¼ cup's worth (see facing page). They can then sprinkle spices, herbs or spicy sauces over the top. It's best to do this right at the table. Then hold the bowl up to the pot and pour in two or three hefty ladles full of soup, stir it up and top it all off with a dab of crème fraiche, a splash of balsamic vinegar or a smattering of peanuts.

Now enjoy the food and make it part of your conversation. Speak up if you find smoked trout, pumpkin seed oil and horseradish to be the absolute best combination you've ever tasted. And if someone tells you that avocado, caviar and lemon juice are at least as good, try it. Which means you should try to take smaller helpings so you'll have room to taste new creations.

# Soup for Eight

**In any case:** 6–8 quarts potato soup (recipe on previous page)

**For seasoning (according to taste):**
Curry powder, nutmeg, pepper, salt; chopped basil, dill, tarragon, chervil, cress, parsley, chives; Harissa or other chile sauce, mustard, soy sauce, Tabasco, Worcestershire sauce; fresh lime and lemon juice

**Veggies for adding (about 1½–2 pounds total):**
Raw veggies such as mushrooms, avocado, green onions, red bell peppers, spinach and tomatoes cut into narrow strips, sliced or diced; pre-cooked veggies such as broccoli, peas, squash, leek, corn; cornichons, capers, pitted olives, sun-dried tomatoes (oil packed variety, drained)

**Meat and fish for adding (About 1 pound total):**
Strips or cubes of cooked: meat, turkey or chicken breast, sausage, ham, bacon, or shrimp; smoked fish: salmon, trout; caviar

**To top it all off (according to taste):**
Olive oil, pumpkin seed oil, balsamic vinegar; crème fraiche, whole milk yogurt, pesto; nuts and seeds, toasted bread cubes, grated Parmesan, diced blue cheese, goat cheese, or feta cheese for crumbling and sprinkling.

**For drinking:** Water, beer, wine (keep it simple)

**For before:** Marinated vegetables (page 64), herb relish (page 44)

**For after:** Apple Charlotte (page 151), poached pears 2 ways (page 148)

# Ratatouille with Cheese Baguette
## A classic from southern France

**Preparation:** No more than two days ahead
**Storage:** In a covered bowl in the refrigerator; prepare cheese baguette just before serving
**Serve with:** Herb relish, lentil salad

Makes enough for 4:

2 eggplants, 2 zucchini

1 red bell pepper, 1 yellow bell pepper

1 large onion

2–4 cloves garlic

$1/3$ cup olive oil

1 can peeled, diced tomatoes (15 oz.)

$1/2$ cup dry red wine (or water or

vegetable stock)

$1/2$ teaspoon dried herbes de Provence

Salt, freshly ground black pepper

8–12 slices baguette

1 wheel of camembert

(or similar soft-ripened cheese)

**1** Rinse eggplant and zucchini, clean and dice. Rinse bell peppers, cut off tops and remove contents. Then quarter and cut into strips. Peel onion and garlic and mince.

**2** In a dutch oven, heat a little more than half the oil. Add eggplant, brown well on all sides and remove. Pour in remaining oil and sauté zucchini and bell peppers. Add onions and garlic and sauté. Pour diced tomatoes with their liquid into pot along with the wine. Add eggplant back in along with herbes de Provence, salt and pepper.

**3** Cover and simmer for about 30 minutes over low heat. Meanwhile, set the oven to 425°F. Lay bread slices on a baking sheet. Cut camembert into slices about $1/8$–$1/4$" thick and place on the bread. Bake in the oven for about 10 minutes until the cheese melts slightly. Serve crispy cheese baguette with hot or warm ratatouille.

Prep time: 1 hour, 30 minutes of which you're actually busy
Calories per serving: 400

# Lentils with Pancetta
## A versatile Italian dish

**Preparation:** No more than 2 days ahead; stir in tomatoes when heating up
**Storage:** In the refrigerator, not in the pot
**Serve with:** Vegetable crostini with almonds, marinated vegetables, cheese rolls

Makes enough for 4:

5–6 oz. pancetta (or bacon), uncooked

2 cloves garlic

Several sprigs fresh thyme and several sprigs

fresh sage (or dried thyme—then omit sage)

2 tablespoons olive oil

$3/4$ cup brown or preferably French green lentils

2 cups of red wine and stock, or just stock

About $1^{1}/_{3}$ lbs. tomatoes

1 bunch basil

Salt, freshly ground black pepper

1 dash vinegar (optional)

**1** Dice pancetta finely. Peel and mince garlic. Rinse fresh herbs. Remove leaves from thyme and sage; chop herb leaves.

2  Pour oil into a dutch oven or deep pan. Add bacon and fry until crispy, turning occasionally. Remove about ¹/₃ to use later in the recipe. Add garlic, herbs and lentils and sauté briefly.

3  Pour in red wine and/or stock, cover and cook lentils over medium heat for 30–50 minutes until they're almost but not quite tender.

4  In the meantime, remove stems from tomatoes and steep in boiling water for about a minute. Rinse under cold water, slip off skins and dice finely. Remove leaves from basil and cut into strips. Stir tomatoes into lentils and simmer another 10 minutes. Season to taste with salt, pepper and, if desired, with vinegar. Sprinkle basil and reserved pancetta over the top.

Prep time: 1–1¹/₄ hours with a 20–40 minute pause
Calories per serving: 520

# Dutch "Stamppott" Stew
## Pork and beans go upscale

**Preparation:** No more than 1 day ahead
**Storage:** Covered in the refrigerator. Store bacon separately so it stays crispy
**Serve with:** Smørrebrød

Makes enough for 4–6:

²/₃ cup dried white beans

(Great Northern, Cannellini or similar)

1 lb. fresh green beans

1 lb. potatoes (firm type)

4 tart apples (Granny Smith, Jonathan)

¹/₂ lemon

1 piece cinnamon stick (about 2" long)

1 tablespoon sugar

Salt

¹/₂ lb. bacon

1  Cover white beans with water and soak overnight. Then pour off water, place beans in a pot with fresh water and bring to a boil. Cover and cook over medium heat for about 1 hour until tender.

2  In the meantime, rinse green beans, snip off ends and cut into pieces 1–1¹/₂" long. Peel potatoes and apples. Remove cores from apples and coarsely dice apples and potatoes. Rinse lemon and slice.

3  Place green beans, apples, potatoes, cinnamon stick, sugar, salt and lemon slices in a pot; just barely cover ingredients with water and heat. Cover and cook over medium heat for about 15 minutes until beans and potatoes are tender.

4  Dice bacon and fry in a pan over medium heat until crispy; set aside. Remove cinnamon and lemon slices from the pot. Coarsely mash a little bit of the potato-apple mixture with a potato masher. Drain cooked white beans (reserve a bit of the liquid) and add to potato-apple mixture; combine well. The liquid in this stew should be a little thick but not as thick as mashed potatoes. If it's too dry, add a little reserved bean liquid. Season to taste, place in a bowl and sprinkle diced bacon over the top.

Prep time: 50 minutes busy, 1¹/₄ hr. total
Calories per serving (6 servings): 410

# Jambalaya
## Not just for Cajun fans

You can put whatever you like most into this stew – chicken, sausage, cooked ham, etc. With or without fish, one pot does it all.

**Preparation:** No more than 1 day ahead but without fish and shrimp. Before serving, bring to a boil again and add stock if necessary (in case the rice soaked up too much). Then cook fish and shrimp and add, sprinkling green onions and parsley on top.
**Storage:** In a covered container in the refrigerator
**Serve with:** Turkey with Cajun salsa, carrot salad with grapes

Makes enough for 4–6:

3 stalks celery

2 green or red bell peppers

2 onions

2 cloves garlic

½ bunch fresh thyme (may substitute 1 teaspoon dried), plus sprigs for garnish

5 oz. prosciutto or serrano ham

2 tablespoons oil

1 cup long-grain rice

1 can peeled, diced tomatoes (15 oz.)

2 cups chicken stock (or vegetable stock)

1 lb. fish fillets (Cod, Sole, etc.)

Salt

½ lb. raw (peeled and deveined) shrimp

Freshly ground black pepper

Cayenne pepper

Tabasco (optional)

1 bunch green onions

¾ cup fresh parsley sprigs

1 Rinse celery and bell peppers; dice. Peel onions and garlic and chop finely. Rinse thyme, shake dry and strip off leaves (it's best to do this against the direction they grow in).

2 Dice ham finely. Heat oil in a large pot. Slightly brown onions, garlic and ham. Add celery, bell peppers, and thyme leaves, then the rice.

3 Add diced tomatoes in their liquid into the pot along with chicken stock. Cover and simmer over low heat for about 20 minutes.

4 In the meantime, cut fish into 1½" chunks and season with salt. Peel each shrimp, slit the back slightly and remove the black vein (or purchase them peeled and deveined).

5 Season tomato mixture to taste with salt, pepper, cayenne and Tabasco. Lay fish and shrimp on top, cover and cook for another 5 minutes or until fish is opaque and flakes a little with a fork.

6 In the meantime, remove roots and wilted parts from green onions, rinse and cut into fine rings. Rinse parsley, shake dry and chop finely. Gently stir fish and green onions into the rice mixture. Add more Tabasco if you want; in either case sprinkle parsley on top and place it on the buffet.

Prep time: 1 hour
Calories per serving (6 servings): 400

## Yet Another Fish Stew

Here's a quicker version from Italy and France: Briefly sauté onions and garlic and season with crushed fennel seeds or herbes de Provence. Add 1 diced fennel bulb or 2 stalks of celery and pour in diced tomatoes from a large 28 oz. can. Pour in 1 cup fish stock and season with salt, pepper and if desired, saffron threads. Dice 1½ lbs. fish fillets (don't be afraid to use inexpensive fish) and lay on top. Cover and let fish stew for 10 minutes. Serve with toasted bread spread with a mixture of mayonnaise and freshly pressed garlic.

# Duck Curry
## Made for digging in

**Preparation:** Marinate and sauté duck 1 day ahead; prepare the rest 1 hour before the party
**Storage:** Marinated duck in a covered, shallow dish in the refrigerator
**Serve with:** Chinese herb rolls, fish cakes, miso soup

Makes enough for 4:

3/4 cup cilantro sprigs

4 cloves garlic

2 tablespoons honey

2 tablespoons soy sauce

Salt, freshly ground black pepper

2 duck breast fillets (about 1 1/2 lbs. or substitute chicken thighs)

1/4 cup canola oil

1/2 lb. small cherry tomatoes

1 small can pineapple chunks

2 teaspoons red curry paste (or more if hotter is desired)

1 can coconut milk (14–15 oz.)

3 tablespoons fish sauce (nam pla)

3/4 cup basil sprigs

**1** Rinse cilantro, shake dry and remove leaves. Peel garlic. Chop cilantro and garlic and then crush in a mortar and pestle. Combine with honey, soy sauce, salt and pepper. Rub into duck breasts and refrigerate covered at least 2 hours.

**2** In a pan, heat 2 tablespoons oil. Starting with the skin side, sauté duck breasts over medium heat for about 5 minutes on each side. Let cool in the pan.

**3** Rinse tomatoes and remove stems. Drain pineapple (discard juice). Cut duck fillets into slices.

**4** Heat pan again. Pour in remaining oil, stir in curry paste and then coconut milk. Simmer briefly. Add sliced duck, tomatoes, pineapple and fish sauce and simmer briefly. Remove basil leaves from stems, stir in and serve.

Prep time: 40 minutes
(+2 hours marinating time)
Calories per serving: 520

## Tip:

Serve duck curry with thoroughly softened, drained cellophane noodles or rice noodles cooked according to their package directions. Each person can put a portion of noodles in their bowl and ladle hot duck curry over the top. This tastes fantastic!

# Colombo
## Not a TV show, not a city, but Caribbean pork stew!

**Preparation:** No more than 1 day ahead
**Storage:** In the refrigerator but not in the pot
**Serve with:** Avocado dip, rice salad with pomegranates, cucumber raita

Makes enough for 4:

1 3/4 lbs. pork shoulder

6 cloves garlic

1 fresh red chile pepper

2 lemons

2 onions

1 cucumber

1 mango (as unripe as possible)

2 tablespoons oil

1 teaspoon dried thyme

2 tablespoons curry powder

1 tablespoon flour

Salt

3/4 cup parsley sprigs

**1** Trim meat from bones and fat; cut into bite-sized chunks. Peel 4 cloves garlic and mince (or press). Rinse chile pepper and chop finely with the seeds (omit seeds and

ribs for less spice). Rinse 1 lemon, zest and squeeze for the juice. Combine all these ingredients and marinate overnight.

2 Then peel and dice onions and remaining garlic. Peel cucumber, quarter lengthwise and cut into pieces ½" thick. Peel mango, cut fruit away from pit and dice to about the size of the cucumber pieces.

3 Drain meat and pat dry (reserve marinade). Heat oil and brown meat thoroughly in 2 portions. Remove meat and stir onions, garlic and thyme into the oil. Add meat, curry and flour; stir and sauté briefly. Pour in marinade and enough water to just cover the meat; stir. Season with salt, cover and simmer for about 15 minutes.

4 Add cucumber and mango and cook for another 30 minutes. In the meantime, peel the second lemon like an orange, cut in half, remove seeds and chop the fruit. Rinse parsley, remove leaves and chop finely.

5 When the meat is tender, stir in chopped lemon (to taste) and parsley; season to taste and pour into a bowl.

Prep time: 1¼ hours
(+ 1 night marinating time)
Delicious with: Rice
Calories per serving: 345

# Chili con Pollo
Every bit as good as its famous relative

**Preparation:** No more than 2 days ahead; don't sprinkle on herbs until after reheating
**Storage:** In a covered container in the refrigerator
**Serve with:** Tomato soup, avocado dip, cheese rolls

Makes enough for 4:

1 lb. chicken breast fillets

2–3 zucchini

1 red bell pepper

1 onion

2 cloves garlic

1 cup drained canned corn

2 tablespoons oil

1 can peeled diced tomatoes (15 oz.)

½ cup chicken stock

Salt

1 teaspoon dried oregano (or marjoram)

½ teaspoon ground cumin

1 teaspoon chili powder (or more)

Tabasco as desired

½ cup cilantro sprigs (or parsley)

1 First cut chicken breasts into thin slices, then into strips, then into ¼" cubes. Rinse zucchini and bell pepper and dice. Peel onion and garlic and chop finely. Pour corn into a colander and rinse under cold water.

2 Heat oil in a pot and brown onion, garlic and chicken until the meat is no longer pink throughout. Add vegetables and corn. Pour in diced tomatoes along with their liquid and the stock. Season with salt, oregano (first crushing gently between your fingers), cumin and chili powder.

3 Cover and stew over low heat for about 20 minutes. Season to taste with Tabasco. If necessary, add a little more salt. Rinse cilantro or parsley, shake dry, chop and sprinkle over the top. Serve with bread— the crustier the better.

Prep time: 1 hour, 40 minutes of which you're actually busy
Calories per serving: 465

# Lunch
# Brunch

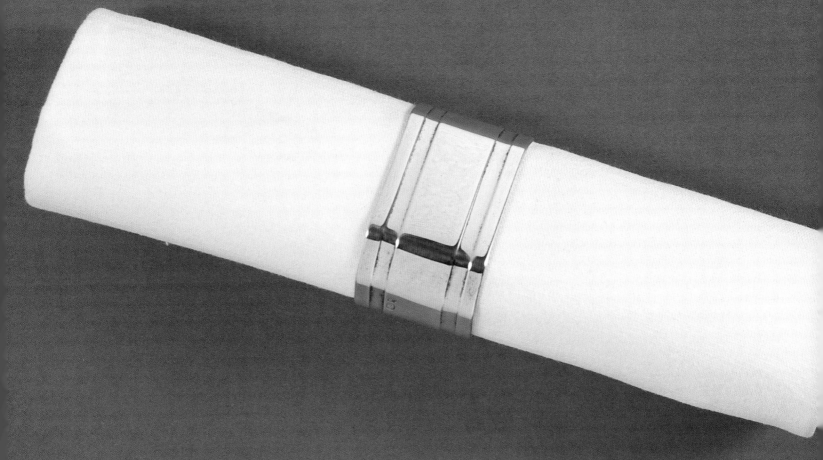

# and
# Food

We'll come straight to the point: What ever happened to a homemade, beautifully prepared lunch, or brunch? Is it being held hostage by fast food chains? Poisoned by cafeteria cooks? Squeezed out by keyboard snacks? Or simply wilted by heat lamps? If this was a game of hide and seek, I'd say we all better look for it.

You say you don't have time, you have too much work, you need to do some writing? You can write as much as Shakespeare but don't forget, even at his house lunch was served daily to friends and family. What do you mean, things were different back then? They were just harder, so today with your state-of-the-art kitchen, what's your excuse for not fixing yourself a nice lunch and setting the table for it?  And why not treat your friends to an elegant time? Especially on the weekends. If you feel like you don't know how, that's why this book was written.

Wouldn't it be great to invite a bunch of people over, enjoy fancy food, and sit around drinking coffee afterwards—all in the middle of the day? Then you have the rest of the day to do something else or clean up after your guests. Can you taste it now—cream-baked salmon, roast lamb, cheese soufflé? Let's turn homemade brunch into a trend…

# 10 Good Reasons for Lunch

### Drink of the Day
# Lassi

Lassi is an Indian drink that's a cross between an ice cream soda and a yogurt shake. It's very refreshing, and not just with a spicy midday curry. Depending on your tastes, you can make it either salty or sweet.

For 4 glasses of a spiced, basic lassi, blend together 1¼ cups yogurt, 2 cups ice-cold water or sparkling water (sparkling foams better), ¼ teaspoon salt and 1 dash cumin powder for several seconds until it foams and then serve over ice (you can also blend the ice with it, coarsely).

For a spiced, sweet lassi, soak ten saffron threads in 1 tablespoon hot milk. Peel 1 mango and 1 small banana. Dice fruit and purée with 1¼ cups yogurt, 1¼ cups ice-cold sparkling water, saffron-milk mixture, ½ teaspoon ground cardamom, 1 tablespoon honey and 1 teaspoon fresh lemon juice. Blend in about 2 cups of ice cubes (about a half tray, or more if desired) until the ice is coarsely chopped. Drink immediately.

All the reason for not grabbing a quick bite on the run.*

1. When breakfast is over, you already have something nice to look forward to.

2. A good lunch can turn a lousy day into a great one. The best dinner can only salvage the last few hours.

3. If you make the decision to knock off work for the rest of the day during lunch, you get more out of it than if you decide during dinner.

4. If you eat well at noon, you'll have more time to enjoy yourself in the evening.

5. If you eat a substantial lunch, you'll reach your low point right when your biorhythm would be low anyway. If you don't, you'll reach your low point just when your mind and body want to perk up.

6. Brunch is kind of like Sunday dinner from childhood—except you can have it any day you want.

7. An invitation to lunch or even brunch is both ordinary and decadent at the same time.

8. In France and Italy, everybody loves lunch! They take long ones and all the shops close.

9. You're hungry! And let's face it, you can do better than fast food.

10. You can follow it up with coffee…or more wine…why not?

* The fact that it's healthier to eat a good meal at noon than in the evening is beside the point

## "Bon appetit!"

Let's deconstruct this phrase. If you wish someone a "good appetite," what are you saying? That they better have a hearty appetite because that's the only way they'll be able to get the food down? Or maybe it means the food is so delicious, you hope they're really hungry for it. Some Americans say, "Let's pray for the meal." That's pretty scary, too, isn't it? Maybe those diner waitresses have the best idea: "Enjoy your meal," they say. Whatever you say, hopefully your guests will realize how lucky they are to be eating your food!

|  |  |
|---|---|
| English | Enjoy! |
| German | Guten Appetit |
| Italian | Buon appetito |
| French | Bon appetit |
| Spanish | Buen provecho |
| Dutch | Eet smakelijk |
| Norwegian | God appetit |
| Swedish | Smaklig maltid |
| Finnish | Hyvää Ruokahalua |
| Polish | Smacznego |
| But not | Mind if I smoke? |

# S.O.S.

## "Was that really necessary?"

Dear Advice Columnist,
Birthdays are always a good excuse for inviting friends over. If only they wouldn't bring gifts! Regardless of whether I say I don't want any or I don't let anyone know it's my birthday, a couple people always bring something. I don't know what to do! Marge from Boise

## Dear Marge:

Try saying "thank you" and be glad that there are obviously people who like you and like giving you things. Don't spoil it for them by acting like some kind of millionaire who can say, "No gifts, please." Nor is it a good idea not to tell them it's your birthday because somebody is bound to know (hopefully) and the rest will just feel out of it. If you don't want any birthday presents, don't celebrate your birthday and invite your friends over on a different day.

But then they might bring flowers. That's okay as long as not everyone does, because that would make a lot of work for you. Otherwise thank them, be glad and put the flowers in water. If they bring wine? That's a little trickier. Is it for drinking now? Warm white wine isn't; cold champagne is. Now, if a true connoisseur shows up at a raucous party with a bottle of '82 Lafite, give him a wink as you hide it away and say, "Let's just us two open this some other time." In any case, polite guests will tell you what it's intended for—or at least they won't be offended if you ask.

You can never get too much wine, but what do you do if it doesn't go with the food you're serving? "I bought Nebbiolo to go with the pasta. If you prefer something Provençal, Dave has been good enough to provide a Bandol Rosé," or use words to that effect. This will also help you avoid getting stuck drinking whatever rotgut other people bring (which is why you should never rely on your guests to provide the drinks).

But back to the issue of presents: "You really shouldn't have!" sounds like "You went to all that trouble for nothing." If you put it aside without unwrapping it, it means "I couldn't care less what's inside." So say thanks, open it as soon as possible and show that you're happy about it. Always. Don't complain if it's yet another box of cheap candy from the all-night gas station or if you know they're recycling it. And don't keep going on and on if someone gives you your absolute favorite – remember you have other guests and gifts to accept.

## Side Dishes Times Five

Every good brunch needs a side dish, or two:

Rustic Mushroom Pancakes
Clean and dice a $1/2$ pound mushrooms. Stir together 3 eggs, a scant $3/4$ cup flour, 8 oz. low-fat sour cream and $1/4$ cup milk and season with salt. Sauté mushrooms in 2 tablespoons butter for 1 minute. Season with salt and pepper and pour batter over the top. Fry until golden, turn and finish frying. Tear into pieces and fry again in 1 tablespoon butter until crispy. Good with roasted meats.

Braised Cucumbers and Potatoes
Peel 1 cucumber, cut in half lengthwise, remove seeds and cut into $1^{1}/4$" slices. Peel and dice 1 onion. Dice 4 oz. smoked bacon. Peel a $1/2$ pound potatoes, cut into quarters and slice to the same size as the cucumber. Sauté bacon and onions in 1 tablespoon oil. Add cucumber and sautée for 1 minute. Season with $1/2$ teaspoon paprika, salt and a little sugar. Add potatoes, $2/3$ cup chicken or vegetable stock and 1 tablespoon red wine vinegar; cover and simmer for 15 minutes. Stir in 1 tablespoon dill and a scant $1/2$ cup sour cream. Serve with fish or poultry.

Pasta with Fennel
Rinse 1 fennel bulb, peel off tough outer layer; quarter and cut into fine strips. Peel 2 shallots, cut in half and cut into strips. Gently sautée both ingredients for 5 minutes in $1/4$ cup good olive oil along with $1/2$ teaspoon ground aniseed and $1/4$ teaspoon sugar. Cook 8 oz. fettucine until al dente; drain and stir into the fennel along with the juice of $1/2$ lemon. Serve alongside salmon.

Corn Cakes
Purée together a scant $2/3$ cup of canned corn, 3 tablespoons crème fraîche and 2 eggs. Add $1/2$ cup flour, $1/2$ teaspoon baking powder and another scant $2/3$ cup canned corn kernels. Season with salt and a dash cayenne powder. Into a hot pan with 2 tablespoons of heated oil, drop tablespoons-full of batter into 2–3" wide circles, smooth them out and fry until golden brown on each side. Good with sausages and steak.

Baked Panzanella
Rinse 1 bunch arugula, 1 head radicchio and $1/2$ cup fresh basil leaves; clean and chop coarsely. Peel and chop 1 clove garlic. Remove crust from 3 slices of white bread and cut into cubes. Bring $1^{1}/4$ cups milk, garlic and $3^{1}/2$ oz. grated Parmesan to a gentle boil and pour over the bread. Let cool, then mix with the arugula, radicchio, and basil, plus 1 tablespoon capers and 4 lightly beaten eggs. Pour into a greased gratin or casserole dish; bake at 300ºF for 25–30 minutes. Good with stewed or braised dishes and fresh greens.

# Fried Chicken with Potato Cucumber Salad

Give the colonel a run for his money

**Before:** Marinated vegetables
**After:** Exotic fruit gelées

Feeds 4:

For the salad:

2 lbs. potatoes (firm type: red, fingerling, or Yukon gold)

1 onion

1¼ cups vegetable or chicken stock

About ½ tablespoon spicy mustard

2 tablespoons white wine vinegar

Salt, freshly ground black pepper

¼ cup canola oil

1 cucumber

**For the chicken:**

1 small whole chicken, cut into 8 pieces

Salt

2 eggs

½ cup flour

1½ to 1¾ cups bread crumbs

At least 1¼ cups vegetable oil for pan frying

Lemon wedges

**1** Start with the salad (ahead of time is fine). Rinse potatoes and place in a pot unpeeled. Add water until potatoes are half covered. Heat and cook at a low boil until potatoes are to a crisp-tender stage (not mushy). Test them with a knife (usually takes about 25 minutes).

**2** In the meantime, peel onion and mince. Bring minced onion to a boil in the stock, then turn off heat and add mustard, vinegar, salt, pepper and oil; mix well.

3 Pour the cooked potatoes into a colander and run cold water over them; or immerse in ice water. When cooled, peel and cut into thin slices. Add to the onion-stock mixture immediately and gently combine all; set aside. Peel cucumber and slice into thin rounds; salt lightly and set aside.

4 And now for the chicken. Ask an obliging butcher to cut the chicken into 8 pieces or do it yourself (divide it up with a knife and poultry shears, preferably always at a joint — so you have 2 thighs, 2 wings, 2 legs [drumsticks], and 2 breasts).

5 Remove the skin. Find a place where you can get your finger or a spoon handle under the skin and loosen it, then pull it off. Sprinkle chicken with salt.

6 Heat oil in a deep pan and place in the oven at 200°F. Break eggs into a shallow dish and whisk lightly. Place flour in a second dish and bread crumbs in a third.

7 First dredge each chicken piece with flour (if too much sticks, brush it off). Then dip it in the egg mixture and finally into the bread crumbs. Move pan with oil to the stove, over medium heat. Place a few pieces in the hot oil at a time and fry for about 7–10 minutes on each side (depending on thickness). Turn the pieces as much as necessary, cooking until chicken is opaque. Remove, place on paper towels to soak up excess oil; then keep warm in the oven. When all the pieces are nice and crispy, place on the table with lemon wedges. For the salad: mix in drained cucumbers, season to taste and enjoy!

Prep time: 1¼ hours
Calories per serving: 780

# Coq au vin
## Use the same wine for cooking and drinking

**Before:** Provençal potato soup
**After:** Orange sorbet

Feeds 4–6:

1 chicken (about 3½ lbs.)

3½ oz. thick cut bacon

1 onion

2 tablespoons butter

2 tablespoons oil

Salt, freshly ground black pepper

½ tablespoon flour

2 cups dry red wine

¾ cup parsley sprigs

6 thyme sprigs

2 bay leaves

8 green green onions

1 lb. small mushrooms (button or cremini)

**For the crostini:**

½ cup parsley sprigs

2–3 cloves garlic

¼ cup oil

12–18 baguette rounds

or 12 slices white bread

1 Cut chicken into 12 pieces: 2 legs, 2 wings and the breasts and thighs (deboned) cut into 2 pieces each.

2 Dice bacon. Peel onion and dice.

3 In a large, deep pan with a lid, heat half the butter and oil. Sprinkle chicken pieces with salt and pepper, brown nicely a few pieces at a time frying on each side and remove (no need to cook through at this point).

4 Add bacon and onions to the pan and sauté briefly. Sprinkle flour over the top and stir quickly. This will help thicken the sauce. Add wine, whisk or stir briefly, and bring to a boil. Rinse herbs and mince parsley; add thyme sprigs, bay leaves, and parsley to pan. Return chicken to the pan, cover and braise (simmer) over medium heat for about 30 minutes.

5 In the meantime, remove roots and dark green parts from the green onions, rinse and cut into pieces. Wipe mushrooms clean with a damp paper towel and cut off stems. Heat remaining oil and butter. Brown mushrooms and green onions over medium heat for about 5 minutes, then add to chicken and braise everything together for about another 30 minutes. Remove thyme sprigs and bay leaves before serving.

6 In the meantime, prepare the crostini. First rinse parsley, shake dry and mince leaves and tender stems. Peel garlic and mince. Stir both ingredients into the oil and brush over the bread slices (crusts trimmed off, unless baguette). Preheat oven to 450°F. Just before the meal, place bread on a baking sheet and toast in the oven for about 5 minutes or until golden. Serve with the coq au vin.

Prep time: 1½ hours, 40 minutes of which you're actually busy
Calories per serving (6 servings): 750

# Pepper Duck Breast with Carrots
## Finesse without stress

**Before:** Vegetable crostini with almonds
**After:** Black and white mini cakes

Feeds 4:

2 duck breast fillets

2–3 teaspoons medium-coarse ground black pepper

Salt

3/4 lb. shallots

1 1/4 lbs. carrots

1 tablespoon butter

1 tablespoon small capers

1/2 cup dry Marsala or Vin Santo

1/2 cup parsley sprigs

1 teaspoon fresh lemon juice

1  Heat oven to 175°F. If you have an older model, verify the temperature with an oven thermometer so the recipe will be sure to work. Place the duck fillets on a cutting board with the skin side up and score the skin with a knife in a grid pattern but don't cut into the meat. Combine salt and pepper and rub into both sides of duck fillets.

2  Peel shallots. Place an ovenproof sauté or frying pan with a handle (not nonstick) on the stove and let it warm up. Place the duck fillets in the pan with the skin side down and brown well. Then turn and brown briefly. Remove fillets from pan and briefly sauté shallots in that same pan.

3  Return duck fillets to the pan with the skin side up. Place pan in the oven and leave for about 40 minutes.

4  Meanwhile: peel, clean and cut carrots into matchstick strips about 1/4 x 2". About 15 minutes before the meat is done, melt butter in a pot. Add carrots and sauté briefly. Add capers, Marsala, salt and pepper. Cover and cook carrots over medium heat for about 8 minutes until crisp-tender.

5  Rinse parsley, shake dry and chop finely. Sprinkle parsley and lemon juice evenly on carrots and toss well. Slice duck breast and place on the table with the carrots.

Prep time: 1 hour, 30 minutes of which you're actually busy
Goes with: French or Italian bread and Nouveau Beaujolais or other light-bodied red wine
Calories per serving: 575

# Rabbit Stew
## It's pure poetry

**Before:** Herb relish
**After:** Lemon chocolate tiramisu

Feeds 4:

1 rabbit (have your butcher cut it into 8 pieces)

Salt, freshly ground black pepper

2 leeks

1 1/2 lbs. potatoes (russet or similar variety)

1 lb. tomatoes

2–3 cloves garlic

1/4 teaspoon red chile flakes

2 sprigs fresh rosemary

1/4 cup olive oil

2–3 bay leaves

1 2/3 cups vegetable or meat stock

1/2 cup dry white wine

1  Rinse rabbit pieces under cold water well to ensure there are no bone splinters. Pat dry with paper towels and season with salt and pepper on all sides. Remove roots and dark green parts from leeks, and cut in half lengthwise. Rinse very thoroughly and cut into 1/4" slices.

2  Peel potatoes and slice thinly (put in salted water until needed). Rinse tomatoes and slice. Peel and chop garlic. Rinse rosemary and remove needles—use about 2 teaspoons of needles (or less if desired).

3  Turn on oven to 350°F. Place a large oven-safe dutch oven on the stove and let it warm up.

4  Pour in half the oil and then brown the rabbit pieces in two portions. Remove rabbit and add leeks, then potatoes (remove from water and pat dry first), sautéing each separately in the oil for 3–5 minutes and then removing.

5  Return everything to the pot in layers, placing a little garlic, red chile flakes, and rosemary between each layer and here and there a bay leaf. Salt vegetables. Place tomatoes on top and season with salt and pepper. Finally, combine stock and wine and pour over the top. Cover and place in the oven for about 45 minutes. Remove cover, stir, and bake another 15–20 minutes uncovered until the surface is slightly brown. Before serving, remove bay leaves.

Prep time: 50 minutes active, 1 hour relaxing
Goes with: Baguettes
Calories per serving: 570

# Greek Meatloaf and Garlic Mashed Potatoes
A vacation from complex cooking

**Before:** Eggplant caviar
**After:** Oranges in honey

Feeds 4–6:

1 bread roll (OK if day-old)

6 green onions

1 zucchini

1 red bell pepper

1–2 marinated hot Italian chile peppers

(or pepperoncini)

6 cloves garlic

3 sprigs fresh thyme (or 1 teaspoon dried)

7 oz. feta cheese

1 lb. ground meat (pork, beef, lamb, or mixed)

2 eggs

1 tablespoon tomato paste

Salt, freshly ground black pepper

Paprika

8 roma tomatoes

6 tablespoons olive oil

1 3/4 lbs. potatoes (russet or similar variety)

1  Place the roll in a bowl and pour lukewarm water over the top. Let soak.

2  Remove roots and dark, wilted parts from green onions; rinse and chop very finely. Rinse zucchini and bell pepper and dice finely. Finely chop marinated peppers and 4 cloves peeled garlic. Rinse thyme and strip off leaves. Preheat oven to 375°F.

3  Dice feta. Squeeze liquid from roll and pull apart. Combine these two ingredients with vegetables, garlic, marinated peppers, thyme and ground meat. Add eggs and tomato paste. Season generously with salt, pepper and dashes of paprika and knead it all together until it adheres. Form into a loaf and place in a baking dish. Rinse tomatoes and place around the sides.

4  Pour 2 tablespoons oil over the meatloaf, place it in the oven and roast for about 1 hour.

5  When the meatloaf is about halfway done, peel potatoes, rinse and dice. Boil until tender in salted water. Pour off water and mash together with about 1/2 cup hot water (or hot milk or hot stock). Add salt. Peel rest of garlic, squeeze through a press and heat slightly with remaining oil. Add to mashed potatoes and serve with meatloaf, garnishing with the roasted tomatoes.

Prep time: 1 3/4 hours, 40 minutes of which you're actually busy
Calories per serving (6 servings): 710

# German Lamb Sauerbraten with Austrian "napkin" dumplings
When you're up for an old world adventure

**Before:** A small green salad of some sort
**After:** Stewed apples

Feeds 4–6:

**For the lamb roast:**

1 cup red wine vinegar

1 teaspoon peppercorns

2 whole cloves

1 teaspoon juniper berries

2 bay leaves

2¼ lbs. leg of lamb, de-boned

Salt, freshly ground black pepper

2 onions

3 cups vegetables such as carrots, celery, leeks, etc.

2 tablespoons clarified butter (or Ghee)

½ cup dry red wine

2 tablespoons raisins

1 tablespoon currant, quince or berry jelly

**For the dumpling:**

8 rolls (day-old are fine)

1⅔ cups milk

1 onion

½ cup parsley sprigs

1 tablespoon + 4 tablespoons butter

5 eggs

Salt

½ cup flour

**In addition:**
1 large napkin or 1 dish towel

1 Bring to a boil the following: red wine vinegar combined with 1⅔ cups water, peppercorns, cloves, juniper berries and bay leaves; then let cool until lukewarm.

2 Place lamb in a ceramic bowl and pour vinegar-spice mixture over the top. Place meat in the refrigerator and marinate 3 days, stirring daily.

3 Drain meat (but reserve marinade), pat dry and season with salt and pepper. Peel onions and peel or rinse vegetables; dice all into small cubes.

4 Melt clarified butter in a dutch oven on the stovetop; brown meat well on all sides and remove. Briefly sauté onions and vegetables in that same pan. Pour marinade through a wire mesh strainer and pour 1 cup of the marinade and the wine into the pot. Return meat, cover and braise over low heat (barely simmering) for about 2 hours.

5 After about 30 minutes, cut the rolls into small cubes for the "napkin dumpling." Heat milk until lukewarm and pour over the top. Peel onion, rinse parsley and chop both finely. Sauté briefly in the 1 tablespoon butter.

6 Separate eggs. Using electric mixer, beat the 4 tablespoons butter until smooth and creamy, gradually mixing in egg yolks. Add salt, flour, onion mixture and bread cubes; combine. Season with salt. Beat egg whites until stiff (using very clean and dry electric mixer beaters and a clean and dry bowl) and fold into batter mixture.

7 Wet napkin or non-terry cotton dish towel under hot water and wring out thoroughly. Spread out on the table. Place dumpling mixture in the middle of the cloth, shaping it into a short, thick baguette. Wrap loosely in the cloth and tie each end with kitchen string. Place a mixing spoon over a large pot —a wide and deep pot is ideal (but you can also allow the dumpling to bend). Tie the two ends of the cloth to the spoon ends so that the dumpling is suspended down into the pot. Remove again. Fill pot with water and heat. Don't let it boil—at most there should be small bubbles rising. Suspend the dumpling in the pot by laying the attached spoon over the top again. Cook dumpling gently in the simmering water for about 1 hour.

8 Remove roast from pot. Pour sauce through a wire mesh strainer and return to pot. Heat raisins in the sauce. Season to taste with salt and jelly. Cut roast into thin slices and return to the sauce. Unwrap dumpling and slice. Serve the two together. Garnish with parsley sprigs.

Prep time: 2½ hours, 50 minutes of which you're actually busy, + 3 days marinating time
Delicious with: The red wine used to make the sauce
Calories per serving (6 servings): 850

## Basic Tip
### Above all, let it be sour!
It doesn't really matter what kind of meat you choose for this festive roast—the sauce will provide the sour flavor. The important thing is that you like the cut—choose humanely raised meat or poultry from reputable butchers or health food grocery stores. Beef and veal take the same amount of time as lamb, and turkey takes just under an hour.

# Cream-Baked Salmon with Dill Pasta
Wonderfully extravagant

**Before:** Potato vegetable salad or carrot salad with grapes
**After:** Berry mascarpone or clafoutis

Feeds 4:

1 lb. onions

3 tablespoons butter

1/2 cup whiskey (may substitute Calvados, Marsala or water)

1/2 lemon, zest and juice

4 salmon steaks (about 5–6 oz. each)

Salt, freshly ground black pepper

Several sprigs parsley

1/2 cup fresh dill sprigs

3/4 cup cream

10–12 oz. fettucine or linguine pasta

**1** Peel onions and dice into 1/4" pieces. Melt half the butter in a pot over medium-low heat taking care not to burn the butter. Add onions and sauté over very low heat for about 10 minutes, stirring occasionally. Pour in whiskey and simmer about another 10 minutes.

**2** In the meantime, preheat the oven to 375°F. Rinse lemon under hot water; dry, remove zest and squeeze out juice from half (other half not used in this recipe). Season salmon steaks with salt and pepper and sprinkle with lemon juice.

**3** Season onions with salt and pepper and place in a baking dish large enough so you can then arrange the salmon steaks on top, side by side.

**4** Rinse and dry herbs. Finely chop parsley and half the dill and sprinkle over salmon. Pour cream over the top and place in oven for 15 minutes or until salmon is just opaque.

**5** In the meantime, cook the pasta in a large amount of boiling, salted water until al dente and drain. Finely chop remaining dill and mix with the hot pasta along with lemon zest and remaining half of the butter. Serve cream-baked salmon with dill pasta and a glass of chilled white wine.

Prep time: 1 hour
Also goes with: Cucumber salad or green salad
Calories per serving: 800

# Hazelnut-Celeriac Fish Fillets
Very unusual

**Before:** Creamy mushroom soup
**After:** Pear-banana chocolate squares

Feeds 4:

1 1/3 lbs. rainbow trout skinless fillets

(or other delicate fish fillets)

3 carrots

1 chunk celeriac/celery root (about 1/3 lb.)

3 green onions

1 clove garlic

Salt

1 tablespoon butter

1 tablespoon sugar

1/3 cup crushed hazelnuts

4 tablespoons sour cream

**1** Cut fish fillets into 8 pieces total (2 for each person). Peel carrots and celeriac and grate coarsely (use a food processor grating attachment if possible). Remove roots and wilted parts from green onions; rinse and cut into rings. Peel garlic, chop, and pulverize in a mortar and pestle with salt and mix with vegetables.

2  Place vegetable-garlic mixture in a wide pan, barely cover with water and bring to a boil. Cover and cook over medium heat for about 5 minutes.

3  At the same time in another pan, heat and stir together butter and sugar until the sugar melts and turns slightly brown. Add hazelnuts and brown slightly.

4  Salt fish pieces and arrange side by side on top of vegetables. Cover and cook over low heat another 3–4 minutes.

5  Carefully remove fish and keep warm between two plates or covered with tinfoil. Stir nut mixture into vegetables and bring to a boil. Season to taste. Place fish on prewarmed plates and top each piece with vegetable-nut mixture and 1 tablespoon sour cream.

Prep time: 45 minutes
Delicious with: Potatoes, rice or orzo pasta
Calories per serving: 390

# Spring Salad with Grilled Herbed Fish
## Highly sophisticated

**Before:** Tomato soup
**After:** Apple Charlotte

Feeds 4:

**For the fish:**

½ cup fresh parsley sprigs

2–3 cloves garlic

1 tablespoon fresh lemon juice

1 teaspoon lemon zest

¼ cup olive oil

Salt, freshly ground black pepper

4 fish fillets such as halibut or cod
(about 6 oz. each)

**For the salad:**

1 lb. green asparagus

½ lb. sugar snap peas

Salt

½ head romaine lettuce

½ lb. cherry tomatoes

1 bunch arugula

2 tablespoons pitted black olives,
preferably kalamata

2 tablespoons mild vinegar
(preferably white balsamic)

Salt, freshly ground black pepper

¼ cup olive oil

1  Rinse parsley, shake dry and mince. Peel garlic and chop finely, then mix with parsley, lemon juice, lemon zest, olive oil, salt and pepper.

2  Rinse fish under cold water and pat dry. Place in a shallow bowl and distribute garlic-parsley mixture over the top. Marinate about 2 hours or even longer.

3  For the salad, rinse asparagus and cut off about 1 to 1½" from the lower ends. Rinse sugar snap peas and cut off the tips. Bring salted water to a boil. First add asparagus and boil 3 minutes. Remove with a slotted spoon and boil sugar snap peas in the same water for about 2 minutes. Place both vegetables in a colander and rinse under cold water.

4  Turn on oven broiler. Remove leaves from half head of romaine and rinse thoroughly. Pat dry and cut into strips. Rinse and halve cherry tomatoes. Rinse arugula, pat dry and remove thick stems; cut remaining leaves in half. Chop pitted olives.

5  Place fish in a baking dish in the oven under the broiler; broil for about 10 minutes or until it is just opaque throughout.

6  In the meantime, whisk together vinegar, salt, pepper and olive oil. Cut asparagus into 1–1½" pieces. Mix together all salad ingredients with the dressing. Distribute on plates and place fish on top of or next to salad.

Prep time: 30 minutes
+ 2 hours marinating time
Delicious with: Garlic bread
made from baguettes
Calories per serving: 430

# The Great
# Pasta Toss

"It's time to have our close friends over." So what should we eat? "Pasta!" Again? "Why not, since it's all in the sauce!"

## Cooking Pasta

For 16 oz. of dry pasta, bring 4 quarts of water to a boil. Add pasta and stir. Then add 4–5 teaspoons salt (waiting to do so until this point helps it return to a boil faster). Bring back to a boil over medium heat, stirring occasionally. Two minutes before the end of the cooking time written on the package directions, test the pasta. If it's hard and doughy, test it again after 30 seconds. If it's firm but not doughy (this is "al dente"), pour it into a colander but use the cooking water to warm the serving bowl. Done!

## Creating the Right Atmosphere

Think of a piazza in Verona or a courtyard in Little Italy. Picture azure blue, egg-yolk yellow, olive green, beach-sand white, brick-oven red. Paint invitations on lasagna noodles, break them apart and send them out as jigsaw puzzles. Spread packing paper over the tablecloth and write the place names on it. Leave colorful laundry hanging on the line and light dripless taper candles in wine bottles. Listen to Ramazotti, Vivaldi and, as far as we're concerned, even Perry Como—as long as it's Italian, it'll sound right!

It's noon. The doorbell rings, two short and one long, as arranged. Outside the door we find our closest friends and their families who've just survived a perilous journey transporting hot merchandise. "Ciao, grazie, baci," we call out because this is supposed to be a perfectly normal Italian lunch. But "la famiglia" has hardly entered our door when they start bringing out mysteriously wrapped pots from under their coats. As the masterminds of this affair, we silently point the way to the steam-filled laboratory. There, the boss unwraps the packages, removes the lids, tastes and pauses. Then, with a brief nod, he says "Va bene, everything is excellent!" and the whole group rejoices. Brother Martin pops Prosecco corks, Aunt Edna sings the Prisoner's Chorus from Nabucco, and the Jones sisters dance a tarantella. Let the pasta party begin!

## What you need

First of all, here's what you don't need— sauce for the pasta because your guests will bring it with them. The assignment you gave them was simple: Just make your favorite sauces. But you need to make sure it doesn't all turn out to be tomato sauce and that there will be something for vegetarians.

But you do need pots for the pasta. They should each easily hold 5 quarts for cooking a one-pound package of pasta. You have to have at least two and if you don't, you can ask someone to bring them. But if you also lack pasta bowls (wide soup bowls work), forks, spoons, wine glasses and water glasses, maybe you need to put them on your Christmas list and wait until January to have your party. And another thing, in Italy in particular and at parties in general, cooking pots are not placed on the table. So it's good to have large serving bowls for pasta and sauces on hand for your pasta party.

## How to noodle your way into everyone's hearts

Contrary to practices in real Italian families, at this party the pasta and sauce are placed on the table separately. To keep the pasta from sticking together, you can either take the professional route and prepare only enough for one round at a time (which means someone always has to be in the kitchen) or cook all the pasta and after draining, toss it with olive oil or butter (which means the sauce doesn't cling to it as well, but it's more easygoing).

Pour the finished pasta and sauces into pre-warmed bowls and place them on the table where guests are already waiting with giant napkins tucked under their chins. Also put out small bowls full of fine things that everyone can sprinkle lightly over their own pasta and follow up with sauce and Parmesan. After mixing it all together, they can each add more of the other ingredients and it's time to eat! Finally, everybody wipes their plates clean with Italian bread before trying out the next combination.
But there can't be even a trace left behind because "clean plates tell no tales!"

# Pasta for Eight

**In any case:** 3 loaves crusty Italian bread, 3 lbs. pasta (without egg), either spaghetti alone or two or three different types—choose from penne, farfalle, fusilli or filled pasta such as tortellini and ravioli. Any more than two or three types gets confusing.

**Sauces (total of 2 to 3 quarts):** Tomato sauce (e.g. marinara) and cream sauce (such as Alfredo or gorgonzola-cream) as the basics plus at least one special sauce—with meat such as a bolognese or ragout, with fish such as tuna or shrimp, or a special sauce like pesto or ratatouille. For inspiration, we recommend the "Basic Italian" cookbook. Give guests recipes or let them prepare their own favorite recipes.

**To complement the sauces:** Strips or cubes of salami, ham, cooked shrimp, smoked salmon; sun-dried tomatoes, olives, capers, chopped fresh chile peppers (or marinated pepperoncini); chopped basil, dill, tarragon, marjoram, chives, parsley; cubes of mozzarella or fresh mozzarella, gorgonzola, or any semi-hard cheeses.

**To top it all off:** Olive oil, balsamic vinegar; lemon wedges; toasted sliced almonds and toasted pine nuts; grated or shaved Parmesan, pecorino, asiago; roasted garlic

**For drinking:** Prosecco, Chianti, Barolo, Barbera, Barbaresco, Tempranillo, Dolcetto or other Italian red wines; Italian white wines such as Soave; Italian sodas; espresso

**For before:** Ham carpaccio (page 65), marinated zucchini (page 64), green salad

**For after:** Chocolate lemon tiramisu (page 155), fresh fruit and gelato.

# Vegetable Casserole with Tomatoes
Not just for vegetarians

**Before:** Ham carpaccio OR polenta crostini with pesto
**After:** Avocado lemon cream

Feeds 4:

2 kohlrabi, 6–8 green onions, Salt, Paprika

6 sprigs thyme or ½ cup fresh parsley sprigs

10 oz. carrots, 7 oz. mushrooms

Freshly ground black pepper, 2 cloves garlic

1⅓ lbs. potatoes (russet or similar variety)

3½ oz. grated Swiss and/or Gruyere cheese

¾ cup + 2 tablespoons crème fraiche

⅓ cup whole milk, 7 oz. cherry tomatoes

**1** Peel kohlrabi and grate coarsely (vegetable grater or food processor). Remove roots and dark green parts from green onions; rinse and cut into rings. Combine with kohlrabi and season with salt and a few dashes paprika.

**2** Rinse herbs and shake dry. Strip off thyme leaves (against the direction they grow in) or chop parsley. Peel carrots and grate. Wipe mushrooms clean with a damp paper towel, cut off ends of stems and chop rest finely. Mix herb, carrots, and mushrooms together; season with salt and pepper.

**3** Peel garlic and squeeze through a press. Peel potatoes, rinse, cut into thin slices and then into fine sticks. Combine garlic and potatoes and season with salt and pepper.

**4** Preheat oven to 350°F. In a fairly deep baking dish, layer the different vegetable mixtures, sprinkling grated cheese over each layer (reserve some cheese for the top). Stir together crème fraiche, milk and remaining cheese and pour over the top. Rinse and halve tomatoes. With the cut side up, slightly press tomato halves down into the casserole.

**5** Place in the oven and bake for about 1 hour until nicely golden brown.

Prep time: At least 1 hour (+ 1 hour baking time)
Delicious with: A fresh green salad such as the one in the next recipe and a Sauvignon Blanc or dry rosé wine
Calories per serving: 450

# Cheese Soufflé with Green Salad
For punctual guests

**Before:** Hungarian paprika soup
**After:** Poached pears

Feeds 4:

4 tablespoons butter (generous) + butter for the baking dish

Bread crumbs for baking dish

¼ cup flour

1 cup + 1 tablespoon whole milk

5 large eggs

5¼ oz. grated Swiss and/or Gruyere cheese (half of each works great)

2 tablespoons crème fraiche

Salt, freshly ground black pepper

Freshly grated nutmeg

**For the salad:**

1 nice head of lettuce

4 radishes or 6 green onions

8 fresh chive spears

2 tablespoons white wine vinegar

1 dash mustard, Salt and pepper, A little sugar

3–4 tablespoons canola oil

**1** Butter the bottom and sides of a high-sided casserole or souffle dish (7½" diameter or smaller)—lightly coat with bread crumbs. Then, to make the Béchamel sauce, cut butter into bits and heat. As soon as it's completely melted, stir in flour and continue stirring until it's nice and golden. Then gradually whisk in milk. Cook over low heat for about 5 minutes or until thickened.

**2** This leaves you enough time to preheat the oven to 375°F and to separate the eggs. Lightly beat the egg yolks with a fork.

**3** When the sauce has thickened, add crème fraiche. Remove pot from the stove and gradually stir in egg yolks and cheese. Let it all cool until lukewarm, then season with salt, pepper and nutmeg. Beat egg whites until stiff using clean and dry electric mixer beaters and a clean and dry bowl—and fold in: start with just a portion of the whites to "soften" the cheese-egg mixture a bit—then fold in the rest until just barely combined. Pour gently into baking dish. Smooth the top carefully.

**4** Place baking dish in the oven on the bottom rack and bake 25–35 minutes until the soufflé has risen nicely and is brown. (Now no jumping or slamming doors!)

**5** In the meantime, remove leaves from lettuce, rinse, pat dry and tear into pieces. Rinse radishes or green onions and slice. Chop chives. Combine vinegar, mustard, salt, pepper, pinch sugar and oil; mix enough with the salad ingredients just to make the leaves shine. To make sure the soufflé stays inflated, take it straight to the table.

Prep time: 1 hour, 45 minutes of which you're actually busy
Calories per serving: 545

# Artichokes with Sauces
Use of fingers required!

**Before:** Lentil salad
**After:** Ice cream or sorbet of some sort

Feeds 4:
8 meaty artichokes (as big and fat as possible)
Salt

**For the pepper mayo:**
1 red bell pepper, 1 fresh red chile pepper
1 tablespoon olive oil
1/2 cup mayonnaise
Salt, freshly ground pepper
1 teaspoon fresh lemon juice

**For the tapenade-cream:**
3/4 cup sour cream
1 tablespoon prepared olive tapenade
1 teaspoon tomato paste
Salt, freshly ground black pepper

**For the vinaigrette:**
1/2 cup fresh mixed leafy herbs, 1 small onion
1/4 cup white wine (or rice wine) vinegar
2 teaspoons spicy mustard
Salt, freshly ground pepper
Honey, 1/3 cup good olive oil

**1** Remove bottom leaves from artichokes and cut off stems. Trim leaf tops with scissors. Bring a large amount of salted water to a boil and add 4 of the artichokes. Cover and cook for 20–30 minutes. When you can pull off one of the outer leaves easily, they're done.

**2** For the sauces, rinse bell and chile peppers (for less heat, discard ribs and seeds from chile), chop and brown in oil. Cover and cook for 10 minutes; purée and let cool—push pulp through a wire mesh strainer and combine it with mayonnaise. Season with salt, pepper and lemon juice. For the second, combine sour cream, olive tapenade and tomato paste; season with salt and pepper. For the third: rinse herbs, shake dry and mince. Peel onion and chop. Stir together vinegar, mustard, salt, pepper and a little bit of honey. Whisk in oil and add herbs and onion.

**3** Drain artichokes upside-down in a colander. Now cook the other 4 artichokes. You can already start eating the cooked ones—pull off one leaf at a time, dip the bottom end in the sauces and scrape off the meat between your teeth. When you get to the fuzzy part, cut it out. Underneath it you'll find the (very fine) artichoke heart.

Prep time: At least 1 hour, about 40 minutes of which you're actually busy
Delicious with: French bread and white wine
Calories per serving: 500

# Outdo

We can't help it, we just wanna be outside...

ors

We feel bad for the heron standing in a pond by the picnic area on a Sunday afternoon. Really! All these lush green lawns covered over with elegant picnic blankets—he probably thinks we're invading his space. This heavenly blue spring air polluted by the scent of young garlic and fresh rosemary rising from the barbecue. No really, Mr. Heron, we sympathize with you but we just can't help ourselves! We want to be surrounded by nature but we can't fight human nature. We simply MUST eat, drink and celebrate outside if we're going to feel good.

It could be worse, Mr.Heron, we could drink all your pond water, catch all your fish or even you... No, there's no danger.  We don't need all that since we have such fine things as grilled chicken and champagne as well as a few shrimp with lemon on the grill. Would you like to try a little? We know you're a real gourmet!

# Surviving Outdoors

Eating well is a wonderful thing, and so is lying out on the grass, but what about doing the two together? In other words, having a picnic? It's a nice idea but if you don't approach it in the right way, it has as much potential for disaster as breakfast in bed or love on the beach. So here's what you need for the perfect picnic:

* Natural surroundings, good weather; level surfaces; enough shade; personal protection from sun, rain and mosquitoes.

* A blanket or folding table with chairs; a set of small, light eating utensils (see standard set on page 16); dishware, glassware, and napkins; cooler; knife and cutting board, materials for transporting dirty dishes back to your house; a leak-proof container for trash.

* Food that's already made and wrapped that you can eat with your hands, or ones easily eaten with a fork or a spoon; creative sandwiches; baked goods; marinated foods for grilling (without the liquid); salt and pepper.

* Ice-cold soft drinks in plastic bottles; syrups that can be mixed with sparkling water; champagne, wine, and beer kept cold in the ice chest.

And here's what you don't need: Anything that melts, smears, drips, leaks, crumbles or spoils quickly; melons, red wine, soup; suit coats, ties, short skirts, high heels; ants, wasps, bears; bad odors, noise, wind. Otherwise, you'd be better off with snow!

# S.O.S.

## "How do I remove hail from the punch?"

Dear Advice Columnist:
I'd just been promoted and was due to have a barbecue for my boss and colleagues. It started out well, but out of a clear blue sky, thunderclouds appeared. Everybody ran inside but I had to stay behind and rescue Grandma's china. By the time I came in, soaking wet, everyone had left except Henderson from Accounting, asking if I'd lend him an umbrella! Can you believe the nerve of that guy?
Harry from Seattle

## Dear Harry:

Oh, Harry, you only have yourself to blame. Rule No. 1: "There are no disasters!" Rule No. 2: "If you think there are, you deserve what you get." In other words: Do whatever it takes to prevent chaos from erupting. I understand that in Seattle a little clear weather can make you light-headed, but you also need to keep an eye on reality, such as the sky over an outdoor barbecue!

You failed to do so and the result was a thunderstorm minus an awning. But you still could have saved the situation. "There are no disasters" means that if they happen anyway, do all you can to minimize the damage. If you'd really been concerned about your future when you had your party, you'd have been better off taking care of your guests rather than rescuing the family heirlooms. And what were they doing outside in the first place?

In a situation like this, take a lesson from insurance companies: They always manage to come through natural disasters with their heads above water. If you'd still managed to serve a feast fit for a king under such trying circumstances, you'd have been the hero of the day. So always remember to keep enough chilled bottles of bubbly and the name of the finest local caterer handy, then your boss and team won't even think of leaving!

And another thing: Cook only what you can handle. Then have a plan "B" all ready to go—if something still goes wrong, make an immediate decision about how to proceed and stick to it. Bluffing only works if you have an ace up your sleeve. Otherwise pass and apologize. And always keep an extra umbrella because the last department you want to have a bad relationship with is accounting!

## small talk

## "Nice Weather"

People who give outdoor parties are always worrying about the weather. That's why on a dry, sunny holiday, they can never get enough of hearing how lucky they are—they think it's great if everybody stands around oohing and aahing about the beautiful weather. Boring? Nevertheless, everybody can find something to say, and it helps break the ice. Hopefully the host isn't taking advantage of the sunny weather to pass off cheap hotdogs burned to a crisp.

| English | It's a beautiful day |
| --- | --- |
| German | schönes Wetter |
| French | beau temps |
| Italian | bel tiempo |
| Spanish | buen tiempo |
| Dutch | prachtig weer |
| Norwegian | pent vær |
| Swedish | vackert väder |
| Finnish | kaunis sää |
| Welsh | 'N arddun nhywydd? |
| Slovenish | Lepo vreme |
| But not | Can you believe this heat? |

# Edna's Mild Wild Duck

Does anyone remember Cold Duck? You do, Aunt Edna? Lemon, white wine, champagne—that's it exactly, ice cold and no sugar. You know how to make it a little wilder? Tell us!

"Well, supposedly it all started with a Bavarian General who always enjoyed his cold drink made from wine and champagne after meals and made no bones about it. 'When you eat something hot, you need a cold ending.' Because of the similar sounds in his language, eventually 'cold ending' (kalte Ende) became 'cold duck' (kalte Ente) and resulted in Cold Duck Punch. Here's how I make the classic: Rinse 1 lemon and remove zest. Put that zest in a punch bowl and add 3 bottles of good, dry Riesling. Let stand 10 minutes, strain to remove zest and add 1 bottle dry champagne." (serves 8–16)

"I once crossed Cold Duck Punch with Sangria and served it to some macho red-wine drinkers in Australia, just because they make such a wonderful dry sparkling red wine down there. Since that's very hard to get here and the combination of flavors can be shocking to certain more delicate palates, here's a tamer version I call 'Mild Wild Duck': Rinse 1 orange, cut into thin slices and place in a punch bowl. Pour in 2 bottles of ice-cold young, fruity red wine (Nouveau Beaujolais or 1 bottle of rosé and 1 bottle of a fruity red). Let stand 10 minutes and add one bottle of sparkling rosé and 1 bottle of sparkling water. For the Aussie Wild Duck variation: Substitute Shiraz and/or dry, sparkling burgundy for the sparkling rosé and, as far as I'm concerned, for the mineral water as well." (serves 8–16)

## Five steps to lighting a Fire

Are you in a sweat because you don't have any heat? That's what happens when the party's about to start and your grill's not ready yet. Any minute, all your guests are going to show up and tell you exactly what you're doing wrong and they'll all be ravenously hungry! Avoid hungry, cranky people at all costs—here's what you do:

1. Cover the bottom of the grill with aluminum foil; this keeps it clean and reflects the heat.

2. Start well ahead of time, placing a sufficient amount of charcoal in the grill (to judge the amount you'll need: after 20 minutes of heating up, one layer will supply the right amount of heat for a good half hour. Two layers need 45 minutes to heat up and then stay hot for 1 hour).

3. Stack the charcoal in a pile with slightly crumpled paper underneath and mixed in. You can also squirt charcoal lighter over the top. Professionals swear by fruit tree twigs for a fine grilled flavor.

4. Light the paper and wait until the pile is burning evenly and the charcoal slowly starts to glow. Blowing and fanning also help. But absolutely never ever pour additional liquid fuel over the top to speed things up! You could say goodbye to your eyebrows, and maybe more...

5. Spread out the coals, putting fewer on one side for a slightly cooler zone for slower grilling. Let the flames burn down until all the coals are glowing white. Place the rack on top (3–4 inches above the coals depending on thickness of food items) and after 10 minutes, start grilling (to learn more, see page 134 ff. and Basic Cooking, page 119).

# Portable Soft Walnut Breadsticks
No, not sweet!

**Preparation:** Same day or make ahead and freeze
**Storage:** After cooled, in zip-top bag in the freezer
**Serve with:** Roquefort-crème fraiche dip, potato vegetable salad Niçoise, chicken wings

For 8 breadsticks:

3¼ cups flour

1 packet yeast

⅛ teaspoon sugar

1 teaspoon salt

3 tablespoons oil

1 handful walnuts

½ teaspoon dried herbes de Provence

Backing parchment and flour for

working dough

**1** Pour flour into a bowl. Stir yeast well into 1 cup plus 1 tablespoon lukewarm water. Add sugar, salt, water-yeast mixture and oil to flour and knead together thoroughly until smooth and elastic (use electric mixer dough attachment if you can). Place dough in lightly oiled bowl, cover and let rise for about 1 hour.

**2** Chop walnuts. Knead dough once again, then knead in walnuts and herbs. Divide dough into 8 pieces. First form into balls, then into long pieces that narrow at the ends. Cover a baking sheet with baking parchment, place breadsticks on top, cover and let rise another 15 minutes.

**3** Preheat oven to 375°F. Brush water on sticks and spray a little water in the oven. Place sticks in the oven immediately and bake 15–20 minutes until golden brown. Remove from the oven and from the baking sheet and let cool.

Prep time: 30 minutes
(+ rising and baking time)
Calories per stick: 220

# Cheese Quiche
This version is easy to carry

**Preparation:** No more than 2 days ahead
**Storage:** Cut into pieces, covered in the refrigerator
**Serve with:** Marinated vegetables, herb relish

For 30 pieces:

$1/2$ cup + 3 tablespoons cold butter

$3 1/4$ cups flour, $1/4$ cup yogurt, Salt

1 large onion, 2 cloves garlic

18 oz. hard cheese (Swiss, gruyere,

Parmesan, asiago—or combination)

4 eggs, $1 3/4$ cups sour cream

Cayenne powder

16 cherry tomatoes

**1** Dice butter and use a pastry cutter to blend together with flour, yogurt and 2 teaspoons salt (or use an electric mixer). In order to form a smooth dough, add up to $1/3$ cup water just until it all comes together. Shape into a ball and refrigerate for 1 hour.

**2** Peel and chop onion and garlic. Grate cheese. Separate eggs. In large bowl, stir together egg yolks and sour cream. Add onions, garlic and cheese. Season with salt and dashes of cayenne.

**3** Preheat oven to 350°F. Roll out dough into a large rectangle on baking parchment and then flip over into a 9" x 13" pan and press into the bottoms and 1" up the sides.

Refrigerate briefly. Beat egg whites until stiff using clean and dry electric mixer beaters and a clean and dry bowl. Fold stiff egg whites into the cheese mixture and spread evenly over the crust.

**4** Rinse and halve tomatoes. With the cut side up, slightly press tomato halves down into the cheese mixture, arranging them so that when you later cut the quiche into pieces, you won't have to cut through any of the tomatoes.

**5** Bake quiche in the oven for about 45 minutes. It's ready when the cheese mixture is firm and the top is appetizingly brown. Let cool and cut into pieces.

Prep time: 35 minutes (+ 1 hour refrigeration time + 45 minutes baking time)
Calories per piece: 185

# Ham Crescents
Definitely something special

**Preparation:** If beforehand, freeze and then reheat prior to serving
**Storage:** After cooled, in a zip-top bag in the freezer
**Serve with:** Canapés with potato-cheese cream, cheese skewers

For 16 rolls:

3 cups flour, 2 teaspoons baking powder

1 cup cold butter, 1 cup sour cream

1 teaspoon salt

5 oz. cooked ham

1 handful chervil (or a little tarragon, parsley, young garlic, or young spinach)

$1/2$ onion

3 tablespoons crème fraiche

Salt, freshly ground pepper

2 tablespoons cream

**1** Combine flour and baking powder. Cut butter into small bits and add to flour along with sour cream and 1 teaspoon salt. Start with a pastry cutter, then knead together thoroughly. (Use an electric mixer if possible.) The dough will be slightly sticky. Shape into a ball and refrigerate until you're ready with the filling.

**2** Dice ham finely. Rinse chervil or other herbs; pat dry and mince. Chop half an onion finely. Combine ham, herb, and onion with crème fraiche; season with salt and pepper.

**3** Preheat oven to 375°F. Divide dough in half and roll out each portion into a circle with a diameter of about 12–14" (on a piece of baking parchment). Transfer dough circle to a baking sheet covered with parchment. Cut each circle into 8 wedges (like a pie) and place a little filling in the center of each piece. Roll up each from the wide end to the pointed end and bend into a crescent shape. Arrange crescents on baking sheet.

**4** Brush crescents with the cream and bake in the oven (center rack) for 20–25 minutes until nice and brown.

Prep time: A little less than 1 hour (+ 2 x 20–25 minutes baking time)
Calories per roll: 260

# Bavarian Cheese Spread
Traditionally old world

**Preparation:** In the morning
**Storage:** In the bowl in which you'll transport it
**Serve with:** Portable soft walnut breadsticks, bacon rolls

Makes enough for 4:

1 small onion

8 chive spears

10 oz. soft Camembert cheese

3 tablespoons softened butter

3–4 tablespoons pale beer

1 tablespoon paprika

Salt (optional)

**1** Peel and chop onion, the finer the better. Rinse chives, dry and chop.

**2** Cut open Camembert, discarding the rind and using the interior. Combine camembert with butter and beer—mix well. Add onion and paprika and taste. Does it need a little salt? It might need a little to bring out the nice, strong flavor.

**3** Place cheese spread in a bowl or plastic container, sprinkle with chives and it's done. It's best with fresh soft pretzels, or rye or pumpernickel breads—but in any case, spread it on thick!

Prep time: 30 minutes
Calories per serving: 330

## Basic Tip

Obviously, you can't see whether the Camembert is soft inside but you can feel it. Simple press down on the package. It must be easy to make an indentation. Otherwise don't use it.

# Cannellini Bean Spread
Tastes great on crostini and with grilled Italian-style meats

**Preparation:** No more than 1 day ahead
**Storage:** Refrigerated in a plastic container
**Serve with:** Salmon tramezzini, stuffed mushrooms, chicken legs

Makes enough for 4:

8 oz. canned cooked white beans (such as cannellini beans—about ½ can, drained)

2 cloves garlic

5 sun-dried tomatoes (oil-packed type)

1 small bunch arugula (about 1 cup)

1 tablespoon capers

2 tablespoons olive oil

Salt, freshly ground pepper

**1** Drain white beans and purée with 3 tablespoons water. Peel garlic, squeeze through a press and add.

**2** Drain sun-dried tomatoes and chop finely. Remove all wilted leaves and thick stems from arugula. Rinse the rest, dry and chop finely. Also chop capers.

**3** Add all these ingredients plus olive oil to the bean purée and mix well. Season with salt and pepper—you're done!

Prep time: 10 minutes
Calories per serving: 340

# Peanut-Celery Spread
## Hooray!

**Preparation:** No more than 2 days ahead
**Storage:** Refrigerated in a plastic container
**Serve with:** Moroccan cream cheese dip, chicken wings, California club sandwiches

Makes enough for 4:

1 stalk celery

2 sprigs parsley

²/₃ cup natural peanut butter (no-sugar variety)

Salt

A few drops Tabasco

**1** Rinse celery and cut off ends. If any threads are left hanging, remove. Rinse parsley, remove leaves and chop very finely along with celery.

**2** Thoroughly mix natural peanut butter, celery and parsley together. Season with salt and Tabasco. Great on crackers, as a dip for carrots or tucked into celery spears!

Prep time: 10 minutes
Calories per serving: 235

# Tomato & Roasted Pepper Bruschetta
## Super easy

**Preparation:** No more than 1 day ahead
**Storage:** Refrigerated in a plastic container
**Serve with:** Eggplant caviar, rolled roast pork, turmeric cucumbers

Makes enough for 4:

4 roma tomatoes

1 cup roasted red peppers (from a jar)

2 cloves garlic

2 tablespoons + ¼ cup olive oil

4 chive spears, 8 basil leaves

Salt, freshly ground black pepper

1 baguette

**1** Dice tomatoes. Rinse roasted red peppers, pat dry, and chop; peel and mince garlic. Mince chives and basil. Mix all of these with the 2 tablespoons olive oil, salt, and freshly ground black pepper.

**2** Slice baguette and brush olive oil (from the remaining ¼ cup) onto both sides of each slice; season with salt and pepper. Grill bread until crispy (or bake in a 350°F oven for 6 minutes). Top with tomato-roasted red pepper mixture.

Prep time: 20 minutes

# African Eggplant Spread
## Peanutty!

**Preparation:** No more than 2 days ahead
**Storage:** Refrigerated in a plastic container
**Serve with:** Tahini dip, chicken wings, bacon rolls

Makes enough for 4:

1–2 eggplants (about 1 lb. total), Salt

3 tablespoons olive oil

½ cup dry-roasted peanuts

1 clove garlic

2 tablespoons fresh lemon juice

Freshly ground pepper

**1** Peel eggplant (with a vegetable peeler or paring knife) and dice. Salt and let stand 10 minutes.

**2** Wipe off eggplant and sauté in oil in a non-stick pan over medium heat for about 15 minutes. Let cool and purée or chop finely. Chop peanuts very finely. Squeeze garlic through a press. Stir peanuts, garlic and lemon juice into eggplant; mix well and season with salt and pepper. Serve on crackers.

Prep time: 35 minutes
Calories per serving: 160

# Pan Bagnat
For a taste of Cannes and St. Tropez

**Preparation:** Make in the morning, wrap and let marinate until the picnic
**Storage**: In the refrigerator
**Serve with:** Marinated vegetables, Roquefort-crème fraiche dip, potato vegetable salad Niçoise

Makes enough for 4:

1 white onion (mild, otherwise use red)

2 cans tuna (packed in water, 5–6 oz. each)

8 lettuce leaves (nice and large)

2 tablespoons pitted black olives
(kalamata or Niçoise)

4 roma tomatoes

2 tablespoons vinegar

$^1/_3$ cup extra virgin olive oil

Salt, freshly ground pepper

1 baguette

**1** Peel onion, cut in half and place on the cutting board. Cut halves into very fine strips. Drain tuna and shred. Rinse lettuce under cold water, pat dry and cut into strips. Leave olives whole but make sure pits are removed. Rinse and dice tomatoes.

**2** Whisk oil and vinegar until cloudy in appearance. Season with salt and pepper and mix with onions, tuna, olives, and tomatoes. Add more seasoning if necessary.

**3** Slice baguette in half lengthwise and then cut into fourths (for 4 sandwiches). Place lettuce strips and then chopped salad mixture on bottom halves and cover with the top halves. Wrap each sandwich tightly in plastic wrap and refrigerate for at least 1 hour.

Prep time: 25 minutes
(+ at least 1 hour refrigeration time)
Calories per serving: 375

## Variation:
### Shrimp Salad Sandwiches
Cut open 4 bread rolls and spread a thin layer of cream cheese mixed with a little creamed horseradish on the bottom halves. Rinse or peel 1 small cucumber and chop finely. Rinse and finely chop $^1/_2$ cup dill fronds. Mix 10 ounces cooked shrimp (thawed and drained) with $^1/_3$ cup mayonnaise, the cucumber and the dill. Season to taste with salt and pepper and, if desired, a little fresh lemon juice. Distribute on the bottom halves of rolls, cover with the top halves and wrap tightly in plastic wrap; refrigerate.

# Sesame Bagels with Eggplant-Tomato Salad
For the vegetarian in all of us

**Preparation:** Prepare salad the day before; add parsley and feta last minute
**Storage**: Covered in the refrigerator
**Serve with:** Falafel, herb relish

Makes enough for 4:

1 medium eggplant

About 1/4 cup olive oil

2 cloves garlic

4 firm roma tomatoes

2 tablespoons fresh lemon juice

$^1/_2$–1 teaspoon harissa

$^1/_4$ teaspoon ground cumin

Salt

1 bunch parsley

3$^1/_2$ oz. feta

4 sesame bagels
(or Middle Eastern sesame rings)

**1** Rinse eggplant and dice finely. Heat oil in a pan (preferably non-stick). Stir in eggplant cubes and sauté over medium heat for about

5 minutes until they're nice and brown. If they don't turn brown, you'll have to add a little more oil.

**2** Peel garlic and mince. Rinse tomatoes and dice, not too finely but not too coarsely. Combine both ingredients with lemon juice and harissa and add to the eggplant. Season with cumin and salt and let cool.

**3** Rinse parsley and chop finely. Crumble feta. Cut open bagels if not cut already. Mix parsley and feta into eggplant mixture; distribute on the bottom halves and cover with top halves. Wrap up and take with you!

Prep time: 30 minutes
Calories per serving: 310

## Variation: Veggie-Cream Cheese Bagels

Rinse 1 bunch radishes and dice finely. Rinse and chop 8 chive spears. Mix both ingredients with 1/3 cup softened cream cheese and 1/3 cup sour cream; season with salt, pepper and a little ground cumin. Cut open 4 sesame seed bagels. Place 2 slices of a semi-hard white cheese on each one, spread cream cheese mixture on top, salt lightly, and cover with top halves and wrap up.

# California Club Sandwiches
Gourmet style

**Preparation:** Cook chicken the day before. Stir in mayonnaise in the morning. Don't assemble club sandwiches until 3–4 hours before the picnic.
**Storage:** Keep chicken fillets in refrigerator and assembled club sandwiches covered in the refrigerator
**Serve with:** Moroccan cream cheese dip, pasta salad with radicchio, bacon rolls

Makes enough for 4 (8 half sandwiches):

1 lb. chicken breast fillets (3–4 fillets)

Salt, freshly ground pepper

1 tablespoon canola oil

1 avocado

2 teaspoons fresh lemon juice

1 carrot

2 green onions

1/4 cup mayonnaise

12 slices sandwich bread

4 slices smoked or cooked ham

8 leaves arugula or other greens

**1** Rinse and pat chicken fillets dry; season with salt and pepper. Heat oil in a pan and sauté filets over medium heat for 5–7 minutes. Turn and sauté another 5–7 minutes or until opaque and juice runs clear. Cover and let stand; cool to room temperature.

**2** Cut avocado lengthwise to the pit, rotate halves and pull apart. Remove pit, then remove flesh carefully with a large spoon, keeping it intact. Dice avocado flesh, and mix with lemon juice so it doesn't turn brown.

**3** Peel carrot and grate or dice finely. Remove roots and wilting parts from green onions, rinse and slice thinly. Combine carrot, green onions, avocado and mayo. Season with salt and pepper but not too much.

**4** Toast bread. Place ham on 4 slices of bread and spread with half the avocado mixture. Top with another slice of bread. Rinse and pat dry arugula and place on top. Cut chicken fillets into thin slices. Try a slice to make sure it's seasoned enough with and pepper. Place on top of the lettuce, spread with remaining avocado mixture and cover with remaining bread.

**5** Cut club sandwiches in half diagonally. Wrap in plastic wrap and keep in the refrigerator until the picnic.

Prep time: 45 minutes
Calories per serving: 620

# Turmeric Cucumbers
## Simply delicious!

**Preparation:** At least 1, but no more than 4 weeks ahead
**Storage:** Sealed tightly in a screw-top jar in the refrigerator
**Serve with:** Rolled pork roast, cheese quiche, Chinese herb rolls

For two jars of about 2 cups each:

1 large cucumber (about $1^{1}/_{3}$ lbs.)

$1^{2}/_{3}$ cups apple cider vinegar

$^{1}/_{2}$ tablespoon sea salt

$3^{1}/_{2}$ tablespoons sugar

2 teaspoons ground turmeric

Several sprigs cilantro

**1** Peel cucumber, halve lengthwise, scrape out seeds with a spoon and cut into $^{1}/_{4}$"-wide strips.

**2** Bring $^{1}/_{2}$ cup water to a boil with vinegar, salt, sugar and turmeric. Add cucumber and bring briefly to a boil, then marinate 24 hours.

**3** Rinse cilantro and remove leaves. Remove cucumber from the pot with a ladle and place in very clean screw-top glass jars but don't seal. Bring the remaining vinegar-water to a boil once more, let cool until lukewarm, add cilantro leaves and pour over cucumbers. Seal jars and let stand at least 1 week, refrigerated. Should keep for about a month.

Prep time: 20 minutes
(not including marinating time)
Calories per jar: 150

# Variations:

## Mushrooms in Balsamic Vinegar

Wipe off $2^{1}/_{4}$ lbs. mushrooms and cut off ends of stems. Pour $1^{2}/_{3}$ cups water into a pot with 4 peeled garlic cloves, a few sprigs of thyme and $^{1}/_{3}$ cup balsamic vinegar. Add 1 tablespoon salt and $^{1}/_{4}$ cup oil and bring to a boil. Add mushrooms and boil for 3 minutes. Remove mushrooms and place in jars with a few capers but don't close jar. Bring vinegar-water to a boil once again and pour boiling hot over the mushrooms. Seal jars and marinate at least 2 days, in the refrigerator. Use within a couple of weeks.

## Asian-Style Radishes

Peel 1 daikon radish and cut into sticks $^{1}/_{4}$ x $1^{1}/_{2}$" long. Sprinkle with salt and let stand 1–2 hours. Rinse under cold water and pat dry. Peel and slice 1 piece ginger. Combine ginger with 1 stick cinnamon, 1 teaspoon peppercorns, 2 star anise, $2^{1}/_{4}$ cups rice vinegar, $2^{1}/_{4}$ cups water and 2 tablespoons sugar—bring to a boil. Add radish and briefly bring to a boil. Pour boiling hot into jars and seal. Marinate at least 1 week, refrigerated. Should keep for up to a month.

## Spicy Carrots

Peel 1 lb. carrots, clean and cut into pieces about $^{1}/_{4}$ x $1^{1}/_{2}$" long. Combine $1^{1}/_{2}$ cups white wine vinegar, $^{1}/_{2}$ cup water, 1 table-spoon salt, $^{1}/_{3}$ cup sugar and 1 dried chile pepper and bring to a boil. Let cool. Remove leaves from several sprigs of mint. Marinate carrots and mint in the vinegar-water for 24 hours. Then reheat and boil for 2 minutes. Pour into clean jars, seal and marinate for at least 1 week, refrigerated. Should keep for up to a month.

# Bell Peppers in Oil
## A delicacy for your friends

**Preparation:** At least 2 days, no more than 4 weeks ahead
**Storage:** Sealed tightly in a screw-top jar in the refrigerator
**Serve with:** Chicken saltimbocca, stuffed tomatoes, salmon tramezzini

For 1 jar of about 2 cups each:

At least $2^{1}/_{4}$ lbs. red and yellow bell peppers

$^{1}/_{2}$ cup white wine vinegar

1 teaspoon salt

4 cloves garlic

2–3 sprigs fresh rosemary, 2 bay leaves

About $1^{1}/_{4}$ cups good olive oil

**1** Preheat oven to 475°F. Rinse bell peppers, cut in half lengthwise and remove contents and stems. Place on a baking sheet with the cut side down and leave in the oven until the peel has dark brown to black "blisters" (about 20 minutes).

**2** Remove peppers from oven, let cool to room temperature and slip off peels. Cut into strips. Pour vinegar, 1 cup water and salt into a pot and bring to a boil. Place peppers in liquid a few at a time and boil for 30 seconds. Remove with a slotted spoon. Peel garlic and blanch briefly in the boiling water along with herbs.

**3** Drain and dry peppers, herbs and garlic on a large dish towel. Place in a jar and pour in enough oil to completely cover the peppers. Seal and marinate for at least 2 days, refrigerated. Should keep for a couple weeks.

Prep time: 45 minutes
(not including marinating time)
Calories per jar of peppers: 630

# Chicken Wings
## Easy to make on a baking sheet

**Preparation:** Marinate on previous day, then bake in the morning
**Storage:** Store marinated chicken wings covered in the refrigerator; store cooked wings in refrigerator.
**Serve with:** Moroccan cream cheese dip, California club sandwiches, cheese rolls

Makes enough for 4:

12 large chicken wings

4 cloves garlic

3 tablespoons honey

3 tablespoons fresh lemon juice

¼ cup soy sauce

2 teaspoons toasted sesame oil

1–2 teaspoons Tabasco

Salt (optional)

If you like: 2 tablespoons sesame seeds

Also: Baking parchment

**1** Rinse chicken wings and pat dry. Place in a backing dish large enough to lay them all side by side. Peel garlic.

**2** Stir together honey, lemon juice, soy sauce and sesame oil. Squeeze garlic through a press and add. Add a few drops of Tabasco (or more if you like), but don't add any salt yet.

**3** Pour sauce over wings, cover and refrigerate overnight. If you don't go straight to bed, turn them over once a bit later.

**4** On the next day, preheat the oven to 425°F. Cover a baking sheet with baking parchment and place chicken wings on top with the skin side down. Bake wings in the oven (center shelf) for about 10 minutes, then turn them over. If you want, you can sprinkle sesame seeds on top. Bake about another 10–15 minutes or more until wings are crispy. Also, if you pierce the chicken with the tip of a knife, the juices should run clear. If necessary, place under broiler briefly toward the end. Season to taste with salt, if necessary.

Prep time: 35 minutes, 10 of which you're actually busy (+ 1 night marinating time)
Calories per serving: 300

# Chicken Legs
## Spices that get under the skin

**Preparation:** No more than 1 day ahead
**Storage:** Covered in the refrigerator
**Serve with:** Turmeric cucumbers, marinated vegetables, portable soft walnut breadsticks

Makes enough for 4:

4 chicken legs with thighs (i.e. the whole piece, otherwise: 2 legs per person)

¾ cup parsley sprigs

2 cloves garlic

3½ oz. feta

2 tablespoons cream

Freshly ground pepper

2 tablespoons fresh lemon juice

2 tablespoons olive oil

Tabasco

Salt

**1** Rinse legs under cold water and pat dry. Massage the skin on all sides to loosen it from the meat without tearing it. At one spot, detach the skin a little with your finger, then stick a spoon handle between the skin and meat and detach the skin further. But the skin should stay attached, because you're going to slide a filling under it.

**2** Rinse parsley, shake dry, remove leaves and chop finely. Peel garlic and squeeze through a press. Crumble feta with a fork. Stir together feta, cream, parsley and garlic and season with pepper. Now stuff the feta mixture under the skin.

**3** Preheat oven to 425°F. Combine lemon juice and olive oil and season with Tabasco and salt. Brush onto chicken legs.

**4** Place chicken legs in a baking dish and bake in the oven (center shelf) for 40–45 minutes, turning once or twice in the process.

Prep time: 1¼ hours, 30 minutes of which you're actually busy
Calories per serving: 390

## Variation:
## Chicken Legs
## with Fennel
Remove zest from 1 lemon. Chop 1 teaspoon fennel seed very finely or crush in a mortar. Squeeze 2 cloves peeled garlic through a press. Combine all these ingredients with ¼ cup olive oil and a little finely chopped parsley—brush onto the legs. Bake as described above.

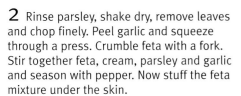

# Rolled Pork
# Roast
## Party animals aren't
## the only ones who love it

**Preparation:** Cook on previous day
**Storage:** Unsliced and wrapped tightly in plastic wrap in the refrigerator; don't slice until the day of the party
**Serve with:** Stuffed tomatoes, bell peppers in oil, pasta salad with radicchio

Makes enough for 6–8:

At least 2½ lbs. pork for a rolled roast

without rind (have an obliging butcher

prepare it but not roll it since you have

to add the filling)

3 slices white sandwich bread

7 oz. uncooked bratwursts

(or other uncooked sausage)

1 bunch green onions (5–6)

2 cloves garlic

1 cup basil sprigs

2 tablespoons pine nuts

1 fresh red chile pepper or jalapeño

¼ cup + 3 tablespoons ricotta or cream cheese

Salt, freshly ground pepper

Zest from ½ lemon

2 tablespoons olive oil

**1** Spread pork out on a board. Briefly soak bread in lukewarm water.

**2** Squeeze contents of bratwursts out of their skins. Remove roots and wilted parts from green onions, rinse and chop rest. Peel garlic and chop. Remove basil leaves and chop finely. Chop pine nuts and fresh chile pepper (without stem—also, omit ribs and seeds for less heat).

**3** Preheat oven to 375°F. Squeeze out bread and combine with sausage, ricotta and everything you just chopped. Season with salt, pepper and lemon zest and spread on top of the meat. Roll meat tightly into a roast and tie with kitchen string.

**4** Rub salt and pepper into the roast on all sides, brush with olive oil and place in a roasting pan. Cook in the oven (center shelf) for about 1¾ hours, occasionally basting with the juice that forms. Afterwards leave in the oven (turned off) for 15 minutes, then remove and let cool to room temperature (then chill in refrigerator overnight). Cut into thin slices. Makes for great sandwiches!

Prep time: 2½ hours, 30 of which you're actually busy (+ 1 night cooling time)
Calories per serving (8 servings): 320

## Sesame Spinach
*Good and green*

**Preparation:** 1–2 hours ahead of time but grilled right before eating
**Storage:** In small aluminum foil packages
**Serve with:** Chicken legs, lemon trout, Indian potato salad

Makes enough for 4:

About 1¹/₂ lbs. spinach

4 cloves garlic, 3 tablespoons soy sauce

2 tablespoons sesame seeds

A couple drops chile oil

Salt, freshly ground pepper

**1** Rinse spinach thoroughly; drain, remove thick stems and wilted leaves.

**2** Cut 4 large pieces of aluminum foil and distribute spinach on top, evenly among them. Peel garlic and squeeze 1 clove through the press and add a little to each pile of spinach. Top each with a little soy sauce, a generous sprinkling of sesame seeds and a few drops of chile oil. Season with salt and pepper. Seal up well.

**3** Heat barbecue. Place packages on top and grill on medium heat for about 4 minutes.

Prep time: 20 minutes (+ BBQ time)
Calories per serving: 100

## Cheese-stuffed Red Peppers
*In Greece, often served as an appetizer*

**Preparation:** Clean bell peppers and brush insides with oil mixture in the morning
**Storage:** Covered at room temperature
**Serve with:** Greek potato purée, stuffed mushrooms, California club sandwiches

Makes enough for 4:

4 red bell peppers (preferably smallish long ones rather than large and round)

1 cup parsley leaves and tender stems

1 tablespoon fresh lemon juice

2 tablespoons olive oil

Salt

Freshly ground pepper

7–8 oz. feta (in a block)

**1** Rinse bell peppers, cut out stem and remove contents.

**2** Rinse parsley, shake dry, remove tough stems and chop rest finely.

**3** Mix together parsley, lemon juice and olive oil and season with salt and pepper. Brush onto the inside of peppers. Cut feta block into 4 pieces and place 1 piece inside each pepper.

**4** Prepare grill. Place peppers on top and cook over medium coals for about 10 minutes on each side.

Prep time: 20 minutes (+ 20 BBQ time)
Calories per serving: 175

# Bacon Mushrooms
Worth fighting over!

**Preparation:** 4–5 hours before wrapping up
**Storage:** Covered with plastic wrap in the refrigerator
**Serve with:** Spareribs, peanut-celery spread, frittata cubes

Makes enough for 4:

½ lb. oyster mushrooms

½ cup parsley or basil sprigs

2 cloves garlic, 2 tablespoons olive oil

Salt, freshly ground pepper

5 oz. sliced bacon

**1** Separate oyster mushrooms and wipe off with paper towels. Cut off and discard thick stems.

**2** Remove parsley leaves and chop finely along with peeled garlic. Combine with oil, salt and pepper and spread over mushrooms. Wrap each mushroom in a piece of bacon.

**3** Heat barbecue. Place mushrooms on top and grill for about 10 minutes, turning at least once. Use skewers if you're worried about them falling through the cracks.

Prep time: 15 minutes (+ BBQ time)
Calories per serving: 275

# Grilled Stuffed Eggplant
Meatless and satisfying

**Preparation:** Salt eggplant and chop filling ingredients in the morning
**Storage:** Covered in the refrigerator
**Serve with:** Herb relish, lamb chops, marinated vegetables

Makes enough for 4:

1 medium eggplant
(Japanese or Italian types work great)

Salt

8 sun-dried tomatoes (oil-packed type)

1 tablespoon pine nuts

¾ cup basil sprigs

A couple fresh mint leaves (optional)

2 cloves garlic

2 tablespoons breadcrumbs

2 tablespoons freshly grated Parmesan

4 tablespoons olive oil

Cayenne pepper

**1** Soak a bunch of toothpicks in water. Peel eggplant (with a vegetable peeler or sharp paring knife) and cut lengthwise into slices about ¼" thick. Sprinkle with salt and let stand for about 30 minutes.

**2** Drain sun-dried tomatoes and chop finely along with pine nuts. Remove leaves from basil and mint and cut into strips. Peel garlic and squeeze through a press. Combine all these ingredients with bread crumbs, Parmesan and 2 tablespoons of the oil and season with salt and a dash cayenne.

**3** Pat eggplant slices dry. Spread mixture thinly on one side, fold over and secure with a soaked toothpick. Season exterior with salt and brush with remaining oil. Heat barbecue. Place eggplant slices on top and grill for about 10 minutes, turning at least once.

Prep time: 20 minutes
(+ 20 minutes standing + BBQ time)
Calories per serving: 220

# Come try the new BBQ

If your vanity plate read "VGBBQ4U," would other people be able to decode it?  Well, it's time for "Veggie Barbecue For You" ...and me!

## Marinating Vegetables

Pierce firmer vegetables with a fork and marinate for 8 hours (only 2–3 hours for tender vegetables). Don't salt.

**Mediterranean marinade** (for 2 lbs. vegetables: eggplant, fennel, carrots, peppers, mushrooms, tomatoes, zucchini): 2 sliced garlic cloves, 1 diced onion, 1 julienned chile pepper, 1 bay leaf, 1 sprig rosemary, $2/3$ cup olive oil, 1 teaspoon fresh lemon juice.

**Asian marinade** (for 2 lbs. vegetables: squash, green onions, carrots, mushrooms, asparagus): 1 chopped garlic clove, 1 grated walnut-sized piece of ginger, $1/3$ cup soy sauce, 3 tablespoons sake or mirin, 3 tablespoons oil, 1 tablespoon honey.

## Creating the Right Atmosphere

Envision Vietnamese street food vendors, a Grecian village square, Caribbean vegetable gardens, an American suburban backyard with flags and overstuffed coolers. Picture sky blue, grass green, dandelion yellow, ember red. Send postcards of your town as invitations—or anything that says "community." Rely on nature to provide the setting but shoot for shade in the daytime and beautiful lighting at night. Listen to birds singing, leaves rustling, hoses spraying, children laughing, Harold playing his guitar—and don't be afraid to sing along! But please, no boom box.

Barbecues are changing. Blade roasts and T-bone steaks still appear on the grill but the alpha wolf no longer controls the fire. Vegetables are coming into their own as a grill star—without meat, without fish but with the color, flavor, and creativity. Yeah, sure, it's also very healthy. But above all, it has a taste of variety instead of the same ol' same ol' (i.e. frozen burger disks and cheap hot dogs). And if anything accidentally stays on the grill too long, it's no big deal because it's also cheaper than that New York Strip. So let's do it!

## What You Need

The most important ingredient for a barbecue is fresh air all around you, which you can't get just by opening the kitchen window. A balcony with room for a grill and the grill master plus tolerant neighbors is more like it. If you have a yard, that's great! If not, go out into nature but do so where charcoal grilling is allowed.

The minimum grill size for a barbecue for four people is about 11" x 15". If you have more people, you either have to use a bigger grill or more than one. Whether you use charcoal or gas is a question of your philosophy, cost and comfort but, even more, of convenience—whatever is available to you. Before you can even start, you need some kind of cooking tool for each grill-master, either a metal grill spatula, tongs or a grill fork, plus brushes, foil, and skewers. You'll need utensils to eat with, silverware and glasses from home or paper and plastic if you don't have a dishwasher. Sitting down directly on the grass with your feast is a little too close to nature so you'll need some sort of seat and table for each guest—or a big blanket. You don't need tablecloths but you do need napkins—paper is fine. You'll need a buffet for the vegetables—a tree stump will do. Use either a large colorful platter for everything or a lot of small plates. Take anything marinated out of its liquid before transporting it outside, to avoid dripping later.

## How to Barbecue

When it's time to start, the barbecue has to be hot, which it will be 10 minutes after you switch on the gas or at least 30 minutes after you light the charcoal (for more on this, see page 123). Season the already-marinated vegetables with salt and pepper on the grill, with the rack no more than about 4 inches above the coals. When foods take on a roasted, wrinkled look and seem tender when you poke them, they're done. If this takes longer than 10–15 minutes, either the coals aren't hot enough or the rack is too high. Sensitive foods such as cheese or narrow objects such as green onions can also be cooked in foil or foil containers. And for the more experimental among you, try smaller chunks of vegetables for making skewers.

# A Grill Party for Twelve

**In any case:** Oil, salt, pepper, and a total of about 11 pounds vegetables, including:

**For fast grilling (5–10 minutes):** Eggplant and zucchini cut diagonally into ¼" slices; oyster mushrooms, white mushrooms, shiitakes; cleaned green onions, halved Belgian endives

**For normal grilling (10–15 minutes):** Carrots cut lengthwise into ¼" slices; pieces of fennel bulb; bell pepper quarters; squash slices (¼" thick including rind); green asparagus; potato slices; par-boiled corn cobs

**For cooking in foil containers:** Cherry tomatoes, garlic cloves, leek slices, onions cut into rings

**Fruit for grilling:** Pineapple, apples and pears (in ¼" slices including seeds and peel); mango halves and bananas in the peel; lemon and lime halves for roasting and sprinkling on top

**Cheese for grilling:** Camembert, feta, mozzarella, goat cheese

**Plus:** Various dips (pages 42–45) and pasta, rice, potato and/or special salads (pages 72–79); green leafy salad; bread

**For drinking:** Citrus soft drinks over ice, fruit syrups with ice-water or sparkling water, ice tea, punch, beer, summery wine

**For after:** Exotic fruit gelées (page 150), trifle (page 155), melon in coconut milk (page 151)

# Lemon Trout
## Quick and easy

**Preparation:** Stuff and season in the morning but don't yet wrap in foil
**Storage:** Covered in the refrigerator
**Serve with:** Bell peppers in oil, chicken legs, tahini dip

Makes enough for 4:

4 trout (about ¾ lb. each)

2 lemons

4–8 green onions

1 cup dill fronds

Salt, freshly ground pepper

¼ cup oil

**1** Rinse trout inside and out and pat dry. Rinse lemons under hot water and slice with the peels on. Remove roots and wilted parts from green onions, rinse and cut in half lengthwise. Rinse dill, shake dry and discard any tough stems; tear or chop into pieces.

**2** Season trout inside and out with salt and pepper. Fill cavity with lemon slices, green onions and dill and brush each fish with 1 tablespoon of the oil.

**3** Now you have two choices: Wrap the trout in aluminum foil or place in a fish grill-basket. You can't put them directly on the grill rack because they'll stick and you won't be able to turn them.

**4** In any case, heat up your grill. Medium hot coals are the best. Or simply place the fish towards the edge of the rack if your coals are hotter. They'll take about 15 minutes. Whether they're in foil or in a basket, you should turn them at least once.

Prep time: 30 minutes (+ grill time)
Delicious with: Crusty white bread
Calories per serving: 300

## Tip:
Tradition has it that in German beer gardens whole fish are often grilled on a stick—like s'mores, only crazier! Often mackerel or other whole fish are skewered on a stick and grilled over a charcoal fire. If you want to make them yourself, season the inside of a cleaned, whole fish with salt and pepper. Sharpen a stick to a point and insert it into the fish's mouth, almost all the way to the tail. Salt a little of the cavity and generously on the outside (you won't be eating the skin anyway). Suspend the stick over the grill (over very hot coals), or even a campfire, until the skin is crispy. It will be quite the conversation starter!

# Cilantro Shrimp
## A touch of elegance

**Preparation:** Marinate the night before or in the morning
**Storage:** In a bowl in the refrigerator
**Serve with:** Tomato dip, avocado dip, chicken wings

Makes enough for 4:

1 piece lemon grass

1 fresh red chile pepper

3 green onions

1 piece ginger (about ½" long)

½ cup cilantro sprigs

Juice from 1 lime or lemon

1 teaspoon sesame oil

2 teaspoons canola oil

About 1½ pounds raw shrimp, peeled & de-veined, tail on

Salt

**1** Rinse lemon grass; remove and discard tough outer layer and cut rest into ⅛" slices. Rinse chile pepper, remove stems and cut into rings with the seeds (omit seeds for less heat). Remove roots and dark tops from

green onions, rinse and cut rest into rings. Peel ginger and chop. Rinse cilantro under cold water, shake dry, discard any tough stems and chop coarsely.

**2** Combine all chopped ingredients with lime juice and oils. Rinse and dry shrimp. Mix with marinade and let sit for at least 4 hours, refrigerated.

**3** Then heat your grill. Cover the rack with aluminum foil. Drain shrimp of all the liquid and spread out on foil. Grill for a total of 8–10 minutes, turning at least once. After cooking, season with salt.

Prep time: 20 minutes
(+ 4 hours marinating time + BBQ time)
Delicious with: Flatbread
Calories per serving: 180

# Grilled Tuna Skewers
## Absolutely delicious

**Preparation:** Place on skewers in the morning
**Storage:** Covered on a plate in the refrigerator
**Serve with:** Tahini dip, carrot salad with grapes, lamb chops

Makes enough for 4:

1$\frac{1}{3}$ lbs. fresh tuna

2 tablespoons fresh lemon juice

$\frac{1}{2}$ teaspoon harissa

1 tablespoon tahini (sesame-seed paste)

1 tablespoon oil + oil for brushing

Salt

$\frac{1}{2}$ lb. cherry tomatoes

$\frac{1}{2}$ lb. shallots or small onions

$\frac{1}{4}$ cup fresh mint

12 wooden or metal skewers

(soak wood skewers in water)

**1** Rinse and pat tuna dry and cut into bite-sized pieces. Combine lemon juice, harissa, tahini and oil; season with salt and mix with tuna. You can either place the fish and the other ingredients on skewers immediately or marinate them first. Either way is OK.

**2** Rinse cherry tomatoes. Peel shallots. Cut large shallots in half. Place tuna, cherry tomatoes and shallots on skewers, placing 1 mint leaf between the pieces. Salt the skewers and brush with a little oil.

**3** Then heat up your grill. Grill skewers for a total of about 10 minutes, preferably over medium coals, turning at least once.

Prep time: 30 minutes (+ grill time)
Delicious with: Flatbread or olive ciabatta
Calories per serving: 400

## Variation:
### Eel Skewers
Eel is very fatty, which is why it tastes especially good grilled, and it doesn't dry out. Have a fishmonger (try an Asian market) skin fresh eels (about 1$\frac{1}{2}$ lbs.). Cut into pieces $\frac{1}{2}$" long. Place on skewers with onions or mushrooms, here and there adding a fresh bay leaf. Season with salt and pepper, sprinkle with lemon juice and grill for about 15 minutes, turning as often as possible. Discard bay leaves before serving.

# Tandoori Chicken
So red, so Indian, so good

**Preparation:** Marinate the day before
**Storage:** Covered in the refrigerator
**Serve with:** Cucumber raita, Indian potato salad, meatballs

Makes enough for 4:

4–6 chicken breast fillets (depending
on the size—about 5–8 oz. per person)

Juice from 1 lemon

Salt

1 piece fresh ginger

2 cloves garlic

1 teaspoon ground turmeric

1 teaspoon ground cumin

$\frac{1}{2}$ tablespoon chili powder

$1\frac{3}{4}$ cups yogurt

Drops red food coloring

**1** Rinse and pat chicken breast fillets dry and cut in half. Score each piece a few times with a knife, about $\frac{1}{8}$" deep. Pour lemon juice over the top and season with salt.

**2** Peel ginger and garlic and squeeze both through a press. Combine with spices and yogurt. Dye bright red with food coloring. Slather meat with red yogurt mixture and refrigerate overnight.

**3** On the next day, remove chicken from red marinade and grill over medium hot coals for about 20 minutes, turning occasionally and brushing on more marinade.

Prep time: 20 minutes
(+ marinating overnight + grill time)
Delicious with: Chapatis—Indian skillet bread (Basic Baking, page 136 or purchased)
Calories per serving: 335

# Spareribs
Fun to gnaw on

**Preparation:** Prepare sauce the day before
**Storage:** Covered in the refrigerator
**Serve with:** Avocado dip, tomato dip, lemon trout

Makes enough for 4:

1 onion

4–6 cloves garlic

$\frac{1}{3}$ cup honey

$\frac{2}{3}$ cup tomato ketchup

2 tablespoons balsamic vinegar

3 teaspoons dijon or spicy mustard

A little Tabasco

Salt, freshly ground pepper

$4\frac{1}{2}$ lbs. spareribs (yep, you really do need this much—it's mostly bone)

**1** Peel onion and garlic and mince. Combine both in a pot with honey, ketchup, balsamic vinegar and mustard; heat. Simmer for about 15 minutes. Season to taste with Tabasco, salt and pepper.

**2** Divide spareribs into pieces with 2–3 ribs each. Wipe with a cloth (to check for any bone splinters).

**3** Heat up your grill. Grill spareribs over medium coals for 10–20 minutes or longer so that meat cooks through (depending on the heat of the barbecue). During this time, brush on the sauce fairly frequently and, of course, keep turning.

Prep time: 25 minutes (+ grill time)
Delicious with: Crusty white bread
Calories per serving: 490

## Basic Tip:
Sauce with sugar (and that's basically what honey is) burns easily. So make sure the coals aren't at their hottest and that the rack is far enough away from them.

# Lamb Chops
## Italian style— simply the best

**Preparation:** Marinate the day before
**Storage:** Covered in the refrigerator
**Serve with:** Marinated vegetables, bacon mushrooms, Roquefort crème fraiche dip

Makes enough for 4:

2 sprigs fresh rosemary

(+ a few rosemary sprigs for the coals)

4 cloves garlic

1 dried chile pepper

1/2 lemon (zest and juice)

1/3 cup olive oil

Freshly ground pepper, salt

12 lamb chops (weighing about 3 oz. each)

**1** Rinse 2 sprigs rosemary, pull off needles and chop coarsely. Peel garlic and cut into thin slices. Crush chile pepper in a mortar. Rinse lemon under hot water, zest and squeeze out juice.

**2** Combine all these ingredients with oil and season with salt and pepper. Wipe off lamb chops with a damp cloth (to check for bone splinters) and place in a ceramic baking dish. Pour marinade over the top and marinate lamb chops overnight. If you think about it, turn them once in a while.

**3** Heat up your grill. Remove the marinade from the lamb chops as much as possible (otherwise it'll burn when you grill them) and grill over medium coals for about 4 minutes on each side. The trick is to throw a few fresh rosemary sprigs onto the coals. It will work magic with the flavor. Season with salt and enjoy!

Prep time: 20 minutes
(+ marinating overnight + grill time)
Delicious with: Crusty white bread
Calories per serving: 560

## Variation:
### Lamb skewers
Cut shoulder or leg of lamb (about 1 1/3 lbs.) into cubes and marinate the same as above. On the next day, place on skewers with zucchini pieces, mushrooms and cherry tomatoes or small onions. Grill for about 10 minutes, turning frequently.

# Sweet

Something to bring a smile to your stomach...

# Food

Toward the end of a meal, guests are bound to be thinking, "I wonder what is for dessert?" A bold sugar-fiend might even ask outright. If you were planning on just throwing some chips in bowls onto the coffee table to munch during the evening's festivities, think again. Because, if you are a dessert-less host(ess), you'll have to deal with a few desertions. Such an omission is unforgivable! And unforgettable.

It doesn't have to be a big deal, nor heavy and complicated, just a little sweet. Something to give people's hearts another little boost and bring a smile to their stomachs just as the party is winding down… They'll see you come through the door with a few bowls of melon in coconut milk or they'll watch you finally fill the empty spot on the buffet with a fresh-baked clafoutis. Also unforgettable—this time with a positive memory.

# When waffling is a good idea

The doorbell rings. Suddenly, the three poker buddies you vaguely remember visiting last night (before you had a little too much to drink) are standing in your hallway. "Hi, you party animal you, here we are!" Huh? "Last night we beat you at vodka poker and we've come to collect our homemade brunch." You did...you are? Oh well, what could be more fun than making big fat waffles for four, because sometimes sweet food can be the main course! (These waffles are also great for dessert, no kidding.)

In a large bowl, mix together 1¾ cup flour, 1 tablespoon baking powder, and ¼ teaspoon salt. In another bowl, mix together 2 eggs, 1½ cup milk, ¼ cup cream (or buttermilk), ½ cup canola oil, and 1 teaspoon vanilla. Then add the egg-milk mixture to the flour mixture all at once and briefly mix just until all the flour is moistened and incorporated. Use a heated Belgian waffle maker, and pour about ⅓ to ½ cup batter for each waffle. Serve with ice cream, fruit, whipped cream or something a little more grown up (see next page).

## Drink of the Day
# Limoncello

We started out the party with Lime Fizz, and now it's time to bring it to a sweet conclusion. What could be more fitting than Limoncello, the Italian lemon liqueur with a taste of summer? It's perfect because it wakes you up while soothing at the same time. Its ice-cold temperature refreshes while the alcohol brings warmth. The only catch is that it takes about a month to make, but it's fun!

For two bottles (one for the freezer and one in reserve), rinse 7 thick-skinned lemons under hot water. Place in a bowl, cover with boiling water and let stand 1 hour. Then zest the lemons, taking only the yellow part. Make sure you don't get any of the white part—it makes the liqueur bitter. (Use the fruit of the lemon for something else.) Place the zest in a large, 2 quart jar that you've rinsed out with hot water (you can also use a saucepan if it has a lid and you won't be needing it anytime soon). Pour 1 bottle of good 40% vodka over the top.

Now melt 1 cup + 2 tablespoons sugar in 1⅔ cups boiling water and add to lemon vodka. Let cool and seal (wrap several layers of plastic wrap around the jar or saucepan). Store in a cool, dark place; the refrigerator is too cold. During the first week, shake up the liqueur once a day, then leave it alone for 3–4 weeks. Finally, pour it through a wire, fine-mesh strainer. Fill two bottles, seal and place at least 1 bottle in the freezer for later. As of the next day, it's time to be stimulated and soothed, warmed and cooled. Serve ice cold. Salute!

## small talk
## "See you soon!"

It's hard to say "I'm sorry," but sometimes it's even harder to say good-bye. The good news is that with close friends, there will always be a next time. Make sure you leave the party at a decent hour (follow the cues of your host and other guests), thank the host personally, and if you mean it—tell them what a great time you had.

| | |
|---|---|
| English | Bye-bye! |
| German | Tschüs |
| Italian | Ciao |
| French | Au revoir; À bientôt |
| Spanish | Adios; Hasta luego |
| Dutch | Tot ziens |
| Norwegian | Hade bra |
| Swedish | Hej da |
| Finnish | Näkermiin |
| Hungarian | Viszlát; Szia |
| Polish | Pa; Do widzenia |
| Personal | I had a really good time |
| Polite | Till next time |
| But not | I'll have my people call your people |

# S.O.S.

## "Sure tastes lemony, doesn't it?"

Dear Miss Manners,
On my last birthday, HIS parents were also invited. I decided to throw together something simple. I'd just make artichokes, with lemon water for rinsing our fingers. It was okay that HIS father wanted to salute "our son's future wife," but when he raised his finger bowl in a toast, all I could do was take refuge in the kitchen. Since then, none of them speak to me anymore, not even HIM. Isn't that the most ridiculous thing you've ever heard?
Laura from Saint Louis

## Dear Laura:

The first time that the owner of our favorite Japanese restaurant offered us sushi, he put little trays of liquid on the table. I confidently dipped in my fingers to rinse off the day's grime and everyone else did likewise, including our Japanese host. At the end of a fabulous evening he said, "Thank you so much and please forgive me for being so stupid as to allow us to wash our hands in the sake." That liquid was the rice wine aperitif!

Many blunders committed by guests can be avoided if the host thinks ahead and stays cool. Artichokes for potential parents-in-law? The red flags immediately go up! And with finger bowls? A clear threat to your love life! If this doesn't occur to you until you're actually seated at the table, take immediate action. Stand up, start the meal on a humorous note and dip your fingers in the finger bowl saying, "Just so nobody tries to drink my bath water!" If HIS father laughs the loudest, it means he has a sense of humor and no breath left for a speech. If he feels embarrassed, he's the only one who'll know.

Did you let your attention wander? Has dad already raised his finger bowl in a toast? If his son means anything to you, you'll raise your own bowl and, throwing caution to the wind, take a sip. Then get rid of those bowls as fast as you can and make sure you never put them anywhere near that man again. And next time, remember to think ahead!

## Waffles Times Five

## Only for Grownups!

Waffling isn't just for breakfast or brunch. Try them out for dessert or as a snack. Here are five waffle toppings and dips with a real kick:

Cream Sherry Topping
Beat 1 3/4 cup cream until almost stiff; stir in 2 tablespoons sugar and beat until stiff. Fold in 1 shot sweet sherry or your favorite liqueur or dessert wine.

Vodka Cherry Topping
In a saucepan, add juice from 1 jar of preserved pitted cherries (not maraschino). Peel and grate one 1/2" piece of ginger and add. Add zest and juice of 1 lime, and 3 tablespoons sugar. Add 1 handful raisins. Simmer mixture for 5 minutes. Stir 1 tablespoon cornstarch into 1 shot vodka and whisk in. Bring to a boil, add cherries (pitted) and let cool.

Zabaglione Caffè
In bowl, combine 4 egg yolks, 1/4 cup sugar, 3 tablespoons espresso and 3 tablespoons Marsala. Whisk mixture vigorously over a double boiler on medium heat (or stainless bowl set over a saucepan with 1" boiling water) until frothy and then creamy (do not boil). Serve hot—pour into cappuccino cups and dip pieces of waffles.

Raspberry Tea-Wine Sauce
Brew 1 cup black tea for 3 minutes in a small pan; while still hot, stir in 2/3 cup frozen raspberries until berries fall apart. Bring to a boil 1 1/4 cups red wine, 1 teaspoon mulling spices and 1/4 cup sugar. Whisk in 2 tablespoons rum, 1 tablespoon cornstarch and raspberry tea mixture; bring to a boil. Strain. Pour into punch glasses; dip waffles.

Spicy Spiked Chocolate Fondue
Heat 1 cup cream and 2 tablespoons sugar to just before a boil; remove from heat and add 5 oz. finely chopped dark chocolate (70%). Whisk in 2 tablespoons rum and then spice it up with dashes of cayenne pepper. Place in bowls or in fondue pot; dip waffles.

145

# Black & White Mini Cakes
You can't buy friendship but this comes close

**Preparation:** Bake the day before or that day
**Storage:** Zip-top bag in the freezer

Makes enough for 6:

1½ cups semisweet chocolate chips

3 tablespoons room temperature butter

⅔ cup sugar

4 eggs

⅛ teaspoon salt

¼ cup almonds

½ cup flour

1 teaspoon cinnamon

1 teaspoon vanilla

Plus: nonstick cooking spray

**For the topping:**

⅔ cup cream

1 tablespoon sugar

½ teaspoon vanilla

¼ teaspoon cinnamon

**1** Melt chocolate with 1 tablespoon of the butter in a double boiler (or stainless steel bowl over a pan with 1" boiling water), or in the microwave on half power for 30 second spurts, stirring each time. Set aside to cool slightly.

**2** Preheat oven to 375°F. In the bowl of an electric mixer, combine rest of butter, sugar, eggs, and salt; mix until frothy then creamy.

**3** Using a food processor or extra grinder, grind almonds into bits (as powdery as possible) and mix them in a separate bowl with the flour and cinnamon.

4 Prepare 6 oven-safe molds (or use a muffin tin with a bit of water in the empty holes)—generously spray non-stick spray into molds. Set aside.

5 Quickly remix the sugar-butter mixture. Add the flour mixture and combine well. Next add the slightly cooled chocolate while mixing vigorously. Scrape down sides of bowl and beat again until everything is combined. Divide batter evenly between molds—about $\frac{1}{2}$ cup in each, give or take. Bake for 15–20 minutes, depending on whether you want a soft center or solid cake center.

6 Let mini-cakes cool slightly in the molds, then loosen sides with a knife and reverse onto plates. Beat cream to the soft peak stage, then add sugar and vanilla. Beat a little bit more, and stir in cinnamon. Pour over the tops.

Prep time: $1\frac{1}{2}$ hours, 30 minutes of which you're actually busy

## Coconut Flan
### Easy the Caribbean way

**Preparation:** No earlier than that morning
**Storage:** Covered in ramekins in the refrigerator

Not worth it for fewer than 6:

zest of $\frac{1}{2}$ lemon or lime

$1\frac{3}{4}$ cup coconut milk

$\frac{1}{4}$ cup grated coconut

$\frac{3}{4}$ cup sugar, divided

2 eggs

2 egg yolks

2 tablespoons white rum

1 Rinse citrus and remove zest from half. In a pot, bring coconut milk to a boil. Switch off the burner and let stand.

2 Preheat oven to 275°F. Select 6 small ovenproof molds or ramekins (each should hold about $\frac{2}{3}$ cup liquid). Scatter grated coconut in the bottom of each.

3 In a pot, mix half of the sugar with $\frac{1}{2}$ cup water; cook over medium heat until it liquefies and turns light brown but not too dark, and resembles a syrup. Stir occasionally. Pour quickly into molds. It will harden.

4 Combine eggs, egg yolks and remaining sugar and beat in an electric mixer until nice and foamy (using a whisk attachment if you have one). Gradually pour warm coconut milk and rum into the egg-sugar mixture while continuing to mix gently. Add citrus zest. Pour slowly into the molds.

5 Place the molds in a large baking dish and pour enough hot tap water around the molds to come halfway up their sides. Place on the middle or bottom shelf of the oven and bake for about 1 hour or until the centers don't jiggle. Important: Make sure the water underneath doesn't start to bubble. If it does, add a bit of cold water. Let flan cool. Loosen sides with a knife and reverse onto plates.

Prep time: $1\frac{1}{2}$ hours, 30 minutes of which you're actually busy (plus cooling time)
Calories per serving: 210

## Dessert Muffins
### ...this time for spooning

**Preparation:** Soak muffins 1 day ahead; whip cream at the last minute
**Storage:** In a cool place, but not necessarily in the refrigerator

Makes enough for 4:

4 large chocolate muffins or lemon muffins (store-bought or homemade; see Basic Baking, page 87)

3 oranges

1 lemon

3 tablespoons sugar

1 tablespoon Cointreau (optional)

$\frac{2}{3}$ cup cream

2 tablespoons sugar

$\frac{1}{2}$ teaspoon vanilla

2 teaspoons cocoa powder

1 Place each muffin in a mug or large ramekin and pierce repeatedly.

2 Rinse 1 orange and the lemon and remove zest (put in a bowl, cover and place in the refrigerator). Juice the oranges and lemon and stir together with sugar and Cointreau until the sugar has dissolved.

3 Drizzle juice mixture over the muffins; cover, refrigerate and let stand at least 12 hours. Bring back to room temperature before serving.

4 Beat cream until soft peaks form; then add sugar and vanilla. Beat just a bit more and then mix in cocoa and citrus zest to taste (add gradually); briefly beat to combine. Pour over the muffins or reverse the muffins onto plates with dollops of cream on top or beside them.

Prep time: 40 minutes
(+ 12 hours marinating time)
Calories per serving: 350)

147

# Poached Pears Two Ways
Excellent with ice cream OR strong cheese

**Preparation:** Cook pears the day before
**Storage:** Overnight in the refrigerator immersed in cooking liquid

Makes enough for 4:

4 large, firm pears

1 lemon

1 cup pear juice

A few threads saffron

2 whole cloves

2 tablespoons Campari (or other liqueur)

½ cup orange juice

3 tablespoons sugar

**1** Cut pears in half lengthwise, remove cores with a small knife and peel. Rinse lemon under hot water, dry and remove a thin layer of zest, if possible in the shape of a long spiral.

**2** Combine pear juice, lemon zest and saffron in a pot. Add cloves. Place 4 pear halves in this liquid, heat, cover and cook over low heat for about 15 minutes until they're fairly tender but not mushy nor falling apart.

**3** At the same time in another pot, heat campari, orange juice and sugar in another pot. Add remaining pear halves and cook for 15 minutes. Let pears cool in the liquid.

**4** And now you have a choice of what to serve with the two types of poached pears—ice cream or a strong cheese such as Roquefort, Brie or Cheddar.

Prep time: 25 minutes
Calories per serving: 180

## Variation:

### Cassis Plums
Rinse 1½ lbs. ripe plums, cut in halves and remove pits. Bring to a boil ½ cup Cassis, ½ cup water, 1 vanilla bean (slit open)—or 1 teaspoon vanilla, 1 cinnamon stick, and ¼ cup sugar. Add zest from half a lemon; simmer for 10 minutes. Add plum halves and 1 pinch black pepper and cook over low heat for 15 minutes. Let cool in the liquid. Delicious with cheese but also with pancakes, waffles, or ice cream.

# Stewed Apples with Ginger Cream
Bavarian-French-Asian alliance

**Preparation:** Prepare apples the day before; make ginger cream at the last minute
**Storage:** Covered at room temperature

Makes enough for 4:

4 tart apples (e.g. Granny Smith type)

1 lemon

⅓ cup sugar

1 tablespoon raisins (optional)

1 piece fresh ginger (about ½" long; you can also add 1 piece candied ginger if you want)

1 scant cup crème fraiche

2 tablespoons cream

2 tablespoons sugar

½ teaspoon vanilla

1 Peel apples, quarter, remove cores and cut into wedges. Rinse lemon. Remove zest; set aside half (covered). Squeeze juice from whole lemon.

2 In a pot, combine apple wedges, 2 cups water, lemon juice, half the lemon zest, sugar and raisins and bring to a boil. Cover and simmer over medium heat for 10–20 minutes until the apple wedges are tender, or to your liking. (How long that will take depends on the type of apple—keep checking periodically.)

3 Place the stewed apples in a bowl and let stand until lukewarm or cold.

4 Peel ginger and chop or grate very finely. If you're using candied ginger, also chop finely.

5 Thoroughly mix crème fraiche, cream, sugar, and vanilla. Stir in ginger and remaining lemon zest. Serve alongside apples.

Prep time: 40 minutes
Calories per serving: 340

# Orange Blossom Soaked Fruit
## A trip to a specialty market is worth it

**Preparation:** No more than 2–3 days ahead
**Storage:** Covered in a cool place—not necessarily in the refrigerator

Makes enough for 4:

½ lb. mixed dried fruit

(e.g. apricots, plums, figs, raisins)

1 cinnamon stick

2 whole cloves

2 tablespoons honey

2 oranges

1 lemon

1 tablespoon orange blossom water

(available from a gourmet market, a Middle-Eastern market or sometimes even the pharmacy)

1 pomegranate (optional)

1 If any of the dried fruit pieces are large, cut into pieces. Then mix with ½ cup water and soak overnight.

2 On the next day, pour fruit into a pot with cinnamon, cloves and honey. Squeeze juice from oranges and lemon and add.

3 Bring fruit to a boil and simmer covered over low heat for 15 minutes. Let cool, then flavor with orange blossom water (OK to add more blossom water to taste).

4 If you want to spend a little more, buy 1 pomegranate, cut it in half and scoop out the red seeds with a knife. Place cooked fruit mixture in individual bowls and sprinkle with pomegranate seeds.

Prep time: 30 minutes
(+ soaking overnight)
Calories per serving: 205

# Exotic Fruit Gelées
Bright as the sun

**Preparation:** No more than 2 days ahead
**Storage:** In individual bowls, covered in the refrigerator

Makes enough for 4:

1 lb. (generous) yellow or orange fruit

(e.g. apricots, peaches, mangos, pineapple,

cantaloupe, etc.—preferably a mixture)

¼ cup sugar

1¼ cups light-colored fruit juice, not

too sweet (you can also make part

of it a sweet white wine)

2 tablespoons fresh lemon juice

2 tablespoons cornstarch

½ cup cream for topping (optional)

1 tablespoon sugar for topping (optional)

**1** Rinse all fruit, then peel if necessary (e.g. mangos or pineapple). Clean all fruit (remove stems and pits), cut into small pieces or dice and combine with sugar in a pot.

**2** Mix fruit juice with lemon juice. Stir cornstarch into 2 tablespoons of the juice mixture (set aside).

**3** Add bulk of juice to fruit in pot and bring to a boil. Simmer briefly. Stir in cornstarch mixture and continue to simmer until the mixture thickens slightly. Pour into four bowls and let cool. Tastes great with softly whipped cream (add 1 tablespoon sugar toward the end of beating); you can also add a little lemon zest or dashes of cinnamon to the whipped cream.

Prep time: 25 minutes (+ cooling time)
Calories per serving: 75

# Oranges in Honey
Nothing could be simpler!

**Preparation:** No more than 1 day ahead
**Storage:** Covered at room temperature

Makes enough for 4:

4 oranges

3 tablespoons honey

1 tablespoon fresh lemon juice

¼ cup port (or other dessert wine)

1 pinch cinnamon

Several sprigs fresh mint

**1** Peel oranges with a paring knife, so as to also remove peel and the white "pith." Cut oranges into thin, round slices and if you want, remove the seeds. Pour any juice that runs out straight into a pan.

**2** To the pan, add honey, lemon juice, port and cinnamon; heat. Let simmer slightly until the mixture thickens a bit. Add oranges, turn off heat, and let stand on the same burner. Cool to room temperature. Rinse mint leaves, pat dry, and scatter over oranges. Goes with plain vanilla ice cream or cinnamon parfait (page 160).

Prep time: 20 minutes
Calories per serving: 95

Tip:
Fresh figs instead of (or in addition to) the oranges are also delicious when prepared in this way.

# Melon in Coconut Milk
### Quickly made, quickly eaten

**Preparation:** No more than 1 day ahead
**Storage:** Covered in the refrigerator

Makes enough for 4:

1 cantaloupe

1 vanilla bean

Zest of ½ lime

1¾ cup coconut milk

¼ cup sugar

2 tablespoons white rum

**1** Cut open melon, scoop out seeds with a spoon, peel and dice rest, or even better: use a melon baller.

**2** Slit open vanilla bean and scrape out seeds. Rinse lime and zest half. Combine zest and vanilla bean seeds with coconut milk and sugar, bring to a boil and stir until the sugar dissolves. Let cool. Add rum (whisk in) and then melon. Let refrigerate for at least 1 hour. Great with Pacific Rim meals!

Prep time: 20 minutes
(+ 1 hour refrigeration time)
Calories per serving: 135

# Apple Charlotte
### Very impressive

**Preparation:** Prepare the day before, reverse onto a plate and garnish just before the party
**Storage:** Covered in the bowl in the refrigerator

Not worth it for fewer than 8:

4 tart apples (e.g. Granny Smith)

½ cup apple juice, ½ cup Riesling

1 tablespoon brandy

1 tablespoon fresh lemon juice

7 tablespoons sugar, divided

2 cups heavy whipping cream, divided

1½ teaspoons gelatin powder

3–4 tablespoons Calvados (or apple juice)

7 oz. ladyfingers

½ teaspoon vanilla

Cocoa powder or grated chocolate

for sprinkling

**1** Peel and core apples; cut into 1" pieces. In a pot, combine apple pieces, apple juice, Riesling, brandy, lemon juice and 2 table-spoons of the sugar and bring to a boil. Cover and simmer over low heat until the apples are soft but not mushy. Then strain

in a colander (with a bowl to catch the liquid!) and let cool. Heat one cup of the cream with 3 tablespoons of the sugar and dissolve 1½ teaspoons gelatin powder in it—chill in refrigerator.

**2** Mix reserved juice with Calvados. Then find a round bowl that can hold about 7 cups of liquid (a soufflé dish works well). Dip some of the ladyfingers in the apple juice mixture and then arrange them tightly along the bottom and sides of the bowl (cut in half if necessary). Use additional apple juice as needed for dipping ladyfingers.

**3** Whisk chilled cream-gelatin mixture and fold cooled cooked apples into it. Pour into the bowl lined with ladyfingers; cover the top with more dipped ladyfingers. Cover the Charlotte with a plate and weight it down (e.g. with cans). Refrigerate for at least 4 hours.

**4** Place serving plate on top of the bowl, turn it over quickly, and in this way, reverse the Charlotte onto the plate. If it doesn't work, rest the bottom of the bowl in hot water and then try to unmold it. Beat the other cup of cream until soft peaks form—then add remaining sugar and vanilla and beat until stiff—spread all over the Charlotte. Garnish with cocoa powder or grated chocolate.

Prep time: 1 hour
(+ at least 4 hours refrigeration time)
Calories per serving: 330

# International Tea Party

Tea time knows no boundaries...a brief respite where all the world's peoples can converge and feel at home.

## Making Tea

The best tea is brewed right when the guests arrive—after 15 minutes, it can turn bitter and overly strong. So it's better to make tea in several shifts than to make it all at once. Here's how: Bring 1 quart fresh, cold water to a boil. Place 4–5 heaping teaspoons of tea (the finer the leaves, the less you'll need) in a tea ball dropped down into an empty serving teapot. If it's black tea, pour the water into the teapot as soon as it boils. For green tea, wait 10 minutes, then pour over leaves. Steeping time: For green tea, 2–3 minutes, for black tea, 2–6 minutes depending on your taste from weak to strong.

## Creating the Right Atmosphere

Think English country estate, Parisian salon, Russian Dacha, Chinese teahouse, Bedouin tent. Picture baronial brocade, hotel silver, porcelain white, evening blue, candlelight yellow, Edwardian pastels. Combine contrasting colors in matching tones. Send teabags with parchment notes attached to the strings as invitations. Drape fabric all around, illuminate chandeliers and tealights; set out wildflowers in old jugs. Play classical dinner music, Russian choirs, jazz or swing – but say no to opera!

Actually, we were planning on inviting you over for coffee and dessert, but now we're in such an international frame of mind, we've decided to change it to a global-style tea. The whole world drinks tea—the queen of England following an afternoon jaunt on the high moors, our Russian friends when they return in the evening from a three-day trek across the tundra, the Chinese even during their journeys—and some Japanese even study for 20 years to master the green tea ceremony. An international tea gathering is perfect for engaging all different types of people—let's experiment with different teas and both sweet and savory foods.

## What You Need

A tea party as we imagine it has a formal quality, as in "high tea" taken at elegant hotels, but there's also something familial about it—imagining a visit to a teahouse or Russian Zakuska where sweet and salty hors d'oeuvres are set out on the table toward the evening along with the tea. Guests longingly gaze out over endless fields with a cup in one hand and a saucer in the other. Or they sit and chat on the divan with a teacup and plate of hors d'oeuvres on an end table. OK, you don't have to have endless fields, and a flea market sofa will do just fine. But a small table of some sort is an absolute must, for resting teacups. Well-placed cardboard boxes with fabric remnants draped over the top can do the job, provided you have enough of them—remember this because balancing a teacup is no less difficult than removing tea stains!

For the large table you'll need: Teapots labeled according to contents, for example, by placing small bowls of tea leaves in front of them. Fine china is great if you have it. Also, glass pots have a certain je ne sais quoi; thermoses don't look so good but work. There's just one thing that is not okay: using the same pot you usually use for coffee. For the same reason, don't offer heavy mugs that say, "Thank God it's Friday"—fine tea goes in fine cups. So use teacups, tea glasses (found at Middle Eastern specialty stores), Asian teacups (ones without handles) and a few champagne glasses, too. Of course you'll need small plates and silverware: spoons, small and large forks, knives and serving utensils. Arrange food on platters and in bowls on the buffet—and if you happen to have a tiered dessert stand for serving or grandma's candelabra for decor, put them out there! The best of what you have is just right for tea parties.

## How to Drink Tea

Your living room becomes a grand hotel when you stand at the buffet pouring tea and asking guests (purists close their ears), "British with milk, Russian with jelly, Russo-British with lemon, Middle-Eastern with honey or sugar, Mongolian with butter, northern German with Rum or Chinese with nothing?" And then: "I recommend the muffins with assam, dim sum with gunpowder, mushroom caviar with caravan, tamago maki with bancha." The rest is just sitting around, talking, looking out the window and sipping tea. Which doesn't rule out more serious drinking later on! (Enter champagne glasses...)

# Tea for Twelve

**In any case:** Loose tea for 4–5 quarts of brewed tea, preferably pure varieties from the tea plant (i.e. black, green or green-black such as Oolong) and only these (i.e. no flavored wild cherry or Christmas blend). Look for variety in where it was made, such as India or Russia, China or Japan, Sri Lanka or other exotic originations.

**For the tea:** Sugar, rock candy sticks, honey and sweetener; lemon, lime and orange for the sour; milk or cream for clouding the tea; rum or liqueur for clouding the mind; berry jelly, butter, chili powder and cinnamon sticks for pizzazz.

**Store-bought goodies:** British such as biscuit cookies or shortbread; French such as eclairs or madeleines; Asian such as fortune cookies or rice crackers; any variety of nuts, cookies and candy for munching.

**Home-made goodies:** For Russian, rye bread with mushroom caviar (page 50); for Middle-Eastern, cheese rolls (page 56) or falafel (page 59); for Asian, vegetable skewers (page 41) or dim sum (page 82); for British, cucumber sandwiches (page 51).

153

**Plus:** Store-bought scones or toast and butter, English clotted cream and lemon curd; champagne and caviar if you can afford it; cognac, whiskey and vodka if you want.

# Avocado Lemon Cream
About as quick as it gets

**Preparation:** Just before the party
**Storage:** If necessary, in the refrigerator

Makes enough for 6:

1 lemon

2 ripe avocados (ones that have

some give when you squeeze 'em)

1/2 cup sugar

3/4 cup + 2 tablespoons yogurt

(whole 4% plain)

3/4 cup + 2 tablespoons sour cream

**1** Rinse lemon and pat dry. Remove a very thin layer of zest with a vegetable peeler and cut into very fine strips (or create long strips with a zester). Squeeze out juice.

**2** Cut avocados to the pit all the way around, rotate halves in opposite directions and pull apart. Scoop out the pit. Spoon out flesh into blender along with sugar, lemon juice, yogurt, and sour cream. Purée, pour into glasses and garnish with lemon peel. Serve shortbread or other elegant cookie alongside. Also works as a dip for pieces of fruit.

Prep time: 15 minutes
Calories per serving: 380

# Berry Mascarpone
Poetry on a spoon

**Preparation:** Make mascarpone cream 1 day ahead, combine with berries just before the party
**Storage:** Covered in the refrigerator

Makes enough for 4:

3 cups (about 11 oz.) mixed fresh berries

(or frozen)

1 tablespoon powdered sugar

8 oz. mascarpone cheese

2 tablespoons honey

1 tablespoon cocoa powder

1 tablespoon lemon or orange juice

1/2 cup cream (or use half-and-half)

**1** Drain berries in a colander, catching the juice in bowl. Combine powdered sugar and 1–2 tablespoons of the berry juice.

**2** Stir together mascarpone, honey, cocoa, lemon or orange juice and cream until very smooth. Gently mix sugar-berry juice mixture with the berries. Fill dessert cups with alternating layers of berries and cream. Garnish with a few berries. Refrigerate for at least 2 hours.

Prep time: 15 minutes
Calories per serving: 420

# Trifle
So sweet, so fine

**Preparation:** Spread jelly on cake the night before, assemble desserts a few hours before the party.
**Storage:** Store finished dessert briefly in the refrigerator, covered

Makes enough for 4:

2 cups (about 11 oz.) fresh raspberries

(or frozen)

7 oz. pound cake

1/2 cup seedless raspberry jelly

2 tablespoons dry sherry

1/2 vanilla bean

2 egg yolks

2 cups + 2 tablespoons milk

2 tablespoons cornstarch

1/3 cup sugar

**1** Sort through fresh berries to make sure they're all nice. Or, if frozen, pour in a colander, place over a bowl and let thaw. In either case: don't rinse them or they'll get mushy.

**2** Cut cake lengthwise into slices around ¼" thick. Mix jelly and sherry. Spread on cake slices and reassemble the cake. Then slice normally (across the width) and arrange strips along the bottom and sides of four dessert bowls (clear glass ones work great).

**3** Slit open half a vanilla bean lengthwise and scrape out seeds. Separate eggs (discard whites). Bring vanilla seeds and vanilla bean to a boil in the milk. Thoroughly whisk together egg yolks and cornstarch into a paste. Remove vanilla bean from milk. Whisk sugar into milk. Take a little of the milk mixture and whisk it into the egg-cornstarch mixture—then whisk all of the egg-cornstarch mixture into milk mixture in pan while mixing constantly and vigorously. Let it bubble up once, then remove from heat and let cool.

**4** Distribute berries over the cake slices on the bottoms of the dessert bowls. Top with cooled vanilla cream (whisk till smooth if necessary first), garnish with more berries, and serve.

Prep time: 50 minutes
Calories per serving: 465

# Chocolate Lemon Tiramisu
### For hosts with a playful streak

**Preparation**: The night before
**Storage**: Loosely covered with plastic wrap in the refrigerator

Not worth it for fewer than 8:

1 ²/₃ cups espresso

3 tablespoons cocoa powder

+ cocoa powder for dusting

2 tablespoons chocolate-nut spread

(e.g. Nutella)

2 lemons

18 oz. (about 2¼ cups) mascarpone cheese

½ cup whole milk

1 cup powdered sugar

2 tablespoons sugar

½ teaspoon vanilla

2 tablespoons hazelnut liqueur (optional)

7 oz. ladyfinger cookies, best from a bakery or homemade (Basic Baking, page 102)

**1** Whisk together thoroughly espresso, cocoa and chocolate spread.

**2** Rinse 1 lemon thoroughly under hot water, dry and remove zest. Squeeze juice from both lemons.

**3** Combine well mascarpone, lemon juice and zest, milk, powdered sugar, sugar, and vanilla. If desired, add hazelnut liqueur to espresso mixture.

**4** Cover the bottom of a square pan with ladyfingers and drizzle espresso mixture over them. Then spread mascarpone mixture over the top. Continue adding layers of ladyfingers, espresso mixture and mascarpone mixture until everything is in the pan. Dust the very top layer of mascarpone with cocoa and refrigerate until the party.

Prep time: 40 minutes
(+ refrigeration time)
Calories per serving: 485

# Stuffed Dates
Tiny tempters

**Preparation:** 1–2 days ahead of time
**Storage:** On a plate covered with plastic wrap in the refrigerator

Makes 25 dates:

1 orange

¼ cup chopped walnuts

7 tablespoons cream cheese

1 tablespoon creamed honey

(or whipped honey)

1 teaspoon cinnamon

1 pinch ground cloves

About 25 dried dates

**1** Rinse orange and zest. Squeeze out juice to equal 1 tablespoon. Chop walnuts.

**2** Combine cream cheese, the 1 tablespoon orange juice, creamed honey, cinnamon, cloves, walnuts and orange zest.

**3** Cut open dates and remove pits. Put cream cheese mixture in a pastry bag or small plastic bag (cut off a small corner) and fill the dates (if the mixture seems too thick, add more orange juice before piping). Arrange side by side on a plate.

Prep time: 30 minutes
Calories per serving: 30

# Banana Muffins
Gone in a flash

**Preparation:** No more than 1 day ahead
**Storage:** Loosely covered with plastic wrap

Makes 12 muffins or 24 minis:

1 banana

1 tablespoon fresh lemon juice

1 tablespoon honey

1 cup flour

7 tablespoons powdered chocolate

pudding mix (not instant)

2 teaspoons baking powder

1 egg

⅓ cup sugar

1 teaspoon vanilla

¼ cup oil

7 tablespoons sour cream

Powdered sugar for dusting (optional)

Plus: paper baking cups

**1** Peel banana and dice. Combine lemon juice and honey and add to banana. Preheat oven to 350°F.

**2** Combine flour, pudding mix and baking powder. Stir together egg, sugar, vanilla and oil, then add sour cream. Stir in flour mixture and milk, then the diced banana and mix just until incorporated.

3 Spoon batter into baking cups filling them ½ to ⅔ full. Bake on center shelf for about 20 minutes (less for minis) or until an inserted toothpick comes out mostly clean. Let cool. If desired, dust with powdered sugar.

Prep time: 35 minutes,
20 of which you're actually busy
Calories per muffin: 100

# Fruit Balls
Sweet finger food

**Preparation:** No more than 1 week ahead
**Storage:** Sealed in a tin (like Christmas cookies)

Makes 50 balls:

½ lb. dried fruit

(preferably a variety, e.g. figs and apricots)

2 cups (or about 7 oz.) nuts

(preferably mixed, e.g. walnuts,

sunflower seeds and almonds)

1⅓ cups grated coconut

**1** Cut larger dried fruit into pieces. Place fruit in in a bowl with ¾ cup + 2 tablespoons lukewarm water and soak overnight.

**2** The next day place fruit, the soaking water (if there's any left) and nuts in a blender or heavy duty food processor and pulse until you have a solid but moldable mass. If it's too wet, add nuts. If it's too dry, add a little water or even Schnapps.

**3** With your hands, form into small balls. Pour coconut flakes onto a plate and roll the balls around in them. Place on the buffet or store in a tin.

Prep time: 30 minutes
(+ soaking time)
Calories per ball: 50

# Baklava
So sweeeeet!

**Preparation:** No more than 1 day ahead
**Storage:** Tightly covered and cool but not in the refrigerator

Not worth it for fewer than 8–10:

1 package filo pastry
(you'll need about a pound)

7 tablespoons butter

4 cups mixed nuts—or a little short of a pound (preferably walnuts, almonds and pistachios—unsalted, of course)

2 egg whites

¼ cup honey

1 teaspoon cinnamon

2 teaspoons rose water (try specialty stores or Middle Eastern markets—sometimes even the pharmacy; or, leave out)

1 cup + 1½ tablespoons sugar

Juice from 1 lemon

**1** Cut butter into cubes and melt in a pot over low heat (or microwave on low power for 30 seconds or until melted). But don't let it turn brown!

**2** Chop nuts finely. Beat egg whites until stiff, then fold in honey, nuts, cinnamon and rose water.

**3** Preheat oven to 375°F. Select a baking pan with sides, about the size of the pastry sheets (e.g. a 9" x 13" or lasagna pan) and grease with butter. Start with filo pastry: carefully separate a pastry sheet and cover rest with a barely damp cloth. Brush butter onto each sheet, stacking 3 sheets of pastry to a layer. Scatter nut mixture on top. Now repeat by alternating layers of pastry and nut mixture. Top the last layer with a stack of pastry sheets; brush top with butter.

**4** Place baklava in the oven (center shelf) and bake for about 30 minutes. This leaves you enough time to make a syrup. Pour sugar and 1½ cups water into a pot, heat and simmer for about 10 minutes until it thickens but isn't quite as thick as a syrup. Remove baklava from the oven. Stir lemon juice into the syrup and gradually drench the hot baklava with the syrup. Let cool and cut into squares.

Prep time: 1 hour and 10 minutes, 45 minutes of which you're actually busy
Calories per square (10 squares): 610

# Pear-Banana Chocolate Squares
Just plain good!

**Preparation:** Bake and cut into squares 1–2 days ahead of time
**Storage:** Covered with plastic wrap

Makes 1 sheet:

10½ oz. semisweet chocolate

2 pears

2 bananas

3 tablespoons fresh lemon juice

9 eggs

8 oz. (2 sticks) softened butter
(+ butter for the pan)

⅔ cup sugar

Salt

1¼ cups flour

5 oz. chopped almonds

2 teaspoons baking powder

3½ oz. semisweet chocolate for drizzling (optional; you can also use tempered chocolate designed for candy-making)

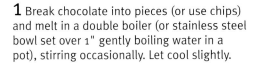

**1** Break chocolate into pieces (or use chips) and melt in a double boiler (or stainless steel bowl set over 1" gently boiling water in a pot), stirring occasionally. Let cool slightly.

**2** Peel pears and cut into quarters; remove core. Peel banana. Dice both fruits and combine with lemon juice.

**3** Separate eggs (if you've forgotten how, see Basic Baking, inside front flap). Cut butter into bits and beat with sugar until frothy. Gradually add egg yolks. Separately, beat egg whites with 1 pinch salt until stiff and refrigerate briefly.

**4** Preheat oven to 375°F. Grease a large rectangular baking sheet with sides. Now add the melted chocolate to butter-sugar mixture. Combine flour, chopped almonds and baking powder and add to that mixture along with fruit. Take egg whites from the refrigerator and fold in until incorporated. Pour batter onto baking sheet and spread out smoothly. Bake in the oven (center shelf) for about 25 minutes.

**5** Let cool. Melt the 3½ oz. chocolate (optional) and drizzle over the chocolate cake. Cut into squares and remove from baking sheet.

Prep time: 1 hour (+ 25 minutes baking time)
Calories per serving (50 squares): 140

# Clafoutis
Bon appetit, mes amis!

**Preparation:** Mix batter and prepare cherries in the morning but bake at the last minute
**Storage:** Keep batter covered in the refrigerator

Makes enough for 4:

1 cup + 2½ tablespoons flour

4 eggs

6 tablespoons sugar

1 teaspoon vanilla

1 pinch salt

1¼ cups milk

1 lb. fresh cherries

Powdered sugar for sprinkling on top

Cognac or brandy for sprinkling on top

(optional)

**1** In a bowl, thoroughly mix flour, eggs, sugar, vanilla, and salt. Gradually stir in milk. Let batter stand for 30 minutes.

**2** Rinse cherries, remove stems, and remove pits with a cherry pitter. Pour cherries into a shallow baking dish.

**3** Preheat oven to 350°F. Stir batter once more and pour over the cherries. Bake clafoutis in the oven (center shelf) for about 40 minutes until the surface is nice and brown. Sprinkle with powdered sugar. Clafoutis tastes best when lukewarm, and many find that it isn't authentically French unless you sprinkle a shot of cognac over the top.

Prep time: 1 hour and 20 minutes, 15 of which you're actually busy
Calories per serving: 285

# Cinnamon Parfait
## For ice-cold enjoyment

**Preparation:** 2–3 days ahead of time
**Storage:** In the freezer

Not worth it for fewer than 10–12:

$\frac{1}{2}$ vanilla bean

1 cup + 1 tablespoon milk

6 very fresh egg yolks

$\frac{2}{3}$ cup sugar

$1\frac{1}{2}$ cups cream

2 teaspoons cinnamon

**1** Lay the half vanilla bean on a board, slit open lengthwise and scrape out seeds with the back of a knife. In a pot, combine milk, vanilla bean and seeds and heat. Switch off the burner and let stand.

**2** Beat egg yolks and sugar until frothy. Remove vanilla bean from milk. Gradually pour milk mixture into egg yolk-sugar mixture while mixing constantly. Pour everything into back into the pan and again heat on the stove until the mixture thickens, while stirring.

3 Pour the entire mixture into a bowl and let cool, stirring frequently to make sure it remains smooth and doesn't form a thick skin on top.

4 Beat cream with cinnamon until stiff peaks form and fold into the main mixture. Pour into a mold (preferably a long rectangular one that holds about 7 cups liquid). Place in the freezer for 3 hours. Then briefly set mold in warm water so you can then reverse the frozen parfait onto a platter; then slice.

Prep time: 20 minutes
(+ 3 hours freezing time)
Calories per serving (12 servings): 190

## And to go with it?

### Some ideas—
### Honey berries:
Thaw 2 cups frozen berries. In a pot, heat up 3 tablespoons honey, 2 tablespoons orange juice and a little fresh lemon juice—simmer until syrupy. Stir in berries, heat and serve with parfait.

### Or a mango sauce:
Peel and coarsely dice 1 ripe mango. Purée with 2 tablespoons coconut liqueur or cream, a little fresh lemon juice, and 1–2 tablespoons sugar.

### Or a hot
### chocolate sauce:
Melt 2 oz. semisweet chocolate in 1 cup + 1 tablespoon milk. Whisk 1 egg, 3 tablespoons sugar and 1 heaping teaspoon cornstarch together. Whisk a little of the hot chocolate milk into it and then pour it all into the hot chocolate milk mixture. Heat while constantly stirring until the sauce thickens. Let cool slightly and, if desired, stir in a little liqueur such as Bailey's Irish Cream.

# Orange Sorbet
## Simple and refreshing

**Preparation**: 3–4 days ahead of time
**Storage**: In the freezer

Makes enough for 8 but not too much for 4:

4 oranges

1 lemon

$^3/_4$ cup + 2 tablespoons sugar

1 tablespoon orange liqueur (optional,

e.g. Cointreau, Triple Sec, Grand Marnier)

1 Rinse 1 orange and the lemon, pat dry and remove zest. Use a zester, a microplane grater, or a vegetable peeler—just avoid getting any of the white part underneath, which imparts a bitter taste.

2 Squeeze juice from all oranges and the lemon.

3 Dissolve sugar in $1\frac{1}{2}$ cups lukewarm water. Add orange and lemon juices, zest, and, if desired, orange liqueur.

4 Place in the freezer for about 4 hours. Stir occasionally: the more often you do, the finer the sorbet will be. (Every $^1/_2$ hour to every hour is sufficient.)

Prep time: 25 minutes (+ 4 hours freezing time with occasional stirring)
Calories per serving (8 servings): 125

# What-Do-I-Do-When-and-How?-Suggestions

The recipes are now behind you and you can hardly wait to start partying. But maybe you still feel like you're missing something. Well, here are a few tips on preparation as well as a couple of ideas about what you can do if you don't have a lot of time...or your wallet is a little light...or you want to get everything ready ahead of time...

## Warming up

Fried foods and baked goods are easy to prepare ahead of time but taste best if you heat them again before the party. Here's how: Preheat the oven to 375°F. Cover a baking sheet with baking parchment, place the baked goods on top and put them in the hot oven. After a few minutes, everything will be nice and crispy on the outside and will also smell great. Take out of the oven, let cool if appropriate and serve.

## Freezing

If you want to avoid stress in the days before your party, make some of the food one or two weeks ahead and freeze it. This works well with soups and stews, with fried items such as cheese rolls, with meat dishes such as rolled roast pork and with baked goods. Take them out of the freezer the night before and put them in the refrigerator. Just before the party, carve (roasts), heat up (soups and stews) or warm up (baked goods).

## Herbs

Sometimes it takes only a simple mint leaf to make a tomato salad into a Middle-Eastern salad. And since you can't always find mint when you need it, consider buying a pot of mint at a weekly market or from a greenhouse and setting it out on your balcony or windowsill. Of course, that doesn't just apply to mint!

## Family Celebrations

Here are some ideas to treat your family very special:

Duck pâté (page 69)
Vegetable crostini with almonds (page 52)
Artichokes with sauces (page 119)
Bell peppers in oil (page 130)
Black & white mini-cakes (page 146)
Plus: Ham, smoked salmon, and a cheese platter

Potato terrine with goat cheese (page 68)
Marinated vegetables (page 64)
Stuffed mushrooms (page 47)
Rolled pork roast (page 133)
Apple Charlotte (page 151)
Poached pears 2 ways (page 148)
Plus: Salami and ham and a platter of spicy cheeses

## Spontaneous Parties

It all has to happen fast and everything has to be readily available. The good news is, these quick dishes go well together:

Cheese skewers (page 41)
Cucumber raita (page 44)
Ham canapés (page 53)
Carrot salad with grapes (page 72)
Peanut celery spread (page 127)
Melon in coconut milk (page 151)
Plus: Salami, cherry tomatoes, cheese

Ham carpaccio (page 65)
Vegetable crostini with almonds (page 52)
Tangy marinated cheese and vegetables (page 71)
Cauliflower salad with capers (page 72)
Provençal potato soup (page 95)
Avocado lemon cream (page 154)
Plus: Tomatoes, cucumbers, radishes and breadsticks

## Stand-up Receptions

Consider any recipe from the finger food chapter, or the following combinations:

Canapés with potato-cheese cream (page 50)
Ham crescents (page 125)
Stuffed tomatoes (page 46)
Chicken legs (page 132)
Fruit balls (page 156)
Stuffed dates (page 156)
Plus: Salami, prosciutto-wrapped breadsticks, cheese platter

Chicken saltimbocca (page 41)
Rye bread with mushroom caviar (page 50)
Meatballs (page 58)
Cucumber raita (page 44)
Cheese quiche (page 125)
Dessert muffins (page 147)
Plus: Cherry tomatoes, radishes, fruit

## Moving Parties

When moving, you have neither time nor dishes. That's when to serve food that can be dipped or eaten out of a large pot. (Your large pot won't fit too well inside a box anyway.) Even better, enlist some volunteers to make a meal:

Moroccan cream cheese dip (page 42)
Tahini dip (page 43)
Avocado dip (page 44)
Peanut celery spread (page 127)
African eggplant spread (page 127)
Plus: Vegetable sticks, tortilla chips, crackers, assorted breads—for dipping or spreading. Purchase a yummy chocolate dessert.

Borscht (page 91)
Chili con pollo (page 103)
Cheese quiche (page 125)
Roquefort-crème fraiche dip (page 42)
Chicken wings (page 132)
Plus: Crackers, radishes, tomatoes and fruit

## Office Parties

All you need is a little bit of food to go with the drinks!

Cheese skewers (page 41)
Bacon rolls (page 57)
Ham carpaccio (page 65)
Stuffed mild banana peppers (page 47)
Meatballs (page 58)
Pear-banana chocolate squares (page 158)
Plus: Tomatoes in oil, breadsticks, grapes or other fruit

Ham crescents (page 125)
Bavarian cheese spread (page 126)
California club sandwiches (page 129)
Turmeric cucumbers (page 130)
Chicken legs (page 132)
Chocolate lemon tiramisu (page 155)
Plus: Radishes, white radishes (dip in salt), cheese, crackers

## Super Parties

For very close friends or a special occasion:

Salmon tramezzini (page 50)
Marinated vegetables (page 64)
Calamari salad (page 65)
Rice salad with pomegranates (page 77)
Duck curry (page 102)
Coconut flan (page 147)
Plus: Melon with prosciutto, salami, sun-dried tomatoes in oil, a well-provisioned cheese platter, fruit, crackers

Mini Cabernet cream puffs (page 52)
Duck paté (page 68)
Tamarind chicken (page 70)
Rolled pork roast (page 133)
Cinnamon parfait (page 160)
Oranges in honey (page 150)
Plus: Cherry tomatoes, cocktail onions, sun-dried tomatoes in oil, cheese and fruit, crackers

## Potlucks

When friends ask if they can bring something, don't automatically say no—better to photo-copy recipes and hand them out. This makes your life easier and keeps you from ending up with five pasta salads on the buffet.

Eggplant caviar (page 66)
Ham salad nouveau (page 71)
Pasta salad with radicchio (page 74)
Bread salad (page 78)
Fish cakes (page 59)
Chocolate lemon tiramisu (page 155)

Stuffed mushrooms (page 47)
Lentil salad (page 78)
Ratatouille with cheese baguette (page 98)
Cheese quiche (page 125)
Baklava (page 158)

## Low-budget Parties

Parties don't have to wipe out your budget. The following combos keep the finances manageable:

Frittata cubes (page 40)
Vegetable crostini with almonds (page 52)
Eggplant caviar (page 66)
Lentil salad (page 78)
Spareribs (page 140)
Clafoutis (page 159)

Cucumber raita (page 44)
Deviled eggs with mango chutney (page 46)
Falafel (page 59)
Tomato soup (page 88)
Chicken wings (page 132)
Avocado lemon cream (page 154)

# Index

165

167

# Credits

## The Authors:

**Sebastian Dickhaut**, text pages

**Cornelia Schinharl**, recipe pages

**Kelsey Lane**, American team editor

## Photography
**Germany and U.S. teams**

**Lime on title page:** StockFood/Bodo Schieren

**Barbara Bonisolli:**
Food photographs (except pages 66 (Chopped Asian Chicken Salad), 68 (Shrimp Terrine Canapés), 127 (Tomato & Roasted Pepper Bruschetta));
17 Things pages 18–19: pencils, blackboard, place cards, place mats, food
16 Dinner Parties pages 30–31: all photos except picnic blanket and olives
Opening pages for recipe sections (except page 13 and Finger Food)

**Alexander Walter:**
People photos of basic models, still-life feature photos pages 3, 14, 15, 22, 25, 26, 27, 28, 38, 39, 41, 51, 59, 63, 119, 122, 134, 141 (cutlery holder), 148
17 Things pages 18–19: shoes, flowers, windows, wall, ceiling, door, chair, table, lanterns, balcony
16 Dinner Parties pages 30–31: picnic blanket, olives
Opening page: Know How pages 4–5,
The Recipes pages 34–35

**Lisa Keenan**
People photos pages 13, 47, 67, 73, 91, 94, 99, 102, 129, 149, 155
Food photographs pages 66 (Chopped Asian Chicken Salad), 68 (Shrimp Terrine Canapés), 127 (Tomato & Roasted Pepper Bruschetta)

**Stock Food Photos**
Studio Bonisolli: pages 77 (lemons), 141 (bread), 145 (lemon), 159 (egg)
Maximilian Stock: page 73 (tomato)
Picture Box: page 139 (onion)
Studio Eising/Martina Görlach: page 36 (cheese skewer)
Peter von Felbert: pages 18, 56, 123 (grass)

**Thank you to:**
Michael Goerden and the Eichlinger family who hospitably placed their beautiful apartments at our disposal for the photo shoots.
**And to:** Catharina Wilhelm for jumping in during an emergency!

## German Team:
Editor: Sabine Sälzer (also production)
Design and layout: Sybille Engels and Thomas Jankovic
Production: Sabine Sälzer and Susanne Mühldorfer
Photography: Barbara Bonisolli (food) and Alexander Walter (people)
Photographers' assistants: Claudia Jurantis, assistant, Studio Bonisolli; and Florian Peljak, photographer's assistant
Recipe stylist: Hans Gerlach
Reader: Susanne Bodensteiner
Photo requisitioning/styling: Sabine Sälzer, Christa Schmedes, and Beate Pfeiffer
Models: Daniel Griehl, Annika Möller, Markus Röleke, Janna Sälzer, Verena Scheibe, Jan Schmedes, Gabi Schnitzlein
Final corrections: Mischa Gallé, Tanja Dusy
Set: Ludger Vorfeld
Repro: Repro Ludwig
Printing and binding: Druckhaus Kaufmann

## U.S. Team:
Editor: Kelsey Lane
Translator: Christie Tam
Production: Patty Holden
Additional recipes: Kelsey Lane: tomato & roasted pepper bruschetta (p. 127); chopped Asian chicken salad (p. 66); black and white mini cakes (p. 146); tankini martini (p. 62).
Photography: Lisa Keenan (food and people)
Recipe stylist: Pouké

Published originally under the title PARTY BASICS: Alles, was man braucht für das beste Fest der Welt © 2001 Gräfe und Unzer Verlag, GmbH, Munich

English translation copyright: © 2002 Silverback Books

ISBN: 1-930603-91-6

Printed in Singapore